WOMEN, THE BOOK
AND
THE GODLY

This book contains a selection of papers on the subject of women and religion, first delivered at a conference held at St Hilda's College, Oxford. Taking a variety of critical approaches, they illustrate clearly the wealth of previously untapped material on this topic, whether in archive, manuscript or early printed sources, using evidence from, for example, books collected by convents, and books left in wills, both by and for women. This volume examines writing by women, writing which excludes women, and writing which ignores them, as well as women readers, women patrons, and women who were read to. Archaeology, canon and civil law, and trial depositions are all represented. The common determinants of marital and social status are, of course, explored, but so also are the problems of women and language, women's various roles as creators, recipients, and objects, and women's positions with regard to the church.

WOMEN, THE BOOK AND THE GODLY

SELECTED PROCEEDINGS OF
THE ST HILDA'S CONFERENCE, 1993

VOLUME I

Edited by
LESLEY SMITH
and
JANE H. M. TAYLOR

D. S. BREWER

First published 1995
D. S. Brewer, Cambridge

ISBN 0 85991 420 8

D. S. Brewer is an imprint of Boydell & Brewer Ltd
PO Box 9, Woodbridge, Suffolk IP12 3DF, UK
and of Boydell & Brewer Inc.
PO Box 41026, Rochester, NY 14604–4126, USA

British Library Cataloguing-in-Publication Data
Women, the Book and the Godly
I. Smith, Lesley J. II. Taylor, Jane H. M.
809.89287
ISBN 0–85991–420–8

Library of Congress Cataloging-in-Publication Data
Women, the book, and the godly / edited by Lesley Smith
and Jane H.M. Taylor.
    p.   cm.
Proceedings of a conference held in Aug. 1993 at St. Hilda's
College, Oxford.
Includes bibliographical references and index.
ISBN 0–85991–420–8 (hbk. : alk. paper)
  1. Monastic and religious life of women – History – Middle
Ages, 600–1500 – Congresses. 2. Women – Religious life –
History – Congresses. 3. Women – Europe – Education–
History – Congresses. I. Smith, Lesley J. II. Taylor, Jane H. M.
BX4210.W65 1995
271.9'0094–dc20   94–44978

The paper used in this publication meets the minimum requirements
of American National Standard for Information Sciences –
Permanence of Paper for Printed Library Materials, ANSI Z39.48–1984

Printed in Great Britain by
St Edmundsbury Press Ltd, Bury St Edmunds, Suffolk

CONTENTS

ABBREVIATIONS

PL	*Patrologia Latina*
CCCM	*Corpus Christianorum Continuatio Medievalis*
CCM	*Cahiers de Civilisation Médiévale*
CSEL	*Corpus Scriptores Ecclesiasticorum Latinorum*
EETS	Early English Texts Society
BL	British Library
BN	*Bibliothèque nationale*
CSS	Cistercian Studies Series
PMLA	Publications of the Modern Language Association of America
TCD	Trinity College, Dublin

INTRODUCTION

This book represents the first selection of papers from *Women and the Book in the Middle Ages*, a conference held at St Hilda's College, Oxford, in August 1993. It comprises papers on women and religion; two others will address women and worldly literature, and women and art. The decision to begin with religious women is not an arbitrary one. For a variety of reasons, many of them argued in essays in this volume, source-material on this topic is less accessible than that for women in secular literature, and wide-ranging surveys are hard to come by: students looking for a comprehensive monograph, with good sources and references and a relatively unpolemical line, still do well to consult Lisa Eckenstein's 1896 classic, *Women Under Monasticism*. Of course, a collection of conference papers can be no substitute for a monograph, but the papers we have gathered here illustrate with particular clarity how great is the wealth of untapped material and how dynamic the new critical approaches which the study of women and religion through archive, manuscript and early printed sources can provide.

It has, after all, been only recently that the separate existence of a history of women has been acknowledged. Even if – and the if is large – women were mentioned in conventional analyses of the past, it was often said that they had left little or no record of themselves: women's worlds of home and children, food and fabric were, in the modern phrase, bio-degradable; they left no traces behind. Degradable, moreover, has too often meant degraded. Historians took no notice of the female contribution to everyday life, valuing it less than grand battles and cunning strategy, law-making and execution, scholastic debate and high culture. From most of these arenas, women were excluded. The few who found their way inside – empresses, queens, abbesses – were subject to a combination of intense scrutiny and benign neglect. The out-of-the ordinary put the others to shame: since some women *could* cut a dash on the male stage, those who did not were evidence of the weakness of the sex. But neither could the celebrities ever be an unqualified success, for they are judged always by male standards, passing the winning post in the wrong race.

But if women were losing a race they had not entered, historians were running in blinkers. Evidence for women's activities is certainly less prolific than for men's, but it does exist, and in much greater quantity than has been allowed. Often it takes a little more looking for, and acknowledgement, than sources for men. One of the strengths of this collection, and of the conference as a whole, is the variety of evidence and of methods that could be encompassed under the general rubric of *Women and the Book*. In this volume we have writing by women and for women, writing which excludes women, writing which ignores them. We have empirical evidence in books collected by convents, and books left in wills – again, both by and for women. We have women readers, women patrons, and women who were read to. Some of our contributors count books that were once physically present; others look for spaces where absent women have been metaphorically deleted. Archaeology, canon and civil law, and trial depositions also provide grist for our mill. And this book is evidence in itself that evidence for women's lives exists – even if it is evidence of absence.

The essays represent something of the variety and range of work being done on women today, chronologically and geographically. They stand as testimony to the impossibility of writing a 'women's history' without the realisation that there are many themes and many histories. The common determinants of marital and social status are, of course, explored, but so also are the problems of women and language, women's various roles as creators, recipients, and objects, and women's positions on the sliding scale between the orthodox, the reforming, and the heterodox churches. What the essays have in common is the pursuit of hard evidence against which to evaluate some of the common-places perpetuated not only in popular, but even, sometimes, in more scholarly histories.

Is it, for instance, the case that literacy levels for women show a steady increase? In which circles, orthodox or heterodox, is one more likely to find educated women? How far are women book-owners, book-readers? The essays collected here, based on the adventurous use of painstaking research, offer some answers, or if not answers, directions for yet more extensive primary research. Dutton's methodologically innovative and rigorous study of devotional books in testamentary bequests in the later Middle Ages demands just such minute analysis of written sources. In her period, of course, women could not make wills without their husbands' permission – and hence evidence is fragmentary and difficult to evaluate. But her conclusions make it clear that for women in mercantile life, with more disposable income, books – in the vernacular – were a prized commodity. Lest this should seem too optimistic a conclusion, however, we might turn to Roy and Ward, both of them studying Anglo-Saxon women whose Latin was skilled, confirming the paradox that education was better and more common for women in England before the Conquest. Ward analyses the presentation of women in Bede's *History*, and paints an encouraging picture of opportunities available to Anglo-Saxon women; Roy, more depressingly, traces a decline in literacy and Latinity even in the short time that elapsed between the Conquest and the *Ancrene Wisse*. And lest we feel inclined to fall back on the commonplace that literate women might have taken refuge in the heretical sects, Biller and McSheffery challenge that too. They consider, from different angles, the use of books by women from heterodox sects, and their conclusions, arrived at separately yet markedly similar, overturn the conventional wisdom that women in heretic movements were more literate, and had greater access to books, than women in the orthodox church. On the contrary: solid archival research offers convincing and depressing evidence of a female oral world and a male textual world, where women listened rather than read, heard rather than preached. Ought we perhaps to relate this to Whalen's exhaustively documented study of Goscelin's hagiographic efforts on behalf of the nuns of Wilton? Whalen finds a very significant drop in the number and population of nunneries in eleventh-century England, by comparison with foundations for men. Goscelin's campaigns on behalf of the nuns, unusually sensitive to women's religious experiences as they are, nevertheless underscore a crisis which he and the nuns hoped to meet by promoting women religious.

Paradoxically in view of prevailing myths, the orthodox churches may have produced more opportunity for women's voices than the unorthodox. Another group of essays recuperates women's voices: the exceptional, of course, but also, to a degree, the day-to-day. We are surprised, perhaps, as modern readers, to find just how far, and sometimes how surprisingly, disruptive women's voices are absorbed into the more orthodox Church. Luongo's study of Catherine of Siena reminds us of the range of unconventionality sanctioned even in such circles. Catherine was given the stamp of approval by the highest of Church authorities, and yet the remarkable fluidity of her imagery is startling, even shocking, to us today. Medieval minds often allowed for a broader, more dynamic symbolism than our too-literal interpretative preferences would desire. Scheepsma, by contrast, looks at women from the other and less dramatic end of the spectrum, records of whose lives are for that very reason rarer and arguably more revealing. He reminds us that women were at the forefront of the orthodox Church as well as those churches outside it. His Schwestern-bücher from the Modern Devotion tell the stories of religious women in remarkable, day-to-day, detail, yet remain a source largely untapped. The nuns themselves recorded the recollections of exemplary and devoted sisters, and even though individuality is to a degree subordinated to community, the particular voices of these women remain identifiable.

But sometimes, of course, even where women did feel called to write or prophesy, they could not use the conventional paths for gaining ecclesiastical approval. Blamires reminds us how widespread was the assumption that women were incapable of scriptural study, how far literate women were in danger of being treated as heretic. The status and authority of women's words and deeds is indeed a key and recurrent issue for religious history. Since they had no common, direct route to being heard, women had to appeal directly to God, claiming a divine mandate for their work. In this, both male and female mystics alike suffered from being excluded from the church hierarchy and intellectual elite. They had no access to the rational debates of the schools, or the councils of the learned, so they had to resort to direct revelation – a strategy, in effect, permitting them to act on their own authority. Yet still their work was as nothing until it had received the imprimatur of the male ecclesiastical leadership. Unlike Hildegard of Bingen, who had the physical as well as mental resources for producing her own works (although even she needed to be endowed with Church authority), other women writers and visionaries relied entirely on men for 'publication', approval, and distribution of their work. As Voaden points out, these women sought to minimise the human element in their writings to remove any taint that association with the female might bring. Murray's paper makes particularly interesting reading in this respect: confessors' manuals in thirteenth-century England, it seems, were sensitive enough to the differing needs of different classes and different professions, but make little attempt to address the specific and individual needs of women. On the contrary: women's needs for moral guidance tend to be subordinated to men's need for spiritual protection against women. Even where women were vastly in the majority, as in the Modern Devotion, which had three women Devout for every one man, men were considered to be the founders and leaders of the movement. Andersen shows how even a respected woman Beguine writer such as Mechthild nevertheless distrusts her self-confidence as being false pride, and lays stress on obedience to ecclesiastical opinion.

Given such pressures, it is remarkable that medieval women found so many, such varied, and such important outlets for their religious experience. And overt expression is by no means the only valid way of detecting women's voices. One point highlighted by this collection is the value of cross-fertilisation between different types of literature by and for women. Innes-Parker and Phillips both juxtapose texts that would conventionally be put into quite separate categories. They show how 'literature' can illuminate a 'religious' text, and vice versa. Innes-Parker, for instance, shows how subtle critical reading of the *Ancrene Wisse* against the topoi of romance makes inroads into the now canonical view of the lady of the former as a passive, helpless victim, and Phillips, reading Julian of Norwich against the *Chevalier des Dames* which also rewrites the myth of the Fall, shows how the two authors' displacement of Eve as sole agent of the Fall, their unusually positive view of the created world, suggest specifically female revisionary voices.

This revelatory breakdown of distinctions in fact mirrors the artificiality of some of the divisions we have had to make in the papers in these volumes. They are distinguished for modern convenience, rather than medieval reality. We have tried to be relatively open-minded, but any distinction is a brisk reminder that all modern readers impose their own expectations on the evidence. This can work both ways, as several writers show: to return for a moment to Innes-Parker, her close reading of a text points out that previous modern readers, *expecting* misogyny, have done the medieval writer a disservice. It is still too common for modern historians to want medieval women to conform to their own images of what women should be, whether they be traditional or feminist. Refreshingly, it was a touchstone of *Women and the Book* as a conference that polemic was set aside in favour of integrity to the texts and cooperative endeavour. We hope this spirit is reflected in the papers in this volume, and that, like the contributors, its readers will be inspired to discover yet more untapped sources, yet more unexpected convergences, for the sake of the medieval women they will thereby bring to light.

For, finally, we have a number of thanks to express, to those people and institutions without which our conference would have been the poorer, and this volume the more inaccurate. We owe most grateful thanks to the Board of the Faculty of Medieval and Modern Languages of the University of Oxford for generous financial and administrative support both for the conference itself and for the publication of this volume; the Board of the Faculty of Modern History gave us valuable help with printing and administrative costs. During the conference, we were greatly helped by our energetic and enthusiastic 'runners': Philip Durkin, Melanie Florence, Rachel Jones and Corinne Saunders. For help with spreadsheets and logos, we must thank John Gurd and David Snelling. Our most heartfelt thanks are also due to our copy editor, Christina Malkowski Zaba; she has battled valiantly with our unprofessional vagaries, and finally, triumphantly, presented us with copy of remarkable accuracy and consistency. Perhaps most of all, we should thank those who read their papers and those who simply came to our conference. We found it heart-warming to gather so many scholars of all ages and stages, and to work together in so friendly and cooperative a spirit.

Lesley Smith
Jane H. M. Taylor

THE LIMITS OF BIBLE STUDY FOR MEDIEVAL WOMEN

Alcuin Blamires

The humanist Heinrich Cornelius Agrippa von Nettesheim reflected that in some cultures, women had once exercised a degree of autonomy; but, by contrast, in contemporary sixteenth-century Europe,

> That is nowe forbydden by lawes, abolished by custome, extincted by education. For anon as a woman is borne even from her infancy, she is kept at home in ydelnes, & as thoughe she were unmete for any hygher busynesse, she is permitted to know no farther, than her nedle and her threede.[1]

Serious study of the Bible was indubitably among those things widely 'extincted' within a medieval European woman's education, for in theory she was 'not permitted to know' the scriptures except at a rudimentary and largely second-hand level. Were she to show signs of biblical expertise, this was a matter (at the least) for surprise:

> Thanne hadde I wonder in my wit what womman it weere
> That swiche wise wordes of Holy Writ shewed.[2]

Of course medievalists are familiar with the general principle of women's exclusion from formal theological – as from legal, and to a lesser extent, medical – study in the period, and readily attribute this exclusion to male monopolization of powerful professions, combined with ingrained masculine contempt for female intellect.[3] But, we might ask, were male monopoly and assumptions about women's intellectual incapacity among the factors recognized by people who discussed women's access to scriptural study at the time? In fact, who did discuss the issue, and what arguments did they use?

---

1 Linda Woodbridge, *Women and the English Renaissance* (Urbana and Chicago, 1984), 43, quoting from Sig. [F8]–[F8]v of Clapham's 1542 translation (*A Treatise of the Nobilitie and Excellencye of Woman Kynde*) of Agrippa's *De nobilitate et praecellentia Foemenei sexus, Opera* (Lyons, 1531).
2 William Langland, *The Vision of Piers Plowman*, ed. A. V. C. Schmidt (London, 1978), i, 71–2.
3 On women's foothold in medical science, see Joan M. Ferrante, 'The Education of Women in the Middle Ages in Theory, Fact, and Fantasy', in *Beyond Their Sex: Learned Women of the European Past*, ed. Patricia H. Labalme (New York, 1980), 9–42 (18–19).

One answer is available in the form of a thirteenth-century scholastic discussion by Henry of Ghent, which will be the main focus of this paper. It will be salutary, however, to recall first the broad lines of medieval opinion as a context for analysis of Henry's engagement with the topic.

With few exceptions, the church actively discouraged laypersons of either sex from 'meddling' with Holy Writ throughout the Middle Ages. Ecclesiasts felt that Holy Writ would not stay holy if released for wide consumption. It would be cheapened and vulgarized; moreover, untrained minds would misunderstand its secrets and drift into error. Transmission of its doctrine to ordinary folk, *simplices*, was the business of professional preaching clergy.

It was the threat of usurpation of this preaching role by evangelizing lay movements which prompted the most substantial official declarations concerning scriptural study. A seminal instance is the reaction of Pope Innocent III to the activities of Waldensians in and around Metz in the 1190s. The Pope was obliged to write a weighty letter of expostulation in 1199 reinforcing the orthodox position. Having heard that 'multitudes of laymen and women' were circulating biblical translations and holding forth about them, he first reassuringly acknowledged that in itself, 'the desire of understanding holy scriptures' is commendable.[4] However, this conciliatory gesture soon gives way to what was to be a standard defence of the exclusivity of biblical study:

> For such is the depth of divine scripture, that not only the simple and illiterate, but even the prudent and learned, are not fully sufficient to understand it. 'For many seek and fail (*defecerunt scrutantes*, Psalm 63:7)', whence it was of old rightly written in the divine law, 'the beast which touched the mount should be stoned' (Hebrews 12:20; Exodus 19:12), lest, apparently, any simple and unlearned person should presume to attain to the sublimity of holy scripture.[5]

The corollary of this position was that scriptural interpretation was reserved for the clergy. They were to *understand* the faith – as the Carmelite Thomas Netter insisted in the fifteenth century – whereas the rest of the people were simply to *believe* it.[6]

Heterodox movements retorted that one could not uphold the 'untouchability' of scripture if its doctrine was at the same time deemed crucial to salvation. Far from merely touching it, all Christians should stretch forth their arms and hands, one Wycliffite later pointedly declared, 'to enbrace to hemsilf the lawe of God [i.e. the Bible]';[7] and Wyclif persistently argued for open

---

[4] Innocent III, *Epistolae*, ii, 141, PL 214:695–98 (695). For partial translation of the letter and comment, see Margaret Deanesly, *The Lollard Bible and Other Medieval Biblical Versions* (Cambridge, 1920), 30–1.

[5] PL 214:696.

[6] 'Vere infra eundem ambitum fidei periti spirituales dicuntur *intelligere*: caeteri populares solum simpliciter *credere*', Thomas Netter of Walden, *Doctrinale Antiquitatum Fidei Catholicae Ecclesiae*, ed. B. Blanciotti (Venice, 1757–9), ii, Chap. 44, col. 277.

[7] From the tract known as *The holy prophet David saith*, in Deanesly, *Lollard Bible*, 445–56 (456).

communication of scripture to everyone, since it contained what was 'necessary for salvation'.[8]

Just what kind of biblical knowledge was necessary for salvation, and for whom, evidently constituted contested ground in the Middle Ages, though rulings on the matter would have varied according to context. Within the bounds of orthodoxy it was possible to justify a woman's right to read, for reasons which sound ostensibly like Wyclif's. I am thinking of the well-known opinion ventured by Geoffroy de la Tour-Landry in the 1370s in his handbook for his daughters, that reading is profitable for all women because 'a woman that can rede may better knowe the peryls of the sowle and her sauement'. But the reading he envisages (to judge from hints scattered in the book) is probably didactic and liturgical rather than scriptural, and in any case his point is expressly made in defiance of a contrary male view that wives and daughters should know nothing of books.[9]

Although estimates of women's literacy in the Middle Ages are currently being revised upwards, there seems no reason to doubt that, even among a laity whose access to scripture was restricted, women were peculiarly 'disenscriptured'.[10] Part of the evidence for this emerges in the nuance of derision with which church officials confronted the prospect of female Bible training. An Inquisitor complained of the Waldensians in the mid-thirteenth century that 'they teach even little girls the words of the gospels and epistles': two centuries later the Archbishop of Mainz was still registering the same dismay when he asked who would enable 'simple and uneducated men, and even women' to understand the sacred books if they were widely available.[11]

Like other unclerical folk, but more definitively, women were expected to gain their salvation on a diet of extracts of scripture and substitute scripture: extracts, available in liturgical books and in moral primers incorporating elementary biblical matter such as the Ten Commandments or the Paternoster; and substitute scripture, in the form of lives of Christ and gospel summaries or paraphrases. The only part of the Bible which was exempted from clerical monopoly, and perhaps considered particularly suitable for women, was the Psalms. Ferrante mentions a thirteenth-century satirist who advises delinquent male students to muster at least a knowledge of the Psalter and the canonical

---

However, the extent to which Lollard, and before them Cathar, women could put such advice into practice as readers has been questioned respectively by Shannon McSheffrey and Peter Biller in their articles below.

[8] E.g. *De Veritate sacrae scripturae*, ed. R. Buddensieg, Wyclif Soc. (London, 1905), ii, 138; and *De Eucharistia*, ed. Iohann Loserth, Wyclif Soc. (London, 1892), 47.

[9] William Caxton (transl.), *The Book of the Knight of the Tower*, ed. M. Y. Offord, EETS, Supplementary Series, 2 (London, 1971), Chap. lxxxix, 122.

[10] Royal and aristocratic women were the most persistent exceptions to the rule; Ferrante, 'Education of Women', 9–11; Deanesly, *Lollard Bible*, 18–22, 278–80.

[11] Respectively David of Augsburg (d.1272), and Berthold of Henneburg (commenting on the availability of printed bibles in 1486); Deanesly, *Lollard Bible*, 63, 125.

hours, which will enable them to fall back on teaching girls if necessary.[12] This jibe is consistent with the prominence of Psalters in wealthy women's wills to the end of the Middle Ages, as well as with the kind of policy which the church had attempted to establish at the synod of Toulouse (1229), prohibiting the laity from owning books of scripture except Psalters and books of divine office.[13] Actually the tradition of female psalm-reading has a long history: Jerome tells us that in Paula's fourth-century monastery at Bethlehem 'none of the sisters was allowed to be ignorant of the Psalms'.[14]

It may be objected that women leading a religious life frequently engaged in biblical study. However, their prospects and facilities for doing so seem to have been generally more substantial in the early church and in the Saxon period than they were to become subsequently. A significant decline in female Latinity has been detected between the eleventh century and the time of the *Ancrene Wisse* (late twelfth or early thirteenth century) whose author has lower expectations of his charges' biblical attainments than had his predecessors in the genre.[15] It can be argued that the availability of Vulgates in nunneries was rather slight, on the evidence of library data and wills;[16] and it has been pointed out that even Dominican sisters, amongst whom some theological ambition might have been predicted, were by no means expected to emulate the academic efforts of their brothers.[17] Finally, it is instructive to discover that the direct knowledge of the Vulgate usually ascribed to so celebrated a holy woman as Julian of Norwich may be open to question as an editorial delusion.[18]

The Wycliffites sometimes spoke in terms of authorities 'stopping' or 'shutting up' scripture so that laypeople could not get at it. By the thirteenth century, women could not get at institutional study of it at all. They were debarred from the universities, which quickly became the most prestigious

---

[12] 'Education of Women', 12.

[13] On Psalters in English women's wills, see Carol M. Meale, ' "... alle the bokes that I haue of latyn, englisch, and frensch": Laywomen and their Books in Late Medieval England', in *Women and Literature in Britain 1150–1500*, ed. Meale (Cambridge, 1993), 128–58 (130–1, 132, 136, 144). On the synod of Toulouse (reacting to heresy in southern France), see Deanesly, *Lollard Bible*, 36–7. Chrétien's Laudine exemplifies the twelfth-century noblewoman reading a Psalter; *Le Chevalier au Lion*, ed. Mario Roques (Paris, 1965), 1418–19.

[14] Jerome, *Epistle* 108; transl. Elizabeth A. Clark, *Women in the Early Church* (Wilmington, 1983), 135.

[15] A point explored in Gopa Roy in Chap. 10 below. See also Charles Jourdain, 'Mémoire sur l'éducation des femmes au moyen âge', *Mémoires de l'Institut National de France: Académie des Inscriptions et Belles-Lettres* (Paris: Imprimerie Nationale, 1974), 79–133.

[16] Deanesly, *Lollard Bible*, 109–16. A more positive impression emerges in Ferrante, citing e.g. the nun Diemud of Wessobrun who listed multi-volume Bibles among books she had personally produced, 'Education of Women', 16.

[17] Edward T. Brett, *Humbert of Romans: His Life and Views of Thirteenth-Century Society* (Toronto, 1984), 77 and 79, referring to details of the Dominican constitutions.

[18] A view persuasively argued by Nicholas Watson in his paper 'How "Learned" Was Julian of Norwich?' given at the conference, 'Women and the Book in the Middle Ages', St Hilda's College, Oxford (August, 1993).

centres for biblical analysis; and it is to the university context that we must turn in order to locate an extended discussion of women's ability to undertake formal biblical study. The discussion occurs as a *Quaestio* of the *Summa quaestionum ordinarium* (a compilation of lectures on theological knowledge, dating from 1276–92) by Henry of Ghent, a secular master whose career at the University of Paris followed shortly after that of Aquinas. The relevant *Quaestio* has been presented before by Alistair Minnis, who has done important pioneering work on Henry of Ghent.[19] However, since Minnis does not set Henry's discussion within the wider context of controversy about access to scripture, and since he does not have space to subject the *Quaestio* to the degree of probing it really invites, I think it worthwhile to take a second look at it here.

Having considered who may teach theology in Article 11 of his *Summa*,[20] Henry proceeds to discuss what categories of people may study it in Article 12: a youth? a sinner? anyone (*omnis homo*)? someone not educated in secular knowledge? Heading the list – for reasons other than courtesy, as I shall later suggest – is the *Quaestio* 'Whether a Woman may learn Sacred Scripture' (*Utrum mulier possit esse auditor sacrae scripturae*).[21]

The terminology used here prompts two observations. One is that Henry's use of *auditor* and *audio* throughout Article 12 is semi-technical,[22] and should be distinguished from the 'listening' implicit in, say, the memorization of sacred text practised by Waldensians and Lollards – and by Margery Kempe. Felicity Riddy (among others) has recently drawn attention to the importance of 'auditory culture', of the 'textuality of the spoken word', among networks of medieval women.[23] Henry, however, has two particular aural circumstances in mind. Primarily he is referring to the formal context of lecturer and listening students in the university theology course, which involved four years of attending lectures on the Bible and two more on the *Sentences* of Peter Lombard. The use of *auditor* has the further advantage that it allows him to encompass an alternative mode of 'listening' to discourse on scripture, namely at sermons. Something of this range of reference can be preserved if we use the translation 'learn/learner' in the present discussion.

The second observation prompted by the Question's terminology is simple

---

[19] A. J. Minnis, 'The *Accessus* Extended: Henry of Ghent on the Transmission and Reception of Theology', in *Ad litteram: Authoritative Texts and Their Medieval Readers*, ed. Mark D. Jordan and Kent Emery, Jr. (Notre Dame, 1992), 275–326 (314–16).

[20] For the text of Henry's refutation of women's right to teach, see Alcuin Blamires and C. W. Marx, 'Woman Not to Preach: A Disputation in British Library MS Harley 31', *Journal of Medieval Latin*, 3 (1993), 34–63 (50–55).

[21] Quotations are from *Magistri Henrici Goethals a Gandavo . . . Summa in tres partes praecipuas digesta*, 3 vols. (Ferrara, 1642–46), i, 208–10. For an alternative edition see *Summa quaestionum ordinarium theologii . . . Henrici a Gandavo* (Paris, 1520).

[22] R. E. Latham, *Revised Medieval Latin Word-List* (London, 1965), *audio*, 'to study, attend lectures' (from c.1180).

[23] ' "Women Talking about the Things of God" ', in *Women and Literature in Britain*, ed. Meale, 104–27 (111–15).

but far-reaching. *Mulier*, 'woman', is used as an essentializing term almost throughout. The issue is absolute. All female eligibility for institutional biblical study is at stake.

Scholastic Questions characteristically open by posing, in their strongest form, arguments which the teacher wishes to challenge or qualify. Henry posits two such arguments (12.1.1–2). First (the point which was to be taken up by Wycliffites), one must learn whatever is necessary for salvation; scriptural knowledge is, according to St Augustine, among the things necessary for salvation; therefore, women should learn it. Second – in effect restating this in abstract terms – nothing imperfect should be prevented from seeking to perfect itself; women and men alike are imperfect in knowledge and virtue, but can improve through learning scriptural knowledge, so should not be prevented from learning it.

A flatly contradictory point, required to set up the debate, is now brought forward (12.1.3). Since the relevant knowledge is formally taught (*legatur*) only at public lectures, women are debarred from it on the basis of the Pauline edict, 'if they would learn anything, let them ask their husbands at home'.[24] (Henry will later query, if not as fruitfully as one would wish, this contradiction's assumptions about where scripture is taught, and about women's marital status.)

The next stage of the *Quaestio* is to indicate the main lines of the teacher's response (12.1.4) to the problem thus posed. Rather disarmingly, Henry intimates agreement with the first proposition. He states that whoever is to be instructed in a subject must in some way (*aliquo modo*) learn it. Whatever aspects (*quaecunque*) of sacred knowledge it is necessary for both man and woman to know in order to be saved, must accordingly be learned. It is therefore necessary to assert that any Christian – *etiam mulier*, 'woman too', 'even woman' – ought to learn this knowledge.

Within this show of agreement Henry has of course reserved crucial exceptions in the small print (everyone must 'in some way' learn 'whatever aspects. . .'). He will now proceed with a series of distinctions based on those reservations, which enable him systematically to curtail woman's scope for investigation of scripture. It is an object-lesson in medieval patriarchy's most notorious art, the art of enclosure.

Henry has been using *scientia*, 'knowledge', as shorthand for 'knowledge of sacred scripture'. Recalling that Augustine has much to say in *De Trinitate* about the hierarchy of wisdom and knowledge, he reproduces (12.1.5) Augustine's distinction between two grades of *scientia*, which I shall designate as an ordinary personal one and a superior executive one:

> One mode of knowing is to know only what ought to be believed and what ought to be done in order to attain eternal life. Another mode is to

---

[24] I Corinthians 14:35.

6

know how this belief itself may both help the pious and how it may be defended against the impious.[25]

The executive mode of knowledge, argues Henry, presupposes a capacity for learning scripture's profundities and for defending them in public. Woman is disqualified on both counts. She cannot teach in public, as has been urged previously in Article 11, Quaestio 2 of the *Summa*. Nor, owing to the weakness of womanly intellect (*debilitas ingenii muliebris*), is it possible for her to reach the perfection in this knowledge required to defend the faith: indeed, rather than making progress by investigating the sacred mysteries, she regresses through error (*potius errando deficeret, quam proficeret*, the verb *deficeret* perhaps recalling the same Psalter text alluded to by Innocent III).

Ingrained masculine contempt for female intellect has made a conspicuous early appearance in the *Quaestio*, eliminating woman from the higher mode of 'knowing'. Not content with bisecting *scientia* once, however, Henry now moves (1.6) to operate the Augustinian distinction again in order to bisect the bisegment into which he has confined woman. He distinguishes two modes of learning what one must believe and do: an ordinary personal mode whereby one discovers what is necessary given one's station (*secundum statum*), and another more expansive mode whereby one learns, in addition, things extrinsic to one's station. Inevitably the consequence of the distinction is to restrict woman's learning so that she will not be instructed in things not proper to her *status*.

It is interesting to note that Henry, normally assiduous in subdivision, refuses to subdivide the female *status*. There would have been some precedent for doing so in contemporary sermons and even in disputations.[26] When the Franciscan Eustace of Arras debated women's right to preach in the 1260s, he distinguished a 'chosen' or 'privileged' category of women not covered by St Paul's prohibition: he suggested that Paul's doctrine extended only to 'married' women, those in the usual position (*in statu communi*) of women.[27] Henry, far from countenancing variations in female *status*, anxiously elaborates his argument for general restriction of woman's biblical education. The shadow of Waldensian, Cathar, and perhaps Beguine, translation activities stirs up underlying misogynistic cliché. He insists that a wise teacher ought to propound to a woman only what she 'needs' to know of scriptural matters, despite women's characteristic curiosity about other things not beneficial to their *status*: it is above all folly to 'unfold the mysteries of scripture to them and translate the sacred books for them to read in the vernacular'.

---

[25] Minnis tries to trace this in *De civitate Dei* ('The *Accessus* Extended', 326, n. 152), but as the Ferrara edition indicates, it is from *De Trinitate*, 14.1.3, PL 42:1037.

[26] Sermon collections addressed separate groups such as wives, widows, orders of nuns and prostitutes; Brett, *Humbert of Romans*, 69.

[27] *Utrum mulier praedicando et docendo mereatur aureolam*, in Jean Leclercq, 'Le Magistère du prédicateur au XIIIe siècle', *Archives d'histoire doctrinale et littéraire du Moyen Age*, 21 (1946), 105–47 (119–20).

A modern reader might be forgiven for suspecting that the *Quaestio* im-
plodes altogether at this juncture. A foregone conclusion that it is stupid to
allow woman anything but a policed trickle of elementary doctrine because of
her intellectually regressive, lowly and private status, has been dressed up as
the consequence – rather than the motive – of a *distinctio* in 'modes of knowing'. But Henry has not finished, for he has not yet altogether cast woman out
of the precincts of formal biblical education; this he remedies by finally introducing a distinction (12.1.7) between the public lecture – in which scripture is
systematically propounded, its profundities analysed – and preaching. Since
we already know that woman cannot cope with biblical profundities and that
she cannot learn in a situation of public debate, her exclusion from formal
theological lectures is now a matter of course. She is very welcome to learn
about scripture by attending sermons instead.

By listening to public or private sermons (a distinction to which we shall
return), women may learn appropriate biblical matter, because preachers
should not aim to expound anything more esoteric than whatever facilitates
the salvation of people of ordinary station (*communem statum*). Henry declares
that this is the sort of learning (still using the language of 'hearing', *audiendi*)
which is referred to in a controversial Old Testament passage:

> thou shalt read the words of this law before all Israel . . . men, women,
> children and strangers . . . so that hearing [*audientes*] they may learn, and
> fear the Lord, and keep and fulfil all the words of this law. (Deuteronomy
> 31:11–12)

One can instantly see how useful such a passage could be to those who wanted
to broaden access to scripture, and how important it is for Henry to accommodate it safely within his own scheme.

Even as the *Quaestio* concludes, more restrictive clauses pile up. While a
woman can learn at a sermon, she is not to question the preacher in public if
she wants to pursue a point he has made, but should ask her husband privately at home – or, alternatively, ask 'whoever ought to occupy a husband's
place in relation to her in such a matter'. Henry's careful diction actually
leaves unclear whether we are to think here in terms of an unmarried or
widowed woman consulting a male guardian, or whether he has in mind the
possibility of personal scriptural education, for any woman, by a spiritual
director. (The latter could also explain his reference to 'private' preaching,
though more likely that expression presupposes a small group gathered in a
private chapel.) To the extent that scriptural tutorials are envisaged, Henry has
tacitly conceded the possibility of advanced study; and to the extent that
tutorials outside as well as inside the marital state are envisaged, he has
momentarily acknowledged what the rest of the *Quaestio* does not, that
'woman' is not an indivisible category.

Such possibilities barely affect the *Quaestio*'s conclusion, which articulates
summary responses to the two initial arguments 'for'. Yes, a woman is

certainly allowed to learn about sacred scripture, but only those aspects which are necessary for her salvation, and only by listening to public or private preaching (12.1.8). And no, it is not ordained that she should be able to perfect herself in knowledge of theology in this life, except to the extent that is sufficient for her to gain eternity, where everything mortal is perfected anyway (12.1.9).

Apart from feeling that the 'perfectibility' argument deserves more than this curt slamming of the door, what are we to make of Henry's conclusions in their immediate and wider context? It is important to stress, first, that the next *Quaestio* (12.2) goes on to justify the exclusion of youth (*iuuenis*) from theological study. Woman is not the only category barred. On the other hand, invidious comparisons can be made between the first and sixth Questions. *Quaestio* 6 asks 'whether every person (*omnis homo*) should learn this knowledge'.[28] Using a procedure similar to that in *Quaestio* 1, it distinguishes one group of people, *quidam hominum*, insufficiently endowed with *ingenium*, intellectual capacity, to engage effectively with scriptural mysteries or to instruct others in them (12.6.5). Therefore these people are responsible only for the care of their own salvation, not that of others, and preachers provide them with appropriate knowledge. However there are other people endowed with excellent natural intellect (12.6.6) who, if no other legitimate business or vocation preoccupies them, are urgently obligated to study scripture because each of us must eventually render an account of the talent entrusted to us (12.6.8, 12.6.10).

At first sight this discussion of 'everyone's' right to learn (*homo* being a gender-inclusive term) seems odd. After all, Henry has dealt with woman: why apparently re-open her eligibility by subsequently broaching a wider category? The situation is nevertheless clarified if we remember that woman's debility of intellect has been decided in *Quaestio* 1, and thus that she is automatically subsumed into the first group (the low-achievers, as it were) in *Quaestio* 6. After the earlier discussion, anyone of strong intellect was going to have to be male anyway, so the obligation to apply intellectual talents to theological study was only going to be a moral imperative for males – even in a debate about 'everyone'.

To today's reader most of this will seem hopelessly perverse: mere confirmation that Henry speaks from the heart of a male-exclusive theological establishment, that he has prejudged absolutely the answer to the question of women's right to study before working out how to reach it, and that he grinds the machinery of scholastic distinctions into action expressly to distinguish woman out of earshot of the lecture room. By the same token Albertus Magnus had asked 'whether the male is more apt at learning good behaviour than the female', knowing that of course the male must be, even though he had to distinguish his way around an influential Aristotelian principle (connecting

---

[28] *Summa*, 218–21.

softness of skin with sensory superiority and intellectual potential) in order to prove it.[29]

None the less, admitting that the *Quaestio* demonstrates that Henry shared the pervasive medieval masculine disdain of female intellect and the pervasive medieval masculine revulsion from female intrusion into the domain of public speaking, and admitting that considerations of logic – the calculus of elimination – as much as any more interesting factors probably catapulted woman into prominence at the head of this section of his *Summa*, there yet remain enough traces of certain extrinsic factors to warrant a tentative historicization of the discussion in the first *Quaestio*. Two interrelated pressures come to mind.

First, the twelfth and thirteenth centuries had seen a large increase in the numbers of female religious. The proliferation of Cistercian, then Dominican and Franciscan sisterhoods had resulted in considerable and vexed discussion about the extent of the male orders' responsibilities towards the women's houses. By the mid-thirteenth century, women religious must everywhere have seemed more visible, more a force to be reckoned with. And by the time Henry was lecturing, the Beguines (though recently favoured in Paris when Louis IX founded a Beguinage there in 1264) were becoming a focus of controversy, since they were among the implicit targets of repressive legislation at the Council of Lyons in 1274.[30] That women themselves did not necessarily agitate about participating more fully in educational and sacerdotal spheres can be inferred from the example of Christina of St Trond, a holy woman (1150–1224) whose *Vita* reveals that she could readily interpret the Vulgate, but who nevertheless considered biblical exposition to be the clergy's prerogative, not hers.[31] However, the latter part of the century shows continuing anxiety to head off the awesome possibility of female competition and reinforce the male clerical hegemony: a persistent rivulet of *quaestiones* deals with women's power to be priests, preachers or, in the present case, theological students.[32]

---

[29] A point excellently demonstrated in J. D. Burnley, 'Criseyde's Heart and the Weakness of Women', *Studia Neophilologica*, 54 (1982), 25–38 (33–5); see also Joan Cadden, *Meanings of Sex Difference in the Middle Ages* (Cambridge, 1993), 185. The issue resurfaces in 1487 when Bartolomeo Goggio 'cites Aristotle's statement that soft flesh is an indicator of intelligence to prove that women are more intelligent than men'; *De laudibus mulierum*, ch. 5, quoted by Pamela Joseph Benson, *The Invention of the Renaissance Woman* (Philadelphia, 1992), 58.

[30] On these developments see R. W. Southern, *Western Society and the Church in the Middle Ages* (Harmondsworth, 1970), 312–31; Brenda Bolton, 'Mulieres Sanctae', in *Women in Medieval Society*, ed. Susan Mosher Stuard (Philadelphia, 1976), 141–58; Sally Thompson, 'The Problem of the Cistercian Nuns in the Twelfth and Early Thirteenth Centuries', in *Medieval Women*, ed. Derek Baker, *Studies in Church History*, Subsidia, i (Oxford, 1978), 227–52; and Brett, *Humbert of Romans*, 57–79.

[31] Brenda Bolton, '*Vitae Matrum*: A Further Aspect of the *Frauenfrage*', in *Medieval Women*, ed. Baker, 253–73 (269); but the opinion is ascribed to Christina by a male, Thomas of Cantimpré.

[32] On the debate about priests see Francine Cardman, 'The Medieval Question of Women and Orders', *The Thomist*, 42 (1978), 582–99, and John H. Martin, 'The Ordination of Women and the Theologians in the Middle Ages', *Escritos del Vedat*, 16 (1986), 115–77; and on preaching see Alcuin Blamires, 'Women and Preaching in Medieval Orthodoxy, Heresy, and Saints' Lives', *Viator*, 26 (1995).

If defensive tactics were called for against pressure (real or imagined) from within the church, a second factor influencing Henry's *Quaestio* was surely pressure from without it. His irascibility concerning the translation of scripture for women, his sniggering about women 'regressing through error' rather than 'progressing' by study, betray a residual nervousness whose roots were in the dismay felt by orthodox circles at the popularization of the Bible attempted by Waldensian and Cathar men and women. Part of the hidden agenda, as Henry's reference to 'error' suggests, is fear of women as consumers and agents of heterodoxy.

It is instructive to go back to a treatise associated with orthodoxy's earliest skirmishes against the Waldensians. It was written by Abbot Bernard of Fontcaude around 1190 as a guide to the refutation of Waldensian errors, soon after a debate with sect leaders in Narbonne.[33] Significantly, Bernard maintains that these heretics 'have regressed rather than progressed' in the faith: *haeretici non profecerunt, imo defecerunt*.[34] In one chapter he deals with their advocacy of female preaching. In another he discusses 'what sort of people the Waldensians chiefly seduce', identifying the first three most vulnerable categories as: 'women; men of womanly rather than manly character; and inexperienced men'.[35] Like many churchmen before him, Bernard equates heretication with feminization. He quotes Proverbs 9:13–16 concerning the 'foolish woman and clamorous, and full of allurements, and knowing nothing at all' who calls 'little ones' to turn to her. The foolish clamorous woman, he claims, signifies 'heretical depravity', and is intellectually stupid and noisily garrulous; so heresy is a specious 'female' lure for naïve males. A variant of this gendering appears some thirty years later in a Vienna manuscript of the *Bible moralisée*. Below one roundel depicting the sons of Eli about to rape some women assembled at the door of the tabernacle[36] is a complementary scene of students swayed by heretical teachers. The marginal interpretation explains that

> the women signify *simplices*, unlearned men who come before depraved philosophers and are deceived by their perverted proofs.[37]

Leaving aside the complication whereby heretics can be rapists, we may conclude that, given an ubiquitous stereotype of the potentially or actually heretical mind as female, and given the anxieties accumulating in the thirteenth century because of women's roles in 'fringe' religious movements, we should

---

33 See *Heresies of the Middle Ages*, ed. Walter L. Wakefield and Austin P. Evans (New York, 1969), 210–13; and *Adversus Waldensium sectam liber*, PL 204:793–840.

34 PL 204:806.

35 'Seducunt ergo mulieres; viros, non viriliter, sed muliebriter agentes; imperitos', PL 204:821.

36 I Kings 2: 22.

37 Vienna, ÖNB cod. 1179, f.86r; reproduced and discussed in Sara Lipton, 'Jews, Heretics and the Sign of the Cat in the *Bible moralisée*', *Word and Image*, 8 (1992), 362–77 (373–4).

11

not expect Henry to do otherwise than eject woman from the theological academy as unsuitable for training. On the other hand, the wonder is that he gives her so much attention – a whole *Quaestio* to herself. This I take to be a symptom of the expanding female confidence at that epoch triggering a strategy of containment, as much as a symptom of habitually repressive male ideology.

THE ABSENT PENITENT: THE CURE OF WOMEN'S SOULS AND CONFESSORS' MANUALS IN THIRTEENTH-CENTURY ENGLAND

Jacqueline Murray

In 1215 the Fourth Lateran Council promulgated a series of canons designed to renew the spiritual life of the Church. Some canons concerned themselves with the education and mode of life of the clergy, while others were more concerned with the laity. Without a doubt the canon that has generally been regarded as having the broadest impact on the subsequent spiritual development of Christendom is Canon 21, *Omnis utriusque sexus*, which states in part that:

> All of the faithful of both sexes shall, after they have reached the age of discretion, faithfully confess all their sins at least once a year to their own (parish) priest and perform to the best of their ability the penance imposed, . . . [1]

In many ways this canon only served to institutionalize and universalize the practice of regular confession which had become common at the local level as part of the resurgence of popular piety in the late twelfth and early thirteenth centuries.[2] Individual confession was as much a grassroots development as it was an requirement imposed on the faithful from above.

The obligation of annual confession placed new responsibilities on the

---

1 'Omnis utriusque sexus fidelis, postquam ad annos discretionis pervenerit, omnia sua solus peccata confiteatur fideliter, saltem semel in anno proprio sacerdoti, et iniunctam sibi poenitentiam studeat pro viribus adimplere . . .' *Conciliorum Oecumenicorum Decreta*, ed. Josepho Algerigo et al., 3rd edn (Bologna: Istituto per le Scienze Religiose, 1973), 245. Translated in H. J. Schroeder, *Disciplinary Decrees of the General Councils: Text, Translations, and Commentary* (St Louis, 1937), 259–60. This study was undertaken while I held a Canada Research Fellowship and I am grateful to the Social Science and Humanities Research Council of Canada for their support. I would also like to thank Dr Joseph Goering and Dr Abigail Young for their intellectual generosity.
2 E.g. the Council of Paris (1198) and the Council of Westminster (1200) both included instructions for the conduct of confessions. See Council of Paris (1198), C. VI, c. 1. in J. Dominique Mansi (ed.) *Sacrorum Conciliorum nova et amplissima collectio*, vol. xxii (Venice, 1776), col. 678; and Council of Westminster (1200), C. 4 in *Councils and Synods with Other Documents relating to the English Church. I. AD 871–1204*, ed. D. Whitelock, M. Brett and C. N. L. Brooke (Oxford, 1981), pt. 2, 1062.

shoulders of the parish clergy, many of whom were ill-prepared to exercise the cure of souls. As Alexander Murray has stated, the parish priest was now 'bombarded daily with individual problems which thirsted for a more realistic, solid guide to ethics than the schoolmen had so far provided'.[3] Thus, in order to prepare the local clergy to undertake their spiritual duties, and especially to hear confessions and enjoin penances, special manuals for confessors began to be written. Starting at the beginning of the thirteenth century, they appeared with greater frequency after the Fourth Lateran Council's legislation.[4] These manuals, with their simplified presentation of canon law and theology, also constructed the parochial clergy's view of sin and the sinner. The information they presented and how they presented it informed to a large degree the conduct of confession at the parish level; and, consequently, through the mediation of the parish priest, they also influenced the individual's experience of the sacrament, in so far as it was constructed by the confessor.[5]

The important relationship between confession, pastoral manuals and the construction of gender has been highlighted by a number of scholars. Jean Longère has compared the attitudes to women found in conciliar and synodal legislation with those in pastoral manuals.[6] Ivan Illich, somewhat eccentrically and idiosyncratically, has condemned confession and pastoral manuals for

---

[3] Alexander Murray, "Confession as a Historical Source in the Thirteenth Century", in *The Writing of History in the Middle Ages*, ed. R. H. C. Davis and J. M. Wallace-Hadrill (Oxford, 1981), 308.

[4] Leonard E. Boyle has written extensively on the development of confessors' manuals. See, in particular, "The Inter-Conciliar Period 1179–1215 and the Beginnings of Pastoral Manuals", in *Miscellanea Rolando Bandinelli Papa Alessandro III* (Siena, 1986); "*Summa confessorum*", in *Les genres littéraires dans les sources théologiques et philosophiques médiévales: définition, critique et exploitation*, Université Catholique de Louvain. Publications de l'Institut d'Etudes Médiévales ser. 2/5 (Louvain-la-neuve, 1982), 227–37; and "The Summa for Confessors as a Genre, and its Religious Intent", in *The Pursuit of Holiness in Late Medieval and Renaissance Religion*, ed. Charles Trinkaus and Heiko A. Oberman, Studies in Medieval and Renaissance Thought, 10 (Leiden, 1974), 126–30; Jean Longère, "Quelques *Summa de poenitentia* à la fin du XIIe et au début du XIIIe siècle", in *Actes du 99e Congrès national des Sociétés Savantes, Besançon, 1974. Section de philologie et d'histoire jusqu'à 1610*, i, *La Piété populaire au Moyen Age* (Paris, 1977), 45–58; Pierre Michaud-Quantin, "A propos des premières summae confessorum: théologie et droit canonique", *Recherches de Théologie ancienne et médiévale*, 26 (1959), 264–306; "Les méthodes de la pastorale du XIIIe au XVe siècle", in *Methoden in Wissenschaft und Kunst des Mittelalters*, ed. Albert Zimmermann, Miscellanea Medievalia 7 (Berlin, 1970), 76–91, and *Sommes de casuistique et manuels de confession au Moyen Age (XII–XVI siècles)*, Analecta Mediaevalia Namurcensia 13 (Louvain, 1962); Thomas N. Tentler, *Sin and Confession on the Eve of the Reformation* (Princeton, 1977); "The Summa for Confessors as an Instrument of Social Control", in *Pursuit of Holiness*, 103–26.

[5] Allen J. Frantzen has presented a challenging reflection of penitential literature and its location at the intersection of oral and textual culture. His points on how the penitentials modified the confessional context can apply equally to this later genre. "Préface à la Traduction de 1990", *La Littérature de la pénitence dans l'Angleterre anglo-saxonne*, transl. Michel Lejeune (Fribourg, 1991), pp. xiii–xxx.

[6] Jean Longère, "La femme dans la théologie pastorale", in *La femme dans la vie religieuse du Languedoc (xiiie–xive s.)*, Cahiers de Fanjeaux, 23 (Toulouse, 1988), 127–52.

blurring traditional gender distinctions, introducing the notion of the gender-less human being and proposing that men and women commit the same sins despite their biological differences.[7] The relative neglect of women of the upper ranks and their particular sins by the authors of English confessors' manuals has been noted.[8] Most recently, Peter Biller has compared pastoral manuals from northwestern and southern Europe to show how they rein-forced the traditional values and gender systems common to each region.[9]

Yet, as we examine pastoral manuals for the information they contain about women, it is important to remember that confession developed originally in a masculine monastic environment.[10] For all that it was embraced by the laity, male and female alike, the sacrament of confession and the literature associ-ated with it ultimately reflected male concerns and values. The fact that the Fourth Lateran Council felt it necessary to state explicitly that both sexes were required to confess suggests that there was some question or perceived an-drocentric bias even then. Thus, we do well to question the very institution of confession and penance and examine the extent to which it was woman-sensitive or even woman-friendly.

Certainly, women appear to have developed early on a particular affinity for confession, and the special relationship which could develop between a woman and her confessor has been attested to in the lives of many medieval saints and holy women. For example, in the early thirteenth century, Marie d'Oignies and Jacques de Vitry developed a close and mutually supportive relationship. Indeed, de Vitry is just one of many examples of confessors who recorded the *vitae* of the holy women to whom they ministered and served as confessors and spiritual directors.[11]

The later example of Margery Kempe, however, ought to caution us against idealizing the relationship between confessor and female penitent. Margery's experience of confession was frustrating, as she reports at the beginning of her book:

> And when she came to the point for to say that thing which she had so long concealed, her confessor was a little too hasty and began sharply to reprove her, before she had fully said her intent, and so she would no

---

7 Ivan Illich, *Gender* (New York, 1982), 153.
8 Mary Flowers Braswell, "Sin, the Lady, and the Law. The English Noblewoman in the Later Middle Ages," *Medievalia et Humanistica*, (n.s.) 14 (1986), 81–101.
9 P. P. A. Biller, "Marriage Patterns and Women's Lives: A Sketch of a Pastoral Geography", in *Woman is a Worthy Wight. Women in English Society c.1200–1500*, ed. P. J. P. Goldberg (Stroud, 1992), 60–107. My own work has stressed the diversity in the understanding of gender found in these manuals. See Jacqueline Murray, "Thinking About Gender: The Diversity of Medieval Perspectives", in *Power of the Weak?*, ed. Sally-Beth MacLean and Jennifer Carpenter (forthcom-ing, Univ. of Illinois Press).
10 Emile Amann, "Pénitence privée; son organisation; premières spéculations à son sujet", *Dictionnaire de Théologie Catholique* xii, pt. 1, cols. 851–3.
11 Jacques de Vitry, *The Life of Marie d'Oignies*, transl. Margot H. King (Toronto, 1993).

more say for aught he might do. Anon, for the dread she had of damnation on the one side, and his sharp reproving of her on the other side, this creature went out of her mind . . .[12]

Elsewhere, she complains to her regular confessor that 'He that is my confessor in your absence is right sharp with me; he will not believe my feelings, he setteth naught by them; he holdeth them but trifles and japes, and that is great pain to me, for I love him well and would fain follow his counsel'.[13] Thus Margery describes confessors who were so critical, inattentive, impatient and disbelieving that not only was she left spiritually bereft but was also driven to mental breakdown.

We might be tempted to dismiss these complaints as the exaggerations of a particularly difficult woman who would have tried the patience of the most sympathetic confessor. Margery's complaints, however, take on a more insistent and ominous tone in the light of advice given by Humbert of Romans in his *Instructiones de Officiis Ordinis*, written in the mid-thirteenth century, while he was Master General of the Dominicans. In his discussion of the office of confessor Humbert includes a short section entitled 'Concerning Women', which advises:

> Let him restrain those [women] who are called beguines, and wish to confess frequently, let [the confessor] restrain them from this excessive and almost useless frequency, and let him assign to them a set time for confession, outside of which he will not hear them, nor let him make himself available to them ever in other frequent conversations, and always let him use rather harsh and rigid words towards them, rather than soft ones.[14]

This suggests that Margery's problem with an unsympathetic confessor might reflect not the experience of an individual, difficult personality, but rather a

---

[12] '&, whan sche cam to þe poynt for to seyn þat þing whech sche had so long conselyd, hir confessowr was a lytyl to hastye & gan scharply to vndyrnemyn hir er þan sche had fully seyd hir entent, & so sche wold no mor seyn for nowt he mygth do. And a-noon, for dreed sche had of dampnacyon on þe to syde & hys scharp repreuyng on þat oþer syde, þis creatur went owt of hir mende . . .' *The Book of Margery Kempe*, ed. Sanford Brown Meech and Hope Emily Allen, EETS 212 (London, 1940), 7. The modern translation is from William Butler-Bowdon (ed.), *The Book of Margery Kempe* (London, 1936), 23–4.

[13] 'He þat is my confessowr in 3owr absens is rygth scharp vn-to me. He wyl not levyn my felyngys; he settyth nowt by hem; he heldyth hem but tryfelys & japys. & þat is a gret peyn vn-to me, for I lofe hym wele & I wold fawyn folwyn hys cownsel.' Meech and Allen, *Margery Kempe*, 44. The modern translation is found in Butler-Bowdon, *Margery Kempe*, 75. For a discussion of Margery's experience of confession see Clarissa W. Atkinson, *Mystic and Pilgrim. The Book and the World of Margery Kempe* (Ithaca, NY, 1983), 116–17.

[14] 'Illas vero, quae vocantur *Beghinae*, et frequenter volunt confiteri, temperet ab hujusmodi nimia et quasi inutili frequentatione, et certum tempus eis assignet ad confitendum, extra quod ipsas non audiat, nec in aliis collocutionibus frequentibus se eis exponat unquam; et semper potius duris et rigidis verbis utatur ad eas, quam mollibus.' Humbert de Romans, *Opera de vita regulari*, ed. Joachim Joseph Berthier, 2 vols. (Torino, 1956), ii, 368.

harsh and critical attitude towards female penitents which was more systemic and misogynistic.

Humbert also provides us with a little information about how the confession of women ought to be conducted:

> Henceforth let the confessor take care where women are concerned not ever to hear their confessions, except in public, and where he may be seen by some person or persons.
>
> But in hearing them, let them never be face to face, nor let him tarry except for such time as the necessity of the confession requires.[15]

Thus, within forty years of the promulgation of *Omnis utriusque sexus*, the canon which explicitly pertained equally to men and women, the formal requirements for hearing confession, as set out by the Master General of the Dominicans, established a distance and a distrust between the confessor and the female penitent. This distance and distrust, which could easily hamper a woman's experience of the sacrament, as seen so clearly in the case of Margery Kempe, was further exacerbated by the androcentric construction of sin which was set out in confessors' manuals. An examination of some manuals of English provenance, which appeared in the first half of the thirteenth century, will serve to illustrate this point.

Many of the earliest confessors' manuals, such as those by Thomas of Chobham,[16] Richard Wetheringsett,[17] Walter de Cantilupe,[18] Alexander Stavensby[19] and Magister Serlo,[20] appear to address the needs of both male and female penitents. There is, however, no question that in these manuals the male is the universal norm and the female is the marked category of penitent. Consequently, serious questions must be asked about how these works

---

[15] 'Porro circa mulieres cavere debet ne unquam audiat earum confessiones, nisi in publico, et ubi ab aliquo, vel ab aliquibus videatur. Audiendo vero eas, nunquam habeat faciem contra faciem, nec multum immoretur, nisi quantum necessitas confessionis requirit.' Ibid.

[16] Thomas of Chobham, *Thomae de Chobham. Summa Confessorum*, ed. F. Broomfield, Analecta Mediaevalia Namurcensia 25 (Louvain, 1968).

[17] *Summa "Qui bene presunt"*, London, BL Royal 9.A.XIV. and Oxford, New College 94. The author would like to thank Professor Joseph Goering (Univ. of Toronto) for sharing his transcriptions of these manuscripts. Professor Goering is preparing a critical edition of this work.

[18] Walter's *summula, "Omnis etas"*, is printed in *Councils and Synods with other Documents Relating to the English Church. ii. AD 1205–1313*, ed. Frederick Maurice Powicke and Christopher Robert Cheney (Oxford, 1964), 1061–77. For the identification of this work with Walter de Cantilupe, see Joseph Goering and Daniel S. Taylor, "The *Summulae* of Bishops Walter de Cantilupe (1240) and Peter Quinel (1287)", *Speculum*, 67/3 (1992), 576–94.

[19] Alexander Stavensby's two treatises, *"De septem criminalibus"* and *"De confessionibus"*, are printed in *Councils and Synods, ii*, 214–26.

[20] Joseph Goering, "The *Summa de penitentia* of Magister Serlo", *Mediaeval Studies*, 38 (1976), 1–53, presents an ed. of the manual. He discusses the work in some detail in "The *Summa* of Master Serlo and Thirteenth-Century Penitential Literature", *Mediaeval Studies*, 40 (1978), 290–311.

gendered sin, given the (by now well-recognized) limitations of the notion of the 'universal man'.[21]

Robert of Flamborough's *Liber poenitentialis* proclaims its overtly androcentric bias in its very structure.[22] The discussion is presented in the form of a dialogue between a confessor and a model penitent – a male penitent – in the course of which the sacraments are discussed and sins are expounded. All of the information is presented from a male perspective as it pertained to a male penitent. On occasion Flamborough appears to be aware of the limitations of this approach and its *de facto* exclusion of women. He states, for example, in his discussion of lust, that 'Just as I asked of a man whether he [committed sexual acts] against nature, so I ask of a woman, . . .'[23] There are, however, only a handful of these little concessions to the female penitent. Robert of Flamborough's vision remains firmly focused on his archetypical male penitent.

In his *Summa de penitentia* John of Kent, who also adopts the rhetorical device of the dialogue, occasionally switches the gender of the penitent when it becomes necessary to discuss something as it pertains specifically to women.[24] For example, in the midst of a discussion with his paradigmatic male penitent about the prohibition of sex in holy places and during sacred times, John of Kent abruptly changes the sex of the penitent.[25] This should not, however, mislead us into thinking that this manual is necessarily more 'woman-friendly' than that of Robert of Flamborough. For example, in his discussion of how to question a woman about the sins associated with lust John of Kent writes:

> I advise, however, if it is a woman who is confessing and especially if she is young and if the priest himself fears lest he be moved by her carnal words or his fragile sensibility, let him intermingle questions concerning avarice and other sins. Or let him ask about an entirely different topic so

---

21 Sandra Harding, "The Instability of the Analytical Categories of Feminist Theory", *Signs*, 11 (1986), 645–64, esp. 646–7. For a medieval debate about whether the term "man" included "women", see Gregory of Tours' account of the Council of Mâcon (585) in *The History of the Franks*, transl. Lewis Thorpe (Harmondsworth, 1974), viii. 20, 452. Some of the scholastic debates about whether woman was made in the image of God or if she did not in fact reflect the divine image but was solely human in form and nature are summarized in Ian Maclean, *The Renaissance Notion of Woman. A Study in the Fortunes of Scholasticism and Medical Science in European Intellectual Life* (Cambridge, 1980), 7–14.

22 Robert of Flamborough, *Liber Poenitentialis*, ed. J. J. Francis Firth, Studies and Texts 18 (Toronto, 1971).

23 'Sicuti etiam quaesivi de masculo si contra naturam aliquid egerit, ita quaero de muliere, immo de omni genere fornicandi.' Robert of Flamborough, *Liber Poenitentialis*, IV.viii.24, 197.

24 John of Kent, *Summa de penitentia*, London, BL Royal 9.A.XIV, ff. 203va–32vb. The only comprehensive discussion of this unpublished manual is found in Joseph W. Goering, "The '*Summa de penitentia*' of John of Kent", *Bulletin of Medieval Canon Law*, 18 (1988), 13–31. The author would like to thank Professor Goering for generously sharing his unpublished transcription of this *summa*.

25 John of Kent, *Summa de penitentia*, iii, "De loco et tempore", f. 226vb.

that by the accustomed practice of conversation, the minds of each being better strengthened, he may proceed more securely later to enquire about the vice of lust.[26]

This passage presents an early expression of the same kind of suspicion and nervousness of female penitents articulated by Humbert of Romans some thirty years later. Women are closely identified with the sin of lust, although the underlying implication of the passage is that the weaker flesh belongs to the confessor who cannot keep his mind on his sacramental duty and who is so prey to his own desires that he becomes sexually aroused while hearing confession. There is no doubt, however, that to the medieval reader this passage would certainly have conjured up a fear of the female penitent as one who arouses both primary lust in her paramour, and secondary lust in her confessor. Whichever way the problem is examined, the woman is responsible for inciting men's lust. We may well wonder about the extent to which a confessor's fear of his own libidinousness would override his pastoral concern for his penitent.

John of Kent's manual also provides us with an example of how potentially frustrating an indirect form of questioning could be. In his discussion of sexual intercourse at forbidden times, John replaces his male penitent with a female one. The confessor asks the woman if she has ever had intercourse at an inappropriate time. She asks for clarification and the confessor replies that women know better than men those times during which sex ought to be avoided. In an aside the author explains that this oblique form of questioning should be employed because women are ashamed when they are questioned more openly. The woman again asks what the confessor is talking about and he replies that she knows very well about that time when women are weakened and do not want their husbands to know about their infirmity. The woman continues to be completely baffled and ultimately forces the confessor to specify that he is talking about menstruation, at which point the woman asks why he is using such vile language.[27]

There is no apparent reason for the woman's almost unbelievable obtuseness and it is most likely that John of Kent was seeking only to illustrate how to conduct an oblique interrogation that respected what he perceived as

---

[26] 'Consulo tamen si sit mulier que confitetur et maxime si iuuenis et ipse sacerdos timeat ne per audita uerba carnalia sui uel illius fragilis sensualitas moueatur, interrogaciones de auaricia uel aliis peccatis intermisceat. Vel de alio integre interroget ut per interloquendi assuecionem utriusque animo melius confirmato procedat securius ulterius ad uicia luxurie inquirenda.' Ibid. f. 225vb.

[27] 'Fecisti aliquo tempore indebito? P. Mulier: Quomodo? Sacerdos: Vos mulieres scitis melius quam uiri tempus illud quo est maxime abstinendum. Hoc dicitur pro tempore menstruorum quia erubescunt cum aperte interrogatur. Mulier: Quid est illud tempus domine? Sacerdos: Bene scitis quod aliquando infirmantur mulieres et infirmitatem illam nolunt sciri a uiris suis, et ideo tunc magis debent abstinere ne ipsi percipiant. P. Mulier dicit maxime si sit domigerosa: Domine que est illa infirmitas? Sacerdos: Non bene noui quem, set a quibusdam uocatur flores. P. Mulier: Domine ut quid de tam uili re loquaris?' Ibid. f. 226vb.

women's natural modesty. Yet the tone of the dialogue also suggests escalating frustration, and it is not difficult to leap from John of Kent's exasperated penitent to Margery Kempe's complaints about her confessor's impatience, inattentiveness and abruptness.

Leaving the area of the conduct of confession, it is possible to present a profile of how women are presented in pastoral literature by an examination of specific sins. One of the most striking features is the perception that women are the means by which the seriousness of a man's sin is exacerbated or diminished. In order to analyse the circumstances of sin, a man ought to be asked if he had fornicated with a virgin, a single woman, a widow, a nun or a prostitute. Richard Wetheringsett's Summa 'Qui bene presunt' presents a representative example of a discussion that appears in some form in all the manuals. Wetheringsett says that fornication with a virgin is more serious because the woman is irrecoverably damaged by the loss of her virginity. In addition, the seriousness of fornication with a prostitute should not be underestimated because the client would not know if she were a married woman, in which case the sin is adultery, or a straying nun, which is sacrilege, or even one of his own relatives, which is incest. In all these circumstances it is the woman's status which renders the man's sin more serious, even if he were ignorant of her status.[28]

Now, logic might suggest that it would be simple enough for a clever confessor simply to invert the respective genders to render such a passage relevant to a female penitent. Thus the fornicating woman could be asked if she had seduced a virgin, a priest, a widower or a male relative. Given the androcentric focus of these manuals, however, it is dangerous to assume that examples were simply reversed and made applicable to women. This is especially so given the medieval evaluation of female sexuality as passive. For example, elsewhere Wetheringsett observes that adultery is defined as the violation of another man's bed, leaving women defined solely in relation to men as the objects which are violated. The reverse, that women can also be the active violators, is not definitionally possible.[29] Thus, it would be equally likely that a less casuistically-inclined confessor, the very kind for whom these

---

[28] 'Simpliciter et proprie dicitur fornicacione in abusu concubinarum quod mortale peccatum est. Set gravius in abusu viduarum et ad huc gravius in abusu meretricum. . . . Contigit enim sepe meretrices fuisse coniugatas solempniter vel privatim per fidei dacionem et carnalem copulam subsequentem. Vel sanctimoniales errabundas vel consanguineas carnaliter vel spiritualiter vel affines . . . Si meretrix cognita aliquando fuit sanctimonialis, sacrilegium est. Si consanguinea vel affinis, incestus. Si coniugata, adulterium. Nec excusatur qui hoc ignorat.' Oxford, New College 94, f. 59r.

'Cum virgine incorrupta quod est dampnum irrecuperabile.' Ibid. f. 73r.

Similar views are expressed, among others, by Walter de Cantilupe, Omnis etas, in Councils and Synods ii, pt. 2, 1068, 1070; Alexander Stavensby, Quidam tractatus de confessionibus, in Councils and Synods ii, pt. 2, 222 and Magister Serlo, Summa de penitentia, in Goering, "The Summa de penitentia of Magister Serlo", 34.

[29] 'Item adulterium proprie est alterius thori violacio.' London, BL Royal 9.A.XIV, f. 62v.

manuals were designed, might well ask a woman if she had occasion to exacerbate the sin of her sexual partner by hiding the fact she was a runaway nun, a virgin, or a married woman! If the male sinner is the main focus and subject of confessors' manuals then this interpretation is certainly as logical and possible as the direct inversion of sins.

Some species of sin were perceived as pertaining more specifically to women. Alexander Stavensby, for example, requires that women especially be interrogated about magic and sorcery.[30] This is not particularly innovative, since most thirteenth-century confessors' manuals simply followed the earlier example of Burchard of Worms, who provided extensive discussions of women's use of magic.[31] Robert of Flamborough provides a unique twist to the discussion, linking women who engage in lesbian sexual activity with those women who mix their beloved's semen into his food in order to enhance his love;[32] and Serlo extends the discussion to consider both women who make love potions from their menstrual blood and those who render men impotent.[33] Both Flamborough and Serlo show that the identification of women with sorcery and magic was ultimately male-defined. It was not the practice of magic *per se* that was stressed, but rather, that it was a means by which women tried to influence or control men. While magic may be a sin that was associated with women specifically, nevertheless it was defined and understood in relation to men.

Something of the same androcentricism can also be seen in Thomas of Chobham's discussion of prostitution, surely a women's sin if ever there were one.[34] Chobham reflects the opinion prevalent in the contemporary schools at Paris that a prostitute worked with her body and thus was entitled to her fee. The logical extension of this conclusion, however, is that a prostitute sinned if she committed fraud. In this case fraud is defined as when a prostitute used cosmetics to appear younger or more beautiful in order to collect a higher fee for her services than she would otherwise have been able to charge.[35] Again, the focus of the discussion is not on the female sinner, but rather on the male client, who might have been tricked into paying for a younger or more beautiful woman than she was in fact, and so did not get his money's worth.

---

30 *Councils and Synods ii*, pt. 2, 221.

31 See the examination by Aron Gurevich, "Popular Culture in the Mirror of the Penitential", in *Medieval Popular Culture: Problems of Belief and Perception* (Cambridge, 1988), 78–103. Burchard of Worms, *Decretum*, Book 19, *Corrector et medicus*, PL 140.

32 'Mulier, si cum muliere fornicata fuerit, septem annos poeniteat. Sic et illa quae semen viri sui cibo miscet ut inde plus ejus accipiat amorem poeniteat.' Robert of Flamborough, *Liber Poenitentialis*, V.iii.272, 229.

33 Magister Serlo, *Summa de penitentia*, cap. 16, 26.

34 The Parisian schoolmen's treatment of prostitution is discussed in John W. Baldwin, *Masters, Princes and Merchants. The Social Views of Peter the Chanter and His Circle* (Princeton, 1970), i, 134–7. A comparative discussion of the treatment of prostitution in confessional literature in found in Biller, "Marriage Patterns and Women's Lives", 87–9.

35 Thomas of Chobham, *Summa confessorum*, 296.

The extent to which male shadows lingered behind the cure of women's souls can be no better illustrated than in the example of married women. One of the fundamental characteristics that distinguished Christianity from other belief systems in the ancient world was the shift from collective to individual salvation; from a culture of shame to a culture of guilt. Individual faith and interior life superseded communal ritual as the path to salvation. Confession and penance developed as a means by which the believer could assess her motivations, enhance her interior life, and expiate her individual sins.[36] In theory, then, in assessing and assigning penances, the confessor should have taken into account only the well-being of the penitent before him. Yet this would appear not always to have been possible in a society based on hierarchy, mutual dependence and obligation. Magister Serlo discusses how the penances enjoined on married women and others who are confined or under the control of superiors must be ones that can be performed easily and secretly, without revealing their sin.[37]

Thomas of Chobham sets out the interconnectedness of married life and individual salvation when he ponders the case of a wife's secret adultery. The woman has committed a mortal sin, one that some theologians held equivalent to homicide. Consequently, she should do lengthy and rigorous penance. In his discussion, however, Chobham appears more concerned with the husband and how he might react. He advises that a discreet confessor must assign to the woman a penance that she can perform without arousing her husband's suspicion or inadvertently revealing to him his wife's sin. It also must be a penance that the woman's husband will *allow* her to perform. If the woman is enjoined to fast but her husband orders her to eat, the woman must eat because she is required to obey her husband rather than her priest.[38] Ultimately, if no suitable penance can be found, the confessor should enjoin the comparatively mild penance of vehement prayer and internal compunction.

This understanding of a wife's ability to perform penance may only reflect the reality of medieval life, with couples living in close quarters, without privacy, in a milieu which allowed a husband to control the least of his wife's actions. Thus, it can be argued that Chobham's advice was designed to protect the wife from the potentially dangerous consequences which might result if her sin were revealed to her husband. Be that as it may, what is important for the present discussion is that Chobham acknowledged that a husband's

---

[36] John F. Benton, "Consciousness of Self and Perceptions of Individuality", in *Renaissance and Renewal in the Twelfth Century*, ed. Robert L. Benson and Giles Constable (Cambridge, Mass., 1982), 271–4.

[37] 'Et notandum quod ita debet semper penitere adultera, ne marito sit suspecta ut alibi dicit canon. Similiter intellige de aliis personis in arto positis sive custodia maiorum. Talibus debent iniungi private orationes et private abstinentie . . .' Magister Serlo, *Summa de penitentia*, 37.

[38] 'Debet igitur discretus sacerdos inquirere ab ipsa muliere penitente quid possit facere sine suspicione viri et de eius permissione, et hoc iniungat ei in penitentia, quia sicut patet ex predictis, si sacerdos iniungeret mulieri ieiunium, et vir eius preciperet ut comederet, teneretur magis obedire viro quam sacerdoti.' Thomas of Chobham, *Summa confessorum*, 363.

whims took precedence over his wife's penance – and, ultimately, her salvation – and that the church was to accede to this and attempt to work around it. He does not address the problem of what happens if vehement prayer and internal compunction were insufficient to expiate the woman's sin.

This is perhaps the most dramatic example of a long series of intrusions by a husband into his wife's confession. In another passage that has become familiar through the work of Sharon Farmer, Chobham urges wives to be preachers to their husbands, dissuading them from evil and trying to compensate for their wrongdoing.[39] Thus, the husband's faults become the principal topic of discussion during the wife's confession, overshadowing and defining her own actions. Chobham requires women to render the conjugal debt to husbands who demand it in inappropriate times or places.[40] The husband's sexual demands take precedence over the wife's desire to observe a holy season continently. Even the blood taboo which required couples to abstain from intercourse from birth until purification could be bent to accommodate a husband's libido. Chobham advises that a woman seek purification as soon as possible, rather than waiting the traditional forty days, in order to render the conjugal debt to a husband who might otherwise seek his pleasures elsewhere.[41] Somehow, the man's desires and well-being again intrude on the woman's physical recuperation, her ability to observe social and religious norms, and perhaps also her desire for continence.

At least Thomas of Chobham concludes that in these cases not the woman but only the libidinous husband sins. In contrast, John of Kent proffers much the same advice, but states that the acquiescing wife's sin is minimized and the husband's is exacerbated.[42] What better example to illustrate the dilemma of a woman caught between her own desire to avoid sin, yet inexorably pulled into it by a husband she must obey? And in the end, her confessor tells her that her sin is only minimized, yet all the while she is obeying the Church which requires her to obey her husband. Together, the confessor and the husband inhibit the woman's ability to choose not to sin, and the ultimate state of her soul is placed in her husband's control. The woman is in double jeopardy, and does not have the ability, nor indeed the right, to control the situation or exercise her free will to choose virtue over vice.

John of Kent thinks that avoiding intercourse during menstruation is more important than during other prohibited times. The female penitent explains

---

[39] Ibid. 375. See the discussion by Sharon Farmer, "Persuasive Voices: Clerical Images of Medieval Women", *Speculum*, 61 (1986), 517–43.

[40] Thomas of Chobham, *Summa confessorum*, 337.

[41] 'Item, prohibendum est ne quis cognoscat uxorem suam in puerperio, sed si vir instanter petat debitum et illa timeat de lapsu eius, statim accedat ad purificationem et sic debitum reddat.' Ibid. 366.

[42] 'P. Mulier dicit: Non possumus prohibere uiris nostris. Sacerdos: Deberes monere et rogare ut pro reuerencia temporis abstineat. Si non potest sine sui periculo, minoratur tua culpa. Si possit et nolit, augmentatur sua culpa et dicas ei quod caueat.' John of Kent, *Summa de penitentia*, iii, f. 226vb.

that even then husbands pursue their wives, and women do not dare reveal to them their condition. Even in this situation, with the fear of conceiving a deformed child, John does not empower the woman to refuse sex. Rather, he advises deception and benign evasion. Feign a headache or some kind of illness, he says, invent whatever kind of story necessary to dissuade your husband, and if that does not work, as a last resort, tell him the truth. Thus, the confessor urges the woman to lie in order to avoid sex during a time considered both sinful and dangerous. If lying does not work, then he assumes that the truth of menstruation will be so repellent that the husband will then certainly stop demanding his rights.[43] Again, the needs of the female penitent seem the least important, while those of her sexually aggressive husband loom large in the discussion.

One final example illustrates the extent to which a woman's sin was male-defined and indeed, how the needs of the penitent wife could be overshadowed by her husband. The example is found in Magister Serlo's exposition of a wife's adultery which goes far beyond the conventional treatment of adultery in confessors' manuals. Serlo discusses the case of a woman who conceives from her adulterous liaison. The confessor is to require her to work to ensure that the legitimate heirs are not defrauded by an illegitimate one. Serlo provides a variety of suggestions about how restitution ought to be made, including exposing the mother's sin to her illegitimate child in the hope that he can be persuaded to make restitution and enter religious life. If that is too dangerous, the woman should try to make restitution from her marriage portion, secretly, through the mediation of her confessor or some other discreet cleric.[44] What is most telling about the attitudes behind this discussion is that all the concerns are secular. There is concern for the deceived husband and the defrauded legitimate heirs. There is little compassion, however, for the innocent illegitimate child, and there is virtually no attention given to the adulterous woman, the circumstances of her sin, the state of her soul, the quality of her contrition, or even the nature of her penance beyond material restitution. Finally, to highlight the heinousness of this sin, perhaps better termed a crime, Serlo remarks, 'And although it may not seem to [the confessor] that such a woman is able to be saved nevertheless penance should not be denied her . . .'[45] There is no question that this severity, this suggestion that the woman's adultery is so serious a sin that it is scarcely able to be forgiven, is a reflection of exclusively male and exclusively secular concerns. There is nothing spiritual or pastoral in this discussion, and there is an almost complete

---

43 'P. Mulier: Tunc uiri nostri magis instant nobis nec audemus eis reuelare. Sacerdos: Finge infirmitatem lateris uel capitis, et si nolit dicas ei si accedat grauiter eum peccaturum esse, et si esset benignus et de te priuatus, posses rei ueritatem timore periculi reuelare. Set tunc temporis quantum potes abstine et finge quicquid uerius poteris allegare ut desistat.' Ibid. f. 227ra.
44 Magister Serlo, *Summa de penitentia*, 36–7.
45 'Et licet sibi non videatur talis posse salvari non est tamen ei deneganda penitenita, . . .' Ibid. 36.

disregard for the female penitent. Magister Serlo's discussion of the adulterous wife is an extreme example, but it nevertheless reflects something of the general disregard for and distortion of women found in manuals for confessors in early thirteenth-century England.

The picture of women and their pastoral care that is presented in the literature available to early thirteenth-century confessors is problematic at best. Women are the means by which men's sins are exacerbated. Women are the conduit by which confessors can influence and reform the behaviour of sinful men. Women practise sorcery in order to control men and to force men to love them or to render men impotent. Women are adulterers who are unfaithful to their husbands. Women are sexually available to their husbands on demand, except during menstruation when they are rendered so repellent as to kill the man's sex drive. Women are prostitutes who compound their immorality by defrauding and tricking their clients. Women are the source of lust: they arouse lust in paramours, husbands, and, worst of all, in their confessors. Women subvert the patriarchal moral and social order; they betray husbands and secretly dispossess legitimate heirs. Women are beings who commit sins that influence men or harm men. Women are not fully present in their own confessions because their sins are measured by their influence on men. Married women are not full participants in the sacrament because their ability to perform penances is controlled by a third party, their husbands. Above all, women are absent penitents, presented in relation to men, ignored or tacked on as afterthoughts.

Despite the theoretical equality of men and women in the order of salvation, reaffirmed so unequivocally by the Fourth Lateran Council, there is no question that in the Middle Ages sin was androcentrically constructed and pastoral care was a gendered experience. Confession in particular served to reinforce women's subordinate and secondary status, and inhibited their ability to fulfill the requirements of the faith. Yet confession was also the sacrament on which much of contemporary popular piety, as well as learnèd discourse, focused. The androcentricism of pastoral writings, however, must to some extent have influenced the female penitent's experience of the sacrament. The extent to which a woman was devastated to find herself peripheral and marginal in her own confession must remain in the realm of conjecture. While the average laywoman's experience of confession remains unrecoverable, we must avoid the temptation to essentialize and extrapolate the experience of some saints and holy women, for whom confession may have been a salutary experience. Given the androcentric construction of sin and the suspicion of the female penitent evident in these early and influential manuals, confession may have been an experience which highlighted not only the soul's alienation from God but also the female penitent's alienation from her patriarchal church.

'FOR HEREBY I HOPE TO ROUSE SOME TO PIETY': BOOKS OF SISTERS FROM CONVENTS AND SISTER-HOUSES ASSOCIATED WITH THE *DEVOTIO MODERNA* IN THE LOW COUNTRIES

Wybren Scheepsma

Since the twelfth century the Christian Church has been confronted with heretical as well as reforming movements, in both of which women usually played an important part. The historical connections between these phenomena are discussed in an impressive study by the German historian Herbert Grundmann.[1] Since interest in women and religion in the Middle Ages has so increased in recent years, Grundmann's insights, developed in the 1930s, have come to the fore again. Grundmann formulated the following, by now famous, thesis regarding the connection between the rise of religious literature in the vernacular and the presence of a female audience: where male clergy acknowledged and appreciated the flourishing of religious fervour among women, conditions were favourable for the rise of religious literature in the vernacular.[2]

Grundmann's survey ends in the fourteenth century, when great Dominican authors such as Meister Eckhart, Heinrich Suso and Johannes Tauler wrote their mystical works and gave shape to what has been called 'German Mysticism'. In the fifteenth century, however, there were also reforming movements in the church, as Grundmann himself points out.[3] At that time the religious climate in the Low Countries and north-west Germany was dominated by the *Devotio Moderna*. This reforming movement, too, fostered an extensive body of religious literature in the vernacular.

I would like to thank Dr W. van Anrooij and Dr Th. Mertens for their valuable comments on this article. It was translated by Drs. I. van Eijk and Drs. F. van Meurs.

[1] H. Grundmann, *Religiöse Bewegungen im Mittelalter. Untersuchungen über die geschichtlichen Zusammenhänge zwischen der Ketzerei, den Bettelorden und die religiösen Frauenbewegung im 12. und 13. Jahrhundert und über die geschichtlichen Grundlagen der deutschen Mystik.* Anhang: *Neue Beiträge zur Geschichte der religiösen Bewegungen im Mittelalter* (2. verbesserte und ergänzte Auflage, Darmstadt, 1961).

[2] Cf. Grundmann 1961, 439–75. For a reappraisal of his thesis, see U. Peters, *Religiöse Erfahrung als literarisches Faktum. Zur Vorgeschichte und Genese frauenmystischer Texte des 13. und 14. Jahrhunderts* (Tübingen, 1988).

[3] Grundmann, 1961, 2.

This article will focus on a form of religious literature associated with the *Devotio Moderna* that will be referred to by the term 'Books of Sisters'.[4] These books are part of a body of vernacular as well as Latin biographies and chronicles written in the Low Countries at the end of the Middle Ages. From this extensive and complex set of texts, which has as yet hardly been studied as an interrelated whole, only those texts that contain lives of devout women from a particular convent or sister-house will be discussed here.

The Books of Sisters and the other biographical literature produced by the *Devotio Moderna* have nearly always been studied as chronicles of monasteries or convents, or at any rate as historiographical texts.[5] Yet historians complain that the authors of the Books of Sisters lack a sense of historical perspective,[6] as these writers focus virtually exclusively on the history of their own convent, concentrating on its spiritual life. One might try to resolve this contradiction by studying such historiographical or biographical literature as a historical genre in itself.[7] However, an approach which recognizes that this form of literature crosses the boundary between historical and religious literature would seem to be more fruitful.[8] The main aim of these texts, as of almost all the texts produced by the Modern Devotion, was to convey spiritual values.[9]

[4] Cf. J. Van Engen, 'The Virtues, the Brothers, and the Schools', *Revue Bénédictine*, 98 (1988), 184, which refers to *Libri sororum*. The Dutch term which has been proposed is *zusterboeken*; cf. L. Jongen and W. Scheepsma, 'Wachten op de hemelse bruidegom. De Diepenveense nonnen- viten in literair-historisch perspectief', in Th. Mertens et al., *Boeken voor de eeuwigheid. Middel- nederlands geestelijk proza*, (Amsterdam, 1993), 295–317 and 467–76 (296).

[5] For this reason, the Devotionalist biographies of both men and women are included in repertories of historical sources. Cf. J. Romein, *Geschiedenis van de Noord-Nederlandsche ge- schiedschrijving. Bijdrage tot de beschavingsgeschiedenis* (Haarlem, 1932), as well as H. Bruch, *Supplement bij Geschiedenis van de Noord-Nederlandsche geschiedschrijving in de Middeleeuwen van dr. Jan Romein* (Haarlem, 1956), numbers 63–86. At present M. Carasso-Kok, *Repertorium van verhalende historische bronnen uit de middeleeuwen. Heiligenlevens, annnalen, kronieken en andere in Nederland geschreven verhalende bronnen* (The Hague, 1981), is the best and most up-to-date survey of Devotionalist historiography.

[6] Romein, 1932, 199.

[7] Cf. B. Ebels-Hoving, 'Nederlandse geschiedschrijving 1350–1530. Een poging tot karakte- risering', in *Genoechlicke ende lustige historiën. Laatmiddeleeuwse geschiedschrijving in Nederland*, eds. B. Ebels-Hoving, C. G. Santing and C. P. H. M. Tilmans (Hilversum, 1987), 217–42 (224).

[8] For a discussion of the various genres to which the Books of Sisters are related, see Jongen and Scheepsma, 1993, 299–301.

[9] See Th. Mertens, 'Lezen met de pen. Ontwikkelingen in het laatmiddeleeuws geestelijk proza', in *De studie van de Middelnederlandse letterkunde: stand en toekomst*, eds. F. P. van Oostrom and F. Willaert (Hilversum, 1989), 187–200; N. Staubach, 'Pragmatische Schriftlichkeit im Bere- ich der Devotio moderna', *Frühmittelalterliche Studien* 25 (1991), 418–61; Th. Mertens, 'Boeken voor de eeuwigheid. Ter inleiding', in Th. Mertens et al., *Boeken voor de eeuwigheid. Middelneder- lands geestelijk proza*, (Amsterdam, 1993), 8–35 en 361–72 (esp. 16–20); Th. Mertens, '*Devotio Moderna* and Innovation in Middle Dutch Literature', in *Middle Dutch Literature in its European Context*, ed. E. Kooper (in press; Cambridge Studies in Medieval Literature).

The Devotio Moderna as a Religious Women's Movement

Before the Books of Sisters themselves are discussed, something should first be said about the Modern Devotion as a religious reforming movement, and especially about women's role in it.[10] It is well-known that in many respects the fourteenth century was a time of malaise, including religious malaise, in Western Europe. As a result, religious reforming movements wishing to restore the spiritual purity that had characterized the initial stages of Christianity sprang up everywhere in the course of the century. In the Northern and Southern Netherlands and in north-west Germany, the most influential of these movements was the *Devotio Moderna*.

The Modern Devotion was established in the last quarter of the fourteenth century by Geert Grote (1340–1384).[11] It spread from Grote's native town of Deventer, and it became an organization with thousands of followers wherever Dutch and German were spoken. The movement can be divided into four branches. The first is that of the Brethren of the Common Life (mostly clerics and priests), who lived together in brethren-houses, and from there provided spiritual care in the world.[12] The second branch is that of their female counterparts, the Sisters of the Common Life.[13] Like the brethren, the sisters did not take vows, and they can therefore be regarded as semi-monastics.[14] The sisters made a living by spinning and weaving. In addition, the *Devotio Moderna* included the Chapter of Windesheim, an Augustinian monastic order, which comprised both monasteries and convents, the movement's third and fourth branches.[15]

Within the bounds set by the lifestyles they had opted for, the Devotionalists

---

[10] Where possible I will refer to works on the *Devotio Moderna* that are written in English: A. Hyma, *The Brethren of the Common Life* (Grand Rapids, 1950); A. Hyma, *The Christian Renaissance. A History of the 'Devotio Moderna'* (2nd edn, Hamden, Conn., 1965); R.R. Post, *The Modern Devotion. Confrontation with Reformation and Humanism* (Leiden, 1968); R. W. Southern, *Western Society and the Church of the Middle Ages* (Harmondsworth, 1972), 331–58; A. G. Weiler, 'Recent Historiography on the Modern Devotion: Some Debated Questions', *Archief voor de Geschiedenis van de Katholieke Kerk in Nederland*, 26 (1984), 161–79. A number of important texts are available in English translation, either in whole or in part, in J. Van Engen, *Devotio Moderna. Basic Writings* (New York, 1988).

[11] The most recent book on Geert Grote is G. Epiney-Burgard, *Gérard Grote (1340–1384) et les débuts de la Dévotion moderne* (Wiesbaden, 1970). See also Hyma, 1950, esp. 15–55; Th. Van Zijl, *Gerard Groote, Ascetic and Reformer (1340–1384)* (Washington, 1963); Hyma, 1965, 9–40; Post, 1968, 51–170; Southern, 1970, esp. 334–7.

[12] Cf. Hyma, 1950, 96–126; Van Zijl, 1963, 232–242; Hyma, 1965, esp. 99–135; Post, 1968, esp. 197–258, 273–92, 343–468 and 551–631.

[13] Their history is still to be written. For some brief discussions, see Van Zijl, 1963, 232–42; Hyma, 1965, 112–14 and 582–9; Post, 1968, 259–72 and 493–501.

[14] On this, see esp. F. Koorn, 'Women without Vows. The Case of the Beguines and the Sisters of the Common Life in the Northern Netherlands', in *Women and Men in Spiritual Culture, XIV–XVII Centuries. A Meeting of South and North*, ed. E. Schulte van Kessel (The Hague, 1986), 135–47.

[15] Cf. Hyma, 1950, 127–44; Hyma, 1965, 136–57; Post, 1968, 293–313, 502–20 and 632–80.

tried to realize their religious ideals. Among other things, they laid greater stress on personal spiritual life than on formal celebrations of the liturgy. The Devout had a practical and pragmatic attitude to life, which manifested itself particularly in the all-important pursuit of virtue. One of the means of achieving this goal was the use of the written word, in a receptive, reproductive and creative sense. The German term *pragmatische Schriftlichkeit* most clearly characterizes this attitude.[16]

So far research into the *Devotio Moderna* has focused especially on the male Devout, particularly on the Brethren of the Common Life.[17] They were considered to be the ideological founders and creators of the movement, while the women were regarded as recipients.[18] In this approach, the fact that the women far outnumbered the men is overlooked: on average, there were three women to every male Devout.[19]

Geert Grote and Johannes Brinckerinck (1359–1419), a priest from Zutphen, were the fathers of the Devout women's movement. In 1392, Brinckerinck was put in charge of the women of the House of Master Geert, which Geert Grote had founded in 1374. Only when Brinckerinck took over was the Common Life introduced there, which meant that from then on the sisters united their funds and shared their expenses.[20] Around 1400, four other Houses of Sisters of the Common Life were founded in Deventer, all of which were led by the inspiring Brinckerinck.[21] This made Deventer the centre of the Devout women's movement. In 1400, Johannes Brinckerinck also founded a house on a moor called Diepenveen, near Deventer. This sister-house joined the Chapter of Windesheim in 1412, and was to become the most important convent of that order. Both Johannes Brinckerinck and the convent of Diepenveen organized reforms at several convents.[22]

The women's movement of the Modern Devotion brought about a peak in the production of manuscripts in the Low Countries in the fifteenth century.[23] Religious and ascetic texts intended for these women are estimated to have amounted to at least three quarters of the total number of extant manuscripts

---

[16] This notion was first applied to the Modern Devotion in Staubach 1992. See also Mertens, *'Devotio Moderna* and Innovation' (in press).

[17] One of Albert Hyma's books about the Modern Devotion was entitled e.g. *The Brethren of the Common Life* (Hyma, 1950).

[18] The first to attack this view was G. Rehm, *Die Schwestern vom gemeinsamen Leben im nordwestlichen Deutschland. Untersuchungen zur Geschichte der Devotio moderna und des weiblichen Religiosentums* (Berlin, 1985), 11–25.

[19] See Post, 1968, pp. 265–72 for some figures.

[20] See Hyma, 1950, 86–7; Post, 1968, 259–65; Koorn, 1986, 141–4.

[21] These were the Houses of Brandes, Kerstenens, Buusken and Lamme van Dieze. Cf. Post, 1968, 266.

[22] Cf. Hyma, 1950, 135–44; Hyma, 1965, 145–57.

[23] For this, see in the first place J.P. Gumbert, *The Dutch and their Books in the Manuscript Age* (London, 1990). See also Mertens, 1993 and Mertens, *'Devotio Moderna* and Innovation' (in press).

containing Middle Dutch texts.[24] Thousands of these manuscripts have survived, the majority of which originate from convents belonging to the *Devotio Moderna*.[25] Most of the texts in them were translated from Latin, but there were also a number of female authors in the Modern Devotion who actually wrote spiritual texts for their fellow sisters.[26] These include the writers of the Devout Books of Sisters.

The Books of Sisters from the House of Master Geert and the Convent of Diepenveen: A Provisional Survey

Up to now the term 'Book of Sisters' has been used without much reservation. It becomes apparent that such reservation is needed when one tries to determine the exact number of Books of Sisters the *Devotio Moderna* produced. At the moment, around fifteen different historiographical or biographical texts from convents or sister-houses are known to us.[27] Given the present state of research, it is not possible to provide an exact definition of the general characteristics of the genre to which these texts belong. However, in order to be able to make a comparison between the various texts, I will attempt a provisional characterization of the genre, based on two important specimens from the centre of the Devout women's movement: the Books of Sisters from Diepenveen and from the House of Master Geert. As far as can be determined, these two books are the most fully developed variants of this genre. Moreover, the texts that have survived are complete and are easily accessible in modern editions. An additional reason for choosing them is that the House of Master Geert and the convent of Diepenveen were highly influential in their respective branches of the movement, and they may have influenced the Books of Sisters or similar texts in other convents.[28]

---

24 Cf. K. Ruh, 'Geistliche Prosa', in *Neues Handbuch der Literaturwissenschaft 8: Europäisches Spätmittelalter*, ed. W. Erzgräber (Wiesbaden, 1979), 565–605.
25 Cf. Gumbert, 1990, 24–51; K. Stooker and Th. Verbeij "Uut Profectus'. Over de verspreiding van Middelnederlandse kloosterliteratuur aan de hand van de 'Profectus religiosorum' van David van Augsburg', in Th. Mertens et al., *Boeken voor de eeuwigheid. Middelnederlands geestelijk proza*, (Amsterdam, 1993), 318–40 and 476–90 (320–23).
26 See W. Scheepsma, 'Onbekende literatuur door onbekende vrouwen', *Literatuur*, 9 (1992), 322–9. The Windesheim canonesses, Alijt Bake (1415–1455) and Jacomijne Costers (d. 1503), and the Utrecht recluse, Suster Bertken (1427–1514), are among the most important of these female writers.
27 These are listed in Jongen and Scheepsma, 1993, 296–99 and 468 n. 10.
28 At present I am aware of two manuscripts whose form and arrangement are very similar to the Books of Sisters discussed here. The House of Lamme van Dieze at Deventer is known to have possessed an MS containing the lives of Rector Egbert ter Beek (d.1483) and at least ten sisters, which unfortunately has gone missing (Carasso-Kok, 1981, n. 133). See O. A. Spitzen, 'Het leven der eerwaardige moeder Andries Yserens, overste van het Lammenhuis te Deventer, overleden in den jare 1502', *Archief voor de geschiedenis van het aartsbisdom Utrecht*, 2 (1875), 178–216, which provides an edition of one of the lives (189–216). The MS of the Book of Sisters of the sister-house of St Agnes at Emmerich was lost during the Second World War, but

The Book of Sisters from the House of Master Geert, known as 'Manuscript G',[29] [30] contains 60 lives of sisters from the convent, and 5 chapters describing episodes from the history of the house. The sisters described all died in the period 1398–1456, and the watermarks suggest that MS G must have been written between 1469 and 1485. None the less, the editor of this Book of Sisters, De Man, assumes that this manuscript was a copy, because it contains a large number of corrections and words that have been crossed out. In his view, the original of this Book of Sisters was written between 1475 and 1485. However, it seems just as logical to assume that MS G was the original, precisely because of the large number of mistakes and deletions it contains.

De Man is convinced that all the texts were written by one person, with one exception: the life of Sister Lutgert van Buderick (d.1453), which was written by Rector Rudolf Dier van Muiden (d.1459).[31] The author of the remaining texts is anonymous, but she must have been a sister from the House; she constantly refers to the community of sisters, and regularly uses the words 'us' and 'we'. The writer, as it were, looks back at the history of her House. Her most important source is the information communicated to her orally by older sisters who had known the deceased sisters personally.[32] As the lives of the sisters who died around 1400 are rather sketchy, what was still remembered about them at the time the lives were written down must have faded to a large extent. This means that the Book of Sisters was probably not begun before c.1450.

The collection under discussion here regularly refers to another book (that is, a manuscript) containing biographies of sisters, which was also available in the House.[33] The practice of writing lives of deceased sisters from this House appears to have continued after 1456, the last year mentioned in the extant Book of Sisters. This is proved by the existence of a Latin life of Sister Ysentrude van Mekeren (d.1470), which was almost certainly translated from

---

fortunately a copy made by the Rev. Wilhelm Richter has survived. See G. Hövelmann, 'Das Emmericher Süsternbuch. Eine verlorengeglaubte Hauptquelle zur Geschichte der Devotio moderna', in *Thomas von Kempen. Beiträge zum 500. Todesjahr 1471–1971* (Kempen, 1971), 43–62, which provides an edition of 4 of the 69 lives (52–62).

[29] MS Deventer, Stads- of Athenaeumbibliotheek, Suppl. 208 (101 F 25); see Carasso-Kok, 1981, n. 134. The MS has been edited by D. De Man, *Hier beginnen sommige stichtige punten van onsen oelden zusteren* (The Hague, 1919). Van Engen, 1988, *Basic Writings*, translates a number of these lives (121–36). Unless indicated otherwise, information about the MS and its author are derived from De Man, 1919, lxix–xciii.

[30] For information about this sister-house, see Hyma, 1965, 41–43 and 582–9; Post, 1968, esp. 259–66; Epiney-Burgard, 1970, 142–58; Southern, 1972, 337–8. The most exhaustive account, however, is provided by De Man, 1919 (see previous note).

[31] Rudolf Dier also wrote the *Scriptum de Magistro Gerardo, domino Florencio et multis aliis fratribus*, a collection of Latin lives of important Devotionalists. For more information, see Carasso-Kok, 1981, n. 361.

[32] Cf. De Man, 1919, lxxii–lxxiii.

[33] Ed. De Man, 1919, ff. 6c, 37c, 79c, 83a and 108b.

Middle Dutch.[34] Unfortunately, the original text from what may have been a second volume of or an appendix to the Book of Sisters from this House has not survived.

To give an impression of what the lives from the Books of Sisters are like, the complete life of Sister Katharina Hughen (d.1411) is as follows. It is fairly short, probably because not much was known about her any more:

> Good sister Katherine was far along in years when she came to the sisters, for she was already over fifty years old. She was an ardent and Devout person and took pains – because she had entered the Lord's vineyard in her eleventh hour – to give herself all the more ardently to the virtues, for she had spent her time in the world foolishly. She tried now therefore to retrieve twice as much: Just as earlier she had served the world with everything that was in her, so now she served our dear Lord with everything that was in her. She had once lived with people who were great in the world's eyes, and there she had grown accustomed to much worldliness and done all to serve her own pleasure. But when she came to join the sisters, she converted herself wholly to God and gave herself over to great humility and lowliness, as if she neither had nor had ever had great possessions in the world. For she saw what she had done and therefore counted as nothing what she now did in turn. Because she had joined fully in the idle pleasures of this world, she possessed all kinds of beautiful jewellery; this she brought along and gave to our Lady or elsewhere, as there was need. She was very loyal to our house. Because she wanted so very much that the sisters should receive her earthly possessions, she held on so powerfully in her final illness that she nearly died without the holy sacrament.[35]

---

[34] The assumption that the Book of Sisters was added to after 1456 seems to be contradicted by the existence of a Latin life of Gertrude ten Venne (d.1444). However, she later became rectress of the House of Lamme van Dieze, which means that her life may also have come from that House (see n. 28). Both the life of Ysentrude van Mekeren and that of Gertrude ten Venne can be found in MS Brussels, Bibliothèque Royale, 8849–8859, ff. 194r–202r and 206r–212r. This codex is dated at around 1500 and originates from the House of Father Florens at Deventer, which provided spiritual care to most of the sister-houses in the town. For a discussion of the ms see M. Schoengen, *Jacobus Traiecti alias De Voecht, Narratio de inchoatione Domus Clericorum in Zwollis* (Amsterdam, 1908), lxxxi–cvii. An edition of the two lives can be found in W. J. Kühler, 'Levensbeschrijvingen van devote zusters te Deventer', *Archief voor de geschiedenis van het aartsbisdom Utrecht*, 36 (1910), 9–33 and 45–65.

[35] MS G, ff. 3d–4b: 'Dese guede zuster Katheryna was al veer op oer dage gecomen, doe si totten zusteren quam, want si was al over oer viftich jaeren. Het was een vuerich ende goddienstich mensche, ende pijnden oer, want si totter elfter uren in den wijngaert ons Heren gecomen was, alsoe veel te vuerichliker totten doechden te geven, als si die tijt, die si in der werlt geweest hadde, versumeliker hadde toegebracht, ende pijnde die nu dubbelt te verhaelen, want gelick dattet voer al der werlt gedient hadde, soe wat in oer was, alsoe diendet nu wederomme, soe wat in oer was, al onsen lieven Heren. Si plach mit groeten luyden nae der werlt te wonen, daer si groeter dertenheit gewoene was, ende daer si oeck seer veel willen hadde. Mer doe si mitten zusteren quam, kierde si oer soe gehelick tot Gode ende gaf oer tot soe groter oetmodicheit ende nederheit, alsof si nye grote dinge nader werlt gehat en hadde; want si mercte wat si gedaen hadde, ende daeromme en ruecte si niet wat si weder dede. Ende

The shorter the period of time that has lapsed since the deaths of the sisters, the longer the lives become. The style and purport of these lives, however, is not very different from those of the life just quoted. After a brief reference to the sister's descent and to her life before she entered the convent, a description of her spiritual life is given. The sisters' good qualities are discussed by means of illustrative anecdotes. For instance, Alijt ten Sande (d.1439) was so chaste and undefiled that at the age of twenty she still thought that children were dug up from holes in the ground.[36] The sisters' shortcomings are also described without reservation, because they are no more than obstacles on the way to virtue. This means that the lives present an ideal which can be attained by ordinary people. This is an essential difference between the lives of sisters and saints' lives, of which they are strongly reminiscent in other respects.[37]

The Prologue at once makes clear the aim of this Book of Sisters:

> We like to tell about the virtues of our poor and humble sisters, so much more the amazing because such are not often to be found among these poor and partly rural folk. Yet they possessed the right and true virtues, so purely indeed as if they had seen and read them right out of Holy Scripture and the saints' lives. But it was the Holy Spirit, who filled them, who had also taught and illumined them; and just as they were illumined, so they continued to illumine others, one in obedience, another in humility, a third in resignation, and a fourth in sisterly love, while the others seemed devoured by the earnestness of the house of God.[38]

This call to virtue and religious enthusiasm should be seen in the context of a general attempt to strengthen spiritual life which took place at the end of the fifteenth century, and which, among other things, appears to have generated the enormous production of manuscripts referred to earlier.[39] By describing the lives of the old sisters, the writer wants to revive the religious zeal that

want si aldus mitter werlde ydelheit ommegegaen hadde, soe hadde si alrehande suverlike cierheit, ende die brachte si altesamen mede, ende gaf si onser liever Vrouwen, of anders daer men die behoefde. Seer trouwe was si onsen huyse. Want ommedat si soe geerne gehad hadde, dat die zusteren oer tijtlike guet gecregen hadden, hielt si oer soe starck in oere lester ziecten, dit si bynae sonder oer hilich Ammet gestorven hadde.' Ed. De Man, 1919, 14–5. Quoted from Van Engen, 1988, *Basic Writings*, 126.

[36] Ed. De Man, 1919, f. 68d.

[37] Cf. Jongen and Scheepsma, 1993, 299–301.

[38] MS G, ff. Cc–d: 'Ons lustet te vertellen onser oetmodiger armen waere doechden, die soeveel te meer te verwonderen sijn, want si myn in soedanigen armen, alse die veel op den lande gewoent hadden, gevonden plegen te worden, ende nochtan alsoe puerlick die rechte waere doechden in hem gehad hebben, alsof si altoes die Heilige Schrift ende der heiligen leven gelesen ende gesien hadden. Mer die Helige Geest, de sie vervullet hadde, die heeft si geleert ende verluchtet. Ende alsoe als si verluchtet weeren, soe hebben si voert geluchtet: die ene in gehorsomheit, die ander in oetmodicheit, die derde in gelatenheit, die vierde in zusterliker minnen ende die ander scheen gegeten te worden vanden eernste des huyses Gods.' Ed. De Man, 1919, 4–5. Quoted from Van Engen, 1988, *Basic Writings*, 121–2.

[39] Cf. De Man, 1919, lxviii. Mertens, 1993, 364 n. 42 sums up a number of possible explanations for this phenomenon.

characterized the early stages of the House. She points out that, in contrast to the present sisters, their exemplary predecessors had indeed been capable of living spiritual lives in the same place and under virtually identical circumstances:

> Let us listen with inner desire to how these Devout maidens of Christ, our fellow sisters, did their exercises, and not imagine it impossible to imitate what they did before us *in this same place and at nearly the same time* [my italics, WFS]. Moreover, when we describe and take in the lives and morals of good people, they seem in a certain sense to go on living after death, and they awaken many from living death to true life.[40]

I will now go on to discuss the Book of Sisters from the Convent of Saint Mary and Saint Agnes at Diepenveen.[41] The mere fact that two vernacular versions of the book have come down to us makes it an exceptional work. One of these versions was owned by the Diepenveen convent itself (MS DV); this manuscript was written by Sister Griet Essink in 1524.[42] The second version was part of the library of the House of Master Geert in Deventer (Manuscript D), and was made in 1534.[43] Both versions contain several dozen lives of sisters of the convent who died between 1407 – the year in which Sister Zwedera van Rechteren, the first sister mentioned, died – and 1494. The Diepenveen version adds a number of lives of sisters who died in the years up to 1504. This version, furthermore, contains a life of Johannes Brinckerinck, which is at the same time a chronicle of the early stages of Diepenveen's history.[44] The length of the lives in the Deventer version is generally only about two-thirds that of the lives in the Diepenveen version. What appears to have been left out in the Deventer version are mainly details concerning the convent of Diepenveen and monastic life in general.[45] The order in which the lives are presented in

---

[40] MS G, ff. Dd: 'Laet ons mit ynniger begeerten hoeren, hoe dat hem die goddienstige megeden Cristi, onse medezusteren, geoeffent hebben, opdat wi niet en vermoeden ons dat onmoegelick toe syn dat nae te doen, dat si voergedaen hebben, die mit ons in die stede ende bynae inden selven tijden hebben geweest. Want overmids datmen gueder menschen leven ende zeeden bescryvet ende die anmercket, soe schijnen si oec in eenre manieren te leven na den doede; ende veel menschen, die levende doot sin, verwecken sie weder totten waeren leven.' Ed. De Man, 1919, f. Dd. Quoted from Van Engen, 1988, *Basic Writings*, 122.

[41] The history of this convent is described by W. J. Kühler, *Johannes Brinckerinck en zijn klooster te Diepenveen* (2nd edn, Leiden, 1914). Cf. Hyma, 1950, pp. 135–57; Hyma, 1965, pp. 87–9 and 145–57.

[42] MS Deventer, Stads- of Athenaeumbibliotheek, Suppl. 198 (101 E 26); Carasso-Kok, 1981, no. 135. For a discussion of this MS, see Kühler, 1914, viii–x and 341–53. The MS has not been published. Modern Dutch translations of a number of these lives can be found in W. Scheepsma, *Hemels verlangen* (Amsterdam, 1993).

[43] MS Zwolle, Rijksarchief, Coll. van Rhemen, inv. no. 1; Carasso-Kok, 1981, n. 136. Ed. D. A. Brinkerink, *Van den doechden der vuriger ende stichtiger susteren van diepen veen ('Handschrift D')* (Leiden, 1904).

[44] MS DV, ff. 1r–46v. The Books of Sisters from Emmerich and the House of Lamme van Dieze also include lives of one or more rectors.

[45] It is striking that Latin passages from the Bible or the liturgy that occur in MS DV are left out

---

this version is also different.[46] For clarity's sake discussion of the complicated relation between the two versions will not be developed further here.[47]

As far as structure is concerned, the Diepenveen lives can roughly be divided into three parts.[48] The first part concerns the period preceding the sister's convent life, and centres on her conversion. This part is told chronologically. The second part concerns the sister's life in the convent and discusses her virtues. Here the story is no longer told in chronological order, but the sister's virtues are usually ordered thematically, and are discussed through anecdotes. In the last part of each life, which deals with the sister's death, chronology is again strictly adhered to. The process of dying is described very precisely, as it is at this point that the languishing sister has proved to be able to persevere in virtue until death.

The fact that the structure of the lives is the same might lead one to suspect that they were all written by one author, but this is not the case. The texts that the Diepenveen and Deventer versions have in common are now supposed to have been written by two anonymous authors;[49] it seems likely that the additions in the Diepenveen version were made by a third author, possibly the copyist Griet Essink.[50] Like the author of MS G, these writers must undoubtedly have been nuns from the same community as the sisters described. This would seem to be indicated by the authors' use of 'we', as well as their knowledge of certain details concerning life at Diepenveen. Both versions are sixteenth-century copies of a collection which was written after c.1470. Separate individual lives may well have been written before the collection was made. At any rate, it had been customary at the convent of Diepenveen to record important statements by rectors and fellow sisters from a very early stage in its existence.[51] Such *dicta* may have formed the basis for the lives.

or translated into Middle Dutch in MS D. Further research would be needed to see whether this adaptation has to do with differences in the level of education and/or of religious practice between Devout women who lived in a convent and those who lived in a sister-house.

[46] MS D e.g. begins with the life of Salome Sticken (d.1449) (f. 1a–21b), whereas the same life is placed somewhere in the middle of MS DV (f. 190r–225r). This is because Salome was rectress of the House of Master Geert (c.1392–1408) before becoming prioress of the convent of Diepenveen (1412–1446).

[47] A Latin translation of part of this Book of Sisters is also extant; it can be found in the MS from Brussels mentioned above (see n. 34). For a discussion of the relation between these three texts, see Kühler, 1914, 341–53; cf. J. van der Veen, 'Het Diepenveense manuscript supplement 198 van de Athenaeumbibliotheek te Deventer', *Verslagen en mededelingen van de vereeniging tot beoefening van Overijsselsch regt en geschiedenis*, 91 (1976), 28–42, which provides a stemma (37–9).

[48] Cf. Jongen and Scheepsma, 1993, 301–10, in which the structure of the lives in MS D is analysed; these findings also hold true for MS DV.

[49] Cf. Sister Marie Josepha (= G.G. Wilbrink), 'De schrijfster van het Diepenveense Hs. D', in *Album philologum voor prof. dr. Theodor Baader* (Nijmegen, 1939), 157–71.

[50] Her name appears on the flyleaf of MS DV. Apparently this copyist is the same as the 'I' who appears in the prologue, the epilogue, and sometimes also in the lives themselves. Cf. Jongen and Scheepsma, 1993, 297–8.

[51] The *dicta* by John Brinckerinck, included in his life in MS DV, bear witness to this (see esp. ff.

Only the Diepenveen version of this Book of Sisters has a prologue and an epilogue.[52] The prologue reads as follows:

> In the name of the Father, the Son and the Holy Spirit I intend to write and compile something on the life and death of our venerable Father Johannes Brinckerinck. I will also write about a number of devout plants that have shot up in his orchard and blossomed there. As it is impossible to describe all, I intend to gather only a few of the many virtues here, so that we may imitate their virtue and example. For Saint Paul says 'For everything that was written in the past was written to teach us' [Rom. 15:4]. What follows now is also intended for the benefit of others who are wiser and more sensitive of disposition than I, so that everyone who reads this or to whom it is read will say a short prayer for me, for hereby I hope to rouse some to piety.[53]

As in the prologue to the Book of Sisters from the House of Master Geert, the moral aim of the book is expressed here and the importance of the virtues described is pointed out. This aim is restated in the epilogue:

> Nobody should think that there are not more sisters whose lives we ought to describe. Many devout sisters have died in this place and amongst them there were many whose virtues would definitely be worth recording. But if I wanted to describe the virtues of all the sisters, then I would not be finished in a hundred years. Let us therefore keep in mind these few things as an example and realize that imitating them will make a great enough demand on our weakness.[54]

32r–46v; on f. 36v he literally instructs a sister that she should try and learn from her fellow sisters' virtues.) Cf. Mertens, 1989, 194–5.

[52] Presumably the prologue and epilogue were only added when MS DV was made in 1524. Could this also be a reason why neither appears in MS D? Or was it perhaps not considered necessary to include them, as the House possessed its own Book of Sisters?

[53] MS DV, f. 1r: 'Inden namen des Vaders, des Soens ende des Hillighen Ghiestes heb ic voer mi ghenamen een weinich toe scriven ende toe vergaderen vanden leven ende starven onses eerwerdighen vaders heer Johan Brinckerincks, ende van sommighen devoeten planten die ghewassen ende opgheghaen sint in sinen bomgoert. Ende want mi onmoghelick weer al die dogheden toe scriven, soe heb ic opghesat een weynich toe vergaderen uut vollen, op dat wy hoer dogheden ende ex[c]empelen na mochten volghen. Want Sancte Pauwel secht: 'Al dat ghescreven is, dat is ghescreven tot onser leren' ende tot verbeterynghe andre die wyse[r] ende subtil[re] van sijnne sij[nt] dan ic sy, op dat voer my sollen bidden een cort ghebedeken alle die dit lesen of horen lesen, want ic hape hier sommighe mede tot devocien toe te verwecken.'

[54] MS DV, ff. 387v–388r: 'Item niemant en darf dencken of mienen dat wi vermoden dat daer niemant goet gheweest en is dan daer wy hoer leven van ghescreven hebben. Deer sijnt alte volle devoter susteren ghestorven ende der leefter noch ghenoch die dusdane dogheden hebben ende meer dogheden daer toe. Solde ic alder suster dogheden scriven, ic en vermetes mi in hondert jaren niet toe doen. Meer laet ons dit weijnich voer ons setten, als een excempelaer na toe leven ende dencken ons dit ghenoch toe wesen na onser crancheit na toe volghen.'

Genre and Function

We have now looked at two important Devout Books of Sisters. On the basis of these two examples, a list of the features that would seem to be characteristic of the genre and its function can be drawn up.[55] Hopefully, this set will serve as a point of reference for the study of similar texts in the future.[56] Six main characteristics can be distinguished:

1. As a rule, Books of Sisters are texts written by, for and about Devout sisters. Occasional exceptions to this basic rule, however, can easily be found, as is shown by the inclusion of the life of Johannes Brinckerinck in the Diepenveen Book of Sisters, as well as by the fact that a life written by Rector Rudolf Dier was included in the book from the House of Master Geert. These texts too, however, were edited and collected by sisters.

2. Books of Sisters are sets of texts in which a number of lives of deceased sisters from one specific convent or house are collected. Just as a train can have any number of carriages coupled to its locomotive, a Book of Sisters can have any number of lives coupled to its prologue.[57] Each of the manuscripts discussed in this paper was written by one copyist. The texts in this books were apparently written in one go. They were made accessible through an index listing the names of the sisters.

3. As a rule, the authors of the Books of Sisters are anonymous, but it is certain that they were part of the community whose history they record. Only in the case of the possible author of the lives that were added to the Diepenveen MS DV after 1494 can a name be suggested: that of the copyist Sister Griet Essink. Nowhere, however, does she claim to be the author. The authors of Books of Sisters put themselves at the service of their convents and wrote their sisters' lives on behalf of the entire community they belonged to.

4. Books of Sisters have usually come down to us in one manuscript only, which was owned by the convent discussed in the book. They aimed at an audience which did not extend beyond the convent's own spiritual community. This meant that they offered the women reading them or listening to them being read a possibility for identification which was realistic and

---

[55] MS D from the House of Master Geert does not conform to most of the characteristics that will be mentioned below. The unique position of this MS can be explained by the fact that the House of Master Geert owned a copy because the Diepenveen convent was founded from this sister-house and so their histories partly overlapped. MS D was adapted to the needs of the House of Master Geert; the order of the lives is different, there is no prologue or epilogue, and an index is lacking.

[56] The characteristics of the genre of the Devout Book of Sisters sketched here are very similar to those of another genre particular to the *Devotio Moderna*: the collation. Cf. Th. Mertens, 'Collatio und Codex im Bereich der Devotio moderna' (to appear in the proceedings of the colloquium 'Der Codex im Gebrauch', 11–13 June 1992, Münster); see also Mertens, '*Devotio Moderna* and Innovation' (in press).

[57] This simile was suggested to me by Dr Th. Mertens (Antwerp).

attainable. The fact that the books were written in the vernacular also clearly points to a female audience, as women usually did not understand Latin.[58]

5. Devout Books of Sisters were all begun shortly after 1470. In its present form MS G was definitely written after c.1456, and most probably a few years later. Although the two versions of the Diepenveen Book of Sisters date from 1524 and 1534, respectively, they go back to an exemplar that was written after 1478. After c.1505 no new lives were added to the Diepenveen Book of Sisters.[59] The late date of the copies of this Book shows that there was still a clear interest in the lives in later years.[60]

6. The function of the Devout Books of Sisters is made very clear in their prologues and epilogues: the virtues of the deceased sisters are described so that they may be imitated by their spiritual heirs. Even though the subject matter of the Books of Sisters is the history of a convent and its inhabitants, their primary goal is parenetic.[61]

These six points obviously only constitute a rough and provisional characterization of the Devout Book of Sisters, which will hopefully be refined and extended in the future. Much more research needs to be done, particularly into the structure and the spiritual concepts that are particular to this extraordinary type of women's literature.[62] It is very likely that a comparison between the Devout Books of Sisters and a parallel phenomenon in the German-speaking areas, the so-called *Schwesternbücher*, would yield significant results in this respect. *Schwesternbücher* are fourteenth-century Books of Sisters from the circles of the Dominican order.[63] Just as the *Devotio Moderna* marked a religious

---

[58] The extent to which female Devotionalists were acquainted with Latin is discussed in C. Lingier, 'Boekengebruik in vrouwenkloosters onder invloed van de Moderne Devotie', in Th. Mertens et al., *Boeken voor de eeuwigheid. Middelnederlands geestelijk proza* (Amsterdam, 1993), 280–94 and 454–66 (282–6).

[59] The last life included in MS DV is that of Cecilia van Marick (d.1504) (ff. 384v–388r).

[60] The Book of Sisters from the House of Lamme van Dieze was started after seven sisters and the rector died in an epidemic in 1483; their lives were the first to be written down. The last life to be included in this collection seems to be that of Andries Yserens (d.1502). Cf. Spitzen, 1875. The year of Rector Cornelis van Mechgelen's death, 1494, is the last one to be mentioned in the Book of Sisters from Emmerich; the book was finished on 5 Jan. 1503 (cf. Hövelmann, 1971, 46–51).

[61] That the Books of Sisters are nevertheless of great historical value was proved by W. J. Kühler, whose history of the convent of Diepenveen was mainly based on them (Kühler, 1914). De Man also praises the reliability of MS G as a source of historical information (De Man, 1919, esp. lxxx–lxxxiii).

[62] Some research has already been done. See L. Breure, 'Männliche und weibliche Ausdrucksformen in der Spiritualität der Devotio moderna', in *Frauenmystik im Mittelalter*, eds. P. Dinzelbacher and D. R. Bauer (Ostfildern bei Stuttgart, 1985), 231–55; L. Breure, *Doodsbeleving en levenshouding. Een historisch-psychologische studie betreffende de Moderne Devotie in het IJsselgebied in de 14e en 15e eeuw* (Hilversum, 1987); F. W. J. Koorn, 'Hollandse nuchterheid? De houding van de Moderne Devoten tegenover vrouwenmystiek en -ascese', in *Ons Geestelijk Erf*, 66 (1992), 97–114 (with a summary in English).

[63] For literature on this subject, see G. J. Lewis, *Bibliographie zur deutschen Frauenmystik des Mittelalters* (Berlin, 1989), sect. C. Without making a claim to be exhaustive, I would also

revival in the fifteenth century, the German Dominicans marked a reformation in the fourteenth century. This so-called 'German mysticism' brought about an explosion of religious literature in the vernacular intended for women. Like the Books of Sisters produced by the *Devotio Moderna*, the nine extant *Schwesternbücher* stand out because they too were written by, for and about women. Even though no research has yet been done into parallels and differences between *Schwesternbücher* and Devout Books of Sisters, such a comparison will be fruitful, especially since most manuscripts of *Schwesternbücher* date from the fifteenth century and were read in convents that had recently been reformed.[64]

Another avenue that should be explored is a comparison between the Books of Sisters and the Latin *Libri Fratrum* or Books of Brothers produced by the *Devotio Moderna*.[65] In particular, a comparison with these texts will shed more light on the specifically female aspects of the Books of Sisters. In this connection, the relation between the Devout Books of Brothers, the old *Vitae Patrum* and the *Libri Fratrum* of reforming orders like the Cistercians, the Dominicans and the Franciscans, are also interesting. All these reforming movements attempted to conform to the religious ideals of the early Christians and drew inspiration from their writings.[66] Research into the Devout *Libri Fratrum* as a literary genre, however, has as yet hardly begun, as the complexity of the Latin historiography of the *Devotio Moderna* is perhaps even greater than that of the vernacular texts.

mention: S. Ringler, *Viten- und Offenbarungsliteratur in Frauenklöstern des Mittelalters. Quellen und Studien* (Munich, 1980); Peters, 1988, esp. 129–35. G. J. Lewis is preparing a study of the *Schwesternbücher* in English, entitled *The Book of Sisters: By Women, For Women, About Women*; cf. G. J. Lewis, 'Die Verfasserinnen der Schwesternbücher des 14. Jahrhunderts', in *Akten des VIII. internationalen Germanisten-Kongress, Tokyo 1990: 'Begegnungen mit dem 'Fremden'. Grenzen-Traditionen-Vergleiche'* (Munich, 1991), 201, n. 1.

[64] Cf. Ringler, 1980, 3.

[65] Cf. Van Engen, 1986, 181–3; Jongen and Scheepsma 1993, 310–14.

[66] Van Engen, 1988, 'The Virtues', 183–5.

PASSING THE BOOK:
TESTAMENTARY TRANSMISSION OF RELIGIOUS LITERATURE TO AND BY WOMEN IN ENGLAND 1350–1500

Anne M. Dutton

Wills have been recognized as one of the most important sources for the study of medieval women's access to literature,[1] providing us with both a considerable number of women who owned books, and a considerable number of texts in the hands of those women.[2] Because religious texts are the most commonly mentioned texts in wills (after liturgical texts such as missals and paraliturgical texts such as primers or books of hours), wills seem to provide the most information about women's access to religious literature and, by extension, about one facet of women's religious lives. However, wills have also been acknowledged as one of the most problematic medieval sources, whose limitations render their contents difficult to interpret. Indeed, modern readers of these documents would do well to imagine that the medieval scribe had prefaced the will with the words *Caveat lector* instead of with the formulaic opening *In nomine dei amen*.

I would like to thank Felicity Riddy and P. J. P. Goldberg for their expert guidance and assistance. Financial support was given by the Social Sciences and Humanities Research Council of Canada.

1 Margaret Deanesly, 'Vernacular Books in England in the Fourteenth and Fifteenth Centuries', *Modern Language Review*, 15 (1920), 349–58; Joel T. Rosenthal, 'Aristocratic Cultural Patronage and Book Bequests, 1350–1500', *Bulletin of the John Rylands University Library of Manchester*, 64 (1982), 522–48; Carol M. Meale, ' "... alle the bokes that I have of latyn, englisch, and frensch": Laywomen and their Books in Late Medieval England', in *Women and Literature in Britain, 1150–1500*, ed. Meale (Cambridge, 1993), 128–58.

2 Although strictly speaking, wills dealt with the devise of real estate and testaments with bequests of moveable goods, in practice many testators did not distinguish between the two, often leaving a 'last will and testament'. In this paper I use the noun 'will' and the adjective 'testamentary' for all documents that deal with the disposal of a deceased person's estate. See Norman P. Tanner, *The Church in Late Medieval Norwich, 1370–1532* (Toronto, 1984), 113, n. 1; Caroline M. Barron, 'The "Golden" Age of Women in Medieval London', *Reading Medieval Studies*, 15 (1989), 37–8; Clive Burgess, 'Late Medieval Wills and Pious Convention: Testamentary Evidence Reconsidered', in *Profit, Piety and the Professions in Later Medieval England*, ed. Michael Hicks (Gloucester, 1990), 30.

This paper is a study of women's ownership of religious literature in England, as recorded in wills and inventories dated between 1350 and 1500.[3] While bearing in mind the imaginary *caveat*, I feel that probate evidence, despite its limitations, can tell us a great deal about the social status of female owners of religious literature, and the effect that social status and religious vocation had on the type of such texts owned by women, as well as indicating changes that occurred over the 150-year period. Nevertheless, to draw conclusions from a single source is unwise indeed. Comparison is therefore made to a study of sixty-seven extant manuscripts, which, through ownership inscriptions, names and armorial bearings, are known to have belonged to or have been used by women.[4] Extant manuscripts, of course, have their own limitations and survival patterns, but as these are different from those of wills, manuscripts provide valuable comparative material against which we can evaluate wills as sources for examining patterns of women's ownership of religious literature.

The wills and inventories used in this study are drawn from across England, although I have used more from York diocese than from any other geographical region. In order to utilize information from a much larger number of wills than could have been read during my time at York, I have used as the basis of my sample the owner index of Susan H. Cavanaugh's unpublished doctoral thesis, 'A Study of Private Book Ownership in England 1300–1450', which is a lengthy index listing individual book owners and their books, drawn from her examination of approximately eight thousand printed wills.[5] I have supplemented Cavanaugh's owner index with my own reading of both printed and unprinted wills from York diocese, the work of both Jo Ann Hoeppner Moran and Jonathan Hughes on wills from York diocese, and Norman Tanner's study of book bequests in the wills of the inhabitants of Norwich.[6] I

---

[3] I have excluded from this study all bequests of religious writings of a set or formulaic nature, i.e. all discrete prayers, and all liturgical and paraliturgical texts including prayer-books, psalters and primers or books of hours. This is for brevity's sake, and because I feel that they may have been intended to be used in a fundamentally different fashion from the texts discussed in this paper.

[4] These manuscripts are listed in the Appendix. In compiling the list of manuscripts in the hands of female religious, Neil Ker's *Medieval Libraries of Great Britain: A List of Surviving Books*, 2nd edn (London, 1964) and the supplement to Ker's volume, ed. Andrew G. Watson (London, 1987) have been invaluable.

[5] Susan H. Cavanaugh, 'A Study of Private Book Ownership in England 1300–1450', Univ. of Pennsylvania, 1980. The use of material drawn from Cavanaugh's thesis has its own limitations: she relies entirely on material in print, the period covered does not correspond exactly to my own, and most importantly, she gives information only about those testators who bequeath books, and no information about her will sample as a whole.

[6] See Jo Ann Hoeppner Moran, *The Growth of English Schooling 1340–1548: Learning, Literacy, and Laicization in Pre-Reformation York Diocese* (Princeton, 1985), 152–8; Jonathan Hughes, *Pastors and Visionaries: Religion and Secular Life in Late Medieval Yorkshire* (Woodbridge, Suffolk, and Wolfeboro, New Hampshire, 1988), *passim*; Norman P. Tanner, *The Church in Late Medieval Norwich 1370–1532* (Toronto, 1984), 111–12, 193–7; York, Borthwick Institute of Historical Research, Probate Register 2.

have extracted all bequests of religious texts to or by women, and bequests of religious texts that are noted as having been borrowed by or formerly in the possession of women, from the wills of both female and male testators, and entered them into a database.[7]

In using the database, I am concerned not with the numbers of actual women, or with the number of actual books appearing in the wills and inventories, but rather with the number of transmissions of books from men to women, from women to women and from women to men. Thus the number of transmissions does not directly correspond to the number of actual people and books involved. For example, Eleanor Roos bequeathed four religious books in 1438; as a result she appears in four separate transmissions.[8] Transmissions of books from a woman to another woman are, in effect, recorded twice, for it is equally significant that a woman bequeathed a book as that another received it. That the two books are indeed one and the same is insignificant. For example, in 1451 Mercy Ormesby bequeathed 'unum librum Anglie vocatum, the Chastesing of goddes children' to the prioress of Easebourne Priory (Sussex). Such a bequest provides information about two female book owners, and it is consequently recorded first for the information it gives about the donor, Mercy Ormesby, and second for the information it gives about the recipient, the prioress of Easebourne.[9]

Social Status

The problems and limitations inherent in the use of probate evidence for any purpose are well-established.[10] None the less, it is worth briefly drawing attention here to those that affect any attempt to determine the social complexion of the female audience of religious literature. First, the representativeness of the evidence provided by wills remains questionable: it appears that only a minority of the population made and registered written wills. Since wills have different survival rates from different periods and geographical regions, it is not known what proportion still survives today.[11] Similarly, there are few extant inventories listing the moveable possessions of women; again, how representative these documents are of their kind cannot be known. Second, evidence drawn from these sources can, of course, tell us only about those

---

7 I have used Borland's Reflex 2.0 (1989), which has, among other merits, the advantage of simplicity.

8 James Raine (ed.), *Testamenta Eboracensia: A Selection of Wills from the Registry at York*, ii, Surtees Soc. 30 (Durham, London and Edinburgh, 1855), 65–6.

9 H. R. Plomer, 'Books Mentioned in Wills', *Transactions of the Bibliographical Society*, 7 (1904), 116. As can be seen from Tables I and II, below, there are 103 transmissions in the database. These transmissions are contained in 31 wills and one inventory.

10 See Burgess, 'Late Medieval Wills and Pious Convention'; P. J. P. Goldberg, *Women, Work, and Life Cycle in a Medieval Economy: Women in York and Yorkshire c.1300–1520* (Oxford, 1992), 366–7; Meale, 'Laywomen and their Books', 130.

11 This is clear from J. S. W. Gibson, *Wills and Where to Find Them* (Chichester, 1974).

people who made and registered written wills, and those whom they mention in their wills. The social status of the will-making population appears not to have been constant in England throughout the 150-year period under consideration; in the middle of the fourteenth century it was largely, although by no means exclusively, aristocratic; by the end of the fifteenth century, however, will-making as an activity had percolated down the social scale to include a far wider cross-section of the population.[12]

The wills of female testators (which for this study are the most important, as they yield the largest number of female owners of religious literature) pose further problems. Throughout the 150-year period, far fewer women than men made written wills, although the smaller number of extant female wills may have resulted partly from fewer of them being registered. Although some female testators were unmarried, the vast majority of women who made wills were widows; married women needed the permission of their husbands to make and register a will.[13] Finally, it can be very difficult to determine the precise social status of a testator, whether male or female, and frequently impossible to determine that of a recipient of a particular bequest.[14] Wills were not drawn up for the benefit of historians! In my database there are twenty-three female owners of religious literature whose precise social status I have been unable to determine; in thirteen of these cases, however, I have been able to place the women into categories of probable status.

Despite these limitations, probate material and inventories suggest that until the first quarter of the fifteenth century, female owners of spiritual literature were predominantly aristocratic or enclosed religious (I would not go so far as to say exclusively, given that my will sample is by no means exhaustive). These two groups, aristocratic laywomen and female religious, were not mutually exclusive: in the database are 13 bequests of religious literature made to individual nuns, of which 9 are to nuns from noble families and 2 are to nuns from gentry families. I have not been able to determine the social background of the 2 remaining individual nuns. The aristocracy and religious continued to predominate throughout the fifteenth century; however, the presence of women of merchant families is noticeable, and is most strongly felt in the last quarter of the century. Table I shows the breakdown, by 25-year periods, of the social status of the women involved in transmissions.

---

[12] It appears that this was the case for York. See P. J. P. Goldberg, *Women, Work, and Life-Cycle*, 366.

[13] See Barron, 'The "Golden" Age of Women in Medieval London', 37–9, 43; Goldberg, *Women, Work, and Life-Cycle in a Medieval Economy*, 266–72. All female testators were laywomen; female religious, in theory, had no personal possessions, and they did not make written wills. This necessarily has implications for my discussion of nuns' ownership of religious literature below.

[14] Clive Burgess evidently had the same difficulty: see his 'Late Medieval Wills and Pious Convention', 15.

TABLE I. TOTALS FOR THE SOCIAL STATUS OF WOMEN INVOLVED
IN THE TESTAMENTARY TRANSMISSION OF RELIGIOUS LITERATURE

CLASS	1350–74	1375–99	1400–24	1425–49	1450–74	1475–1500	TOTAL
Aristocracy + Probable Aristocracy	2	10	10	16	9	9	56
Religious	1	2	2	4	2	11	22
Merchant + Probable Merchant	0	0	0	4	0	6	10
Gentry/ Merchant	0	0	2	3	0	0	5
Unknown	0	0	4	5	0	1	10
TOTAL	3	12	18	32	11	27	103

From 1350 until 1399, the social status of all of the women in my database has been determined: these fourteenth-century owners of religious literature are either aristocratic laywomen (both nobility and gentry) or female religious. The numbers of aristocratic laywomen clearly predominate; this is to be expected, however, for nuns appear in wills only as recipients, giving us a limited view of the book ownership of enclosed women. Throughout the course of the fifteenth century, aristocratic women, along with women most likely to be aristocratic, form the largest percentage in every 25-year period except 1475–1500, where women religious outnumber aristocratic laywomen. Women religious are the second largest group of identifiable women in every period except that of 1400–1424, where their numbers equal those of women who through birth and marriage belong to both gentry and merchant families (these women are described as "gentry/merchant" in Table I), and that of 1475–1500, where, as I have already pointed out, they are the most numerous.

Women connected with merchant families begin to appear in transmissions of religious literature in the first quarter of the fifteenth century, the first transmission occurring in 1408. At first these involve only women who belong to both merchant and gentry families, and it is not until the second quarter of the fifteenth century that mercantile women with no known connections to the aristocracy appear. The number of women from merchant families remains low until the last quarter of the century. The appearance of such women only in the fifteenth century cannot be explained simply through the popularization of will-making outside the ranks of the aristocracy, and a consequent increase in the number of extant wills of female testators from the urban classes. Urban women appear earlier in my database involved in transmissions of other types of books, primarily liturgical and paraliturgical. Nor can it be explained simply through my reliance primarily upon printed wills, which are heavily biased towards the aristocracy and towards male testators. The current work of Sebastian Sutcliffe on unprinted wills of female testators in East Anglia gives a similar picture to that which I have just presented: women from merchant families, or who are most likely to be from merchant families, do not appear to participate in transmissions of religious literature until the second half of the fifteenth century, although they appear earlier as donors and recipients of other types of literature.[15]

I would suggest that what we see here is something new, a change in the pattern of female ownership of religious texts. What originated as a predominantly aristocratic and religious activity begins to embrace a small number of merchant women. It is significant, I believe, that this phenomenon occurs in the fifteenth century, when the urban merchant élite distinguished itself from the less prosperous urban classes and looked towards the aristocracy – primarily the lower aristocracy.[16] It is possible that the ownership of religious literature was part of an originally aristocratic and religious devotional culture that only extended to the non-aristocratic classes when they began to have aspirations to and connections with the aristocracy.

In contrast to the picture of the social status of female owners of religious literature that emerges from a study of probate and inventory evidence, the picture produced by extant manuscripts known to have belonged to or have been used by women in fourteenth- and fifteenth-century England is rather static. Of the 67 manuscripts containing religious treatises, 16, containing 91 religious texts, belonged to laywomen. Of these lay owners, 14 were aristocratic, the majority of whom were of the nobility rather than the gentry; the social status of the other 2 laywomen is unknown. A further 40 manuscripts, containing 105 texts, belonged to female religious (nunneries, individual nuns and one anchoress), and the remaining 14 manuscripts, containing 52 texts, belonged to women whose social status or religious vocation I have been as yet unable to establish.[17] The predominance of aristocratic laywomen and nuns (who were most often from aristocratic families) may in part be the reflection of survival patterns peculiar to manuscripts. It is likely that those manuscripts that survive today were the more expensive ones of their day, first because they would have been produced of higher-quality materials and therefore would have been more durable than their less expensive counterparts, and second because their value may have ensured that later generations kept them. Manuscript evidence therefore confirms part of the evidence contained in wills and inventories – that nuns and aristocratic women were prominent owners of religious literature – but tells us nothing about urban women. Moreover, because of the difficulties in establishing when a particular

15 Personal communication.
16 See Sylvia Thrupp, *The Merchant Class of Medieval London* (1948. Repr. Ann Arbor, 1962).
17 The total number of manuscripts remains 67, as 3 had multiple owners of different religious vocations.

manuscript was owned or used by a particular woman or community of women, manuscripts are less likely than wills to indicate potential changes in the social status of female owners of religious literature.

Types of Texts

I turn now from looking at the social complexion of the women who bequeathed or received spiritual literature to looking at the texts themselves, and determining whether social status or religious vocation affected the types of religious texts used by such women. Again, there are well-known difficulties in using testamentary material to determine a corpus of religious literature in the hands of women. In many wills and inventories, insufficient information is given about the text, making its identification difficult or impossible. More importantly, however, it is widely accepted that wills do not itemize all of a testator's possessions. Because of this, a comparison of the evidence presented in wills and inventories with that presented in the extant manuscripts of medieval women is all the more valuable.

In total, thirty-five separate religious texts appear in the wills and inventories (many appearing more than once), although this number is somewhat arbitrary, as it is sometimes difficult to identify a particular text or to distinguish between two or more texts. For example, an 'English Book of St Bridget' is bequeathed in 1481 to the nuns of Thetford Priory (Norfolk) by Margaret Purdans.[18] Is this a life of St Bridget (perhaps a literary predecessor of the *Lyfe of Seynt Birgetta* attributed to Thomas Gascoigne), or is it the same text as the 'libro compilato in lingua Anglica de Revelationibus Sanctae Brigidae' that appears in the 1468 inventory of Elizabeth Sewerby and as the 'boke of the Revelacions of Saint Burgitte', bequeathed to Anne de la Pole, prioress of Syon Abbey (Middlesex), by her grandmother, Cecily Neville, Duchess of York, in 1495?[19] Similarly, I have six transmissions of texts called 'the Passion'. Although I have grouped these together as the same text, it is possible that they are texts dissimilar enough to warrant separate listings. These thirty-five or so texts form a wide-ranging body of spiritual literature that includes some of the best-known medieval texts, such as *The Golden Legend*, *The Prick of Conscience* and the *Pore Caitiff*, and some of the best-known writers, such as Walter Hilton and Richard Rolle.[20]

Table II shows the types of religious literature owned by women of different social groups and religious vocations.

[18] See Tanner, *The Church in Late Medieval Norwich*, 112.

[19] For the inventory of Elizabeth Sewerby, see Raine, *Testamenta Eboracensia* ii, 161–8; for the will of Cecily, Duchess of York, see John Gough Nichols and John Bruce (eds.), *Wills from Doctors' Commons*, Camden Soc. 83 (1963), 1–8.

[20] Of the 35 texts, 8 are unidentifiable from the titles given in the wills. Over half of the remaining 27 texts also appear in manuscripts belonging to women in 14th- and 15th-century England.

TABLE II. TYPES OF RELIGIOUS LITERATURE USED BY WOMEN
OF DIFFERENT SOCIAL STATUS, AND NUMBERS
OF TRANSMISSIONS OF EACH CATEGORY

CLASS	H	D	M	G	V/M	ML	BIB	UNC	UNK	TOTAL
Nobility + Probable Nobility	14	4	3	0	3	0	0	0	3	27
Gentry + Probable Gentry	5	5	6	2	3	5	1	0	2	29
Religious	6	3	3	1	3	4	0	0	2	22
Merchant + Probable Merchant	3	0	0	1	1	1	0	1	3	10
Gentry/ Merchant	1	0	1	0	0	1	0	1	1	5
Unknown	2	0	1	0	0	1	0	2	4	10
TOTAL	31	12	14	4	10	12	1	4	15	103

N/H = Hagiographic; D = Didactic; M = Meditative; G = Guides to a Spiritual Life; V/M = Visionary or Mystical; ML = Moral; BIB = Biblical Commentary; UNC = Unclassified; UNK = Unknown.

Female religious (including individual nuns, nunneries, and one anchoress) are involved (as recipients) in twenty-two transmissions, involving sixteen different texts. These texts can be grouped into seven fairly broad categories:

1. Narrative or Hagiographic texts, including the *Legenda Aurea*, a *Vitae Patrum*, a *Life of St Katherine*, a *Life of St Margaret* and a *Life of St Katherine of Siena*.

2. Didactic texts, which are designed to instruct the audience in the syllabus of religious instruction as set out in the Lambeth Constitutions of 1281.[21] These include the *Manuel des Péchés*, a work on the Vices and Virtues, and a copy of what appears to be St Gregory's *Cura Pastoralis*.

3. Meditative texts, including a Life of Christ, and a text called 'Bonaventure', presumably the Pseudo-Bonaventuran *Meditationes Vitae Christi*.

4. Guides to leading a spiritual life, whether an interior or exterior life. These include *The Doctrine of the Heart*.

---

[21] F. M. Powicke and C. R. Cheney, *Councils and Synods with Other Documents Relating to the English Church* (Oxford, 1964), ii, part 2, 900. See G. H. Russell, 'Vernacular Instruction of the Laity in the Later Middle Ages: Some Texts and Notes', *Journal of Religious History*, 2 (1962), 98–119.

5. The writings of mystics or visionaries, here including the *Revelations of St Bridget*.

6. Treatises that encourage moral self-scrutiny. Many of these works deal with questions of sin, temptation and tribulation, and offer advice on coping with moral and spiritual dilemmas. Here these include *The Prick of Conscience*, and *The Chastising of God's Children*.

7. Unidentifiable works, such as an unnamed work by Walter Hilton, most probably his *Scale of Perfection*, and a book of prayers and devotions.

All but two of these texts (the *Life of St Katherine of Siena* and the *Manuel des Péchés*) are also found in bequests to or by laywomen.

Noblewomen and those unknown women whom I believe to be members of the nobility are involved in twenty-seven transmissions, involving fifteen different texts. These texts fall into five of the seven categories listed above for women religious. Hagiographic texts include the *Legenda Aurea*, the *Vitae Patrum*, a Life of St Katherine and a text called *Saintz Ryall*.[22] Didactic texts include a book of the Pater Noster, a work on the vices and virtues and what appears to be St Gregory's *Cura Pastoralis*. Meditative texts include a work on the Passion of Christ and what is presumably Pseudo-Bonaventure's *Meditationes Vitae Christi*; and mystical works include 'the Book of St Matilde' and a 'Maulde Buke', both of which are probably the *Liber Specialis Gratiae* of Mechthild of Hackeborn, and the *Revelations of St Bridget*. Three texts remain unidentified: *Grace Dieu* (possibly the *Holy Boke Gratia Dei* or *The Pilgrimage of the Soul*), a book of prayers and devotions and an unnamed work by Hilton.

The religious treatises bequeathed to and by gentry women, and those who are most likely of gentry families, do not differ greatly from those bequeathed to nuns and to and by noblewomen. Gentry women are involved altogether in twenty-nine transmissions, involving eighteen different texts. Hagiographic texts include the *Legenda Aurea* and St Gregory's *Dialogues*; didactic texts include the *Pore Caitiff*, a work entitled 'Credo in Deum' and a work on the vices and virtues. Meditative treatises include works on the Passion, Lives of Christ, 'Bonaventure' (probably the *Meditationes Vitae Christi*) and Richard Rolle's *Meditation on the Passion*, and mystical texts include the writings of Mechthild of Hackeborn and the Revelations of St Bridget. Texts encouraging moral self-scrutiny include *The Book of Tribulation*, *The Prick of Conscience* and *The Chastising of God's Children*. One guide to leading a spiritual life, Book I of Hilton's *Scale of Perfection*, is also found in the hands of gentry women, as is one biblical commentary, on the Gospel of Matthew. Two texts remain unidentified: one entitled *The Visitation of the Virgin Mary*, and a book of prayers and devotions.

Women from merchant families (including gentry/merchant women), or who are likely to be from merchant families, are involved in fifteen transmissions, involving fourteen different religious texts. Four of the texts are

---

[22] From the title, this appears to be a work on royal saints. It may, however, be the *Sain Graal*, and thus not be a spiritual work at all.

hagiographic: the *Legenda Aurea*, the *Life of St Margaret*, *Barlaham and Josephat* and *St Patrick's Purgatory*. One meditative text, a text on the Passion, is found, along with one guide to the spiritual life, *The Doctrine of the Heart*, and one mystical work, the *Revelations of St Bridget*. Two further texts are treatises encouraging moral self-scrutiny: Henry of Lancaster's *Livre de Seyntz Medicines* and *The Prick of Conscience*. Other texts include *The Spirit of Guy*, *Speculum Guy of Warwick*, one named *Gaudes Beate Marie*, an unnamed work by Walter Hilton and a *Book of St Katherine*, which may be a life of St Katherine or the writings of St Catherine of Siena.

The remaining ten transmissions involve women for whom I have been unable to establish social status. There are ten separate texts bequeathed, all but two of which are also found in the wills of women whose social status or religious vocation is known: two hagiographic works, *Barlaham and Josephat* and *St Patrick's Purgatory*; one meditative work on the Passion; and one moral treatise, Henry of Lancaster's *Livre de Seyntz Medicines*. Other texts include *The Spirit of Guy*, the *Speculum Guy of Warwick*, a unnamed work by Hilton, a *Gaudes Beate Marie* and, for the first time, a text entitled *St Gregory*, which may be a life of Gregory or one of his works, and one entitled *St Crisostom*, which again may be a life of the saint or one of his works.

There are thus no clear patterns in probate and inventory material indicating that female religious had access to different spiritual texts from those available to laywomen, or that women of different social classes had access to different types of texts. The evidence from extant manuscripts, moreover, supports this finding: the 91 texts in the hands of (predominantly noble) laywomen fall into the same broad categories as the 105 texts used or owned by nuns and anchoresses; indeed, at least half of the texts in manuscripts owned by laywomen are also found in manuscripts belonging to enclosed women. The similarity of literary material across the boundaries of religious vocation and social status argues for a devotional culture common to nuns and laywomen, regardless of social status. Once an individual woman gained access to that culture, her social status evidently did not limit the texts available to her.

Women's use of religious literature was almost exclusively in the vernacular. Of the 103 transmissions of religious literature in wills and inventories, 41 involve texts written in Middle English, 12 involve texts in French, and only one transmission involves a Latin text.[23] The remaining 49 transmissions involve texts whose language is neither specified nor determinable, although there is no reason to believe that these texts follow a different language pattern. The picture of women's use of vernacular rather than Latin writings is mirrored in the evidence drawn from extant manuscripts. Of the 248 religious texts that appear in the 67 extant manuscripts belonging to women, 210 are in Middle English, 26 are in French, and only 12 are in Latin.

---

[23] The Latin text is a Life of Christ that appears in the 1468 inventory of Elizabeth Sewerby. See above, n. 19.

Evidence from both wills and manuscripts indicate a decline in the use of French religious treatises by women, both religious and lay, during the fifteenth century.[24] This is seen most clearly in wills, where the proportion of French texts decreases, both among those texts whose language is specified or determinable and among all texts, over each 25-year period, until no French texts appear after 1450. Correspondingly, texts in English begin to appear after the turn of the fifteenth century, and their proportion among all texts increases throughout the century. Nevertheless English texts do not oust their French counterparts entirely: at the very end of the fifteenth century Cecily Welles, daughter of Edward IV and Elizabeth Woodville, owned a copy of *La Lumiere as Lais*, while a collection of French religious texts belonged to the nuns of Derby.[25] The decline of French and increasing prominence of English corresponds in time with the appearance in probate evidence of mercantile women as owners of religious literature, of whom only one appears as the owner of a French text. However, as there are also no aristocratic or religious owners of French texts after 1450, the shift in language does not appear to be directly class-related.

Also in the course of the 150-year period under examination, particular texts appear in wills, inventories and manuscripts, which demonstrate women's participation in certain devotional movements in England. The writings of both Richard Rolle and Walter Hilton appear in fifteenth-century wills and manuscripts, as do the writings of Continental women visionaries such as St Bridget of Sweden, Mechthild of Hackeborn and St Catherine of Siena.[26] Interest in spiritual writers from the Low Countries is also evident through women's ownership of manuscripts containing Thomas à Kempis's *De Imitatione Christi*

[24] The relationship between French and English – where, when, by whom and for what purposes each was used in late medieval England – is a matter of immense complexity and the subject of a long-standing debate. See M. Dominica Legge, 'Anglo-Norman and the Historian', *History* (n.s.), 26 (1941), 163–75; William Rothwell, 'The Role of French in Thirteenth-Century England', *Bulletin of the John Rylands University Library of Manchester*, 58 (1976), 445–66; Helen Suggett, 'The Use of French in England in the Later Middle Ages', *Transactions of the Royal Historical Society* (4th ser.), 28 (1946), 61–83; R. M. Wilson, 'English and French in England 1100–1300', *History* (n.s.), 28 (1943), 37–60.

[25] London, BL Royal 15. D. II, which also contains an illuminated French Apocalypse; London, BL Egerton 2710.

[26] For texts by Rolle see Raine, *Testamenta Eboracensia* ii, 161–8; Cambridge, Univ. Library Add. 3042; Cambridge, Univ. Library Ii. 6. 40. For Hilton's *Scale of Perfection* see Raine, *Testamenta Eboracensia* ii, 65–6; Cambridge, Corpus Christi College 268, London, BL Add. 11748; London, BL Harley 2387; London, BL Harley 2397; Oxford, All Souls College 25; Philadelphia, Rosenbach Foundation Inc., H 491 (printed book); New Haven, Centre for British Art; and his *Epistle on Mixed Life* is in London, BL Harley 2254. Bequests of the *Revelations of St Bridget* are listed in Raine, *Testamenta Eboracensia* ii, 161–8; Tanner, *The Church in Late Medieval Norwich*, 112; and Nichols and Bruce (eds.), *Wills from Doctors' Commons*, 1–8. For the writings of Mechthild of Hackeborn, see Raine, *Testamenta Eboracensia* ii, 65–6; Nichols and Bruce (eds.), *Wills from Doctors' Commons*, 1–8; London, BL Egerton 2006; London, BL Harley 494; London, BL Harley 4012; London, Lambeth Palace 3597. For texts by or about St Catherine of Siena, see Nichols and Bruce (eds.), *Wills from Doctors' Commons*, 1–8; and London, BL Harley 2409.

and the translation of Heinrich Suso's *Horologium Sapienciae*, the *Seven Points of True Love and Everlasting Wisdom*.[27]

It is now time to draw together some conclusions. P. J. P. Goldberg remarked that the medievalist is used to making a little evidence work very hard.[28] In this paper I have subjected testamentary material to a series of rigorous exercises in order to elicit information about women's ownership of religious literature from 1350 to 1500. Four main points have emerged. First, there appears to be a change in the social status of women involved in testamentary transmissions: until the first quarter of the fifteenth century, ownership is predominantly an aristocratic and religious activity. However, in the fifteenth century, women of merchant families, first those with connections to the aristocracy and later those without any such apparent connections, appear as owners of spiritual texts, although the majority of women continue to come from the ranks of the aristocracy and the nunnery. Second, religious vocation and social class have no visible effect or influence on the type of religious texts available to women. Third, the corpus of literature in the hands of women is almost exclusively in the vernacular and, as the fifteenth century progresses, in English rather than French. Finally, women's ownership of literature demonstrates their involvement in particular late medieval devotional movements that appeared in England. For the most part, the evidence offered by wills and inventories is supported by that offered by manuscripts owned or used by women themselves. The parallel nature of the evidence indicates that the limitations of probate material are not insurmountable, and, indeed, that wills and inventories have much to tell us. The subject does not stop here; more work needs to be done on women's access to religious literature, to answer questions not only regarding the social complexion of the audience and the texts that they used, but also regarding how such literature contributed to women's devotional lives. 'Books', wrote Milton, 'are not absolutely dead things'; indeed, we can hear their faint voices across an ocean of five centuries.

---

[27] For Kempis's *De Imitatio Christi*, see Glasgow, Hunterian Library 136; and for Suso's *Seven Points of True Love and Everlasting Wisdom*, see Cambridge, Gonville and Caius College 390/610; and Cambridge, Corpus Christi College 268.

[28] Goldberg, *Women, Work and Life Cycle*, 26.

APPENDIX

EXTANT MANUSCRIPTS OWNED OR USED BY WOMEN

Female Religious

Cambridge, University Library Ii. 6. 40
Cambridge, University Library
Additional 8335
Cambridge, Fitzwilliam Museum
McClean 123
Cambridge, Gonville and Caius
College 390/610
Cambridge, Corpus Christi College 268
Cambridge, Trinity College 301 (B. 14.
15)
Cambridge, Sidney Sussex College Bb.
2. 14 (printed book)
Glasgow, University Library
Hunterian 136
Göttingen, University Library (printed
book)
Lincoln, Cathedral Library 199
London, BL Additional 11748
London, BL Harley 994
London, BL Harley 2409
London, BL Harley 2387
London, BL Harley 2254
London, BL Egerton 2710
London, BL Harley 2397
London, BL Royal 7. F. III
London, BL Lansdowne 436
London, BL Cotton Cleopatra C. vi
London, BL Arundel 396

London, BL Additional 10596
London, BL Additional 70513
London, Lambeth Palace 1495. 4
(printed book)
Miss C. Foyle
New York, Public Library 19
New York, Public Library Spencer 1519
Oxford, Bodleian Library Douce 322
Oxford, Bodleian Library Laud 416
Oxford, Bodleian Library Bodley 923
Oxford, Bodleian Library Douce 372
Oxford, Bodleian Library Hatton 18
Oxford, Bodleian Library Rawlinson B.
408
Oxford, Jesus College 39
Oxford, All Souls College 25
Paris, Bibliothèque Nationale Fonds
Français 1038
Philadelphia, Rosenbach Foundation
Inc. H. 419
Stratton-on-the-Fosse, Downside
Abbey 26542
untraced printed book listed in *Catal.
Bibliothecae Harleianae* (1744) iii, no.
1560
untraced manuscript from Meade
Falkner Sale (Sotheby, 12 Dec. 1932),
lot 387

Laywomen

Cambridge, University Library
Additional 3042
Cambridge, University Library Gg. 1. 6
Edinburgh, National Library of
Scotland Advocates 18. 1. 7
London, BL Cotton Vitellius F. vii
London, BL Egerton 2006

London, BL Harley 1706
London, BL Harley 2254
London, BL Harley 4012
London, BL Royal 15. D. II
Oxford, Bodleian Library Douce 288
Oxford, Bodleian Library e Mus. 35
Oxford, Bodleian Library Hatton 73

Oxford, Corpus Christi College 220   Tokyo, Takamiya 8
New Haven, Centre for British Art
Paris, Bibliothèque Nationale Fonds
    Français 1038

Women of Unknown Religious Vocation

Cambridge, University Library Ii. 6. 40   London, BL Sloane 779
Cambridge, University Library Kk. 1. 7   London, BL Stowe 38
Cambridge, Corpus Christi College 142   London, Lambeth Palace 3597
Cambridge, Gonville and Caius   Manchester, John Rylands University
    College 124/61   Library 94
Cambridge, St John's College 29   Oxford, Bodleian Library Digby 99
London, BL Harley 45   Oxford, Bodleian Library Rawlinson
London, BL Harley 494   C. 882
London, BL Harley 2406

GOD'S ALMIGHTY HAND:
WOMEN CO-WRITING THE BOOK

Rosalynn Voaden

Cry out therefore and write thus.[1]

So God commanded Hildegard of Bingen in a vision.

Let your women keep silence in the churches: for it is not permitted unto them to speak.[2]

Thus St Paul established the role of women in the church for two millennia.

Þow merualles þat I speke and shewe þe swilke grete þinges. Hoppes þowe þat I do it for þiself allone? Nai forsothe, bot for þe edificacion of oþir and hele of oþir.[3]

So Christ instructed Bridget of Sweden in her responsibility as a prophet.

Speech can be used in two ways. In one way privately. . . . In this way the grace of speech becomes a woman. The other way publicly, addressing oneself to the whole Church. This is not conceded to women.[4]

Thus Aquinas interpreted Paul's teaching, applying it here specifically to the question of how women who have the gift of prophecy can speak of their prophecies.

Women visionaries in the Middle Ages found themselves in an impossible position. On the one hand, as prophets, they were commanded by God to communicate their revelations. On the other, as women, they were commanded by men to keep silent. The prophetic mandate is to reveal the word of God to the people. The doctrine and tradition of the Church stipulated that

---

[1] Hildegard of Bingen, *Scivias*, transl. Mother Columba Hart and Jane Bishop (New York, 1990), 61.

[2] I Corinthians 14: 34.

[3] *The Liber Celestis of St Bridget of Sweden*, ed. Roger Ellis, EETS 291 (Oxford, 1987), 155. [You wonder that I speak to you, and show you such great things. Do you expect that I do it for you alone? No, in truth, but for the instruction of others, and their salvation.] [My transl.]

[4] Thomas Aquinas, *Summa Theologiae*, ed. Thomas Gilby O.P., 60 vols. (Manchester, 1963–), xlv: *Prophecy and Other Charisms (2a2ae: 171–8)* transl. and ed. Roland Potter O.P. (1970), 133.

women 'are not perfected in wisdom so as to be fit to be entrusted with public teaching.'[5] Preaching and teaching were forbidden to women; for those women who felt impelled to communicate, the only solution was to write, although this was by no means an easy or a safe option. Authors could be – and were – burned along with their books. However, for the kind of global communication usually enjoined on prophets, writing was the only course open to women. Writing disembodied the word, freeing the prophetic message from its association with woman in all her corporeality and corruption. Rather than an emotional, vernacular flow of words issuing from an orifice in the 'grotesque' body of a woman, the Word of God was transmitted through the written *corpus*, which was, undoubtedly, masculine: sealed, rational and Latinate.[6] Recognizing at some level of awareness the restrictions which hedged around their communication, an overwhelming majority of medieval women visionaries who were involved in the writing and/or editing of their own representations of visionary experience included in their works some account of their divine call to write.[7] In this way they claimed for themselves divinely authorized access to the one form of communication which was not closed to them by tradition and culture, and thereby established their mandate to write their revelations.

This paper will explore the representations, and the significance, of the divine call-to-write vision of a number of women, as well as varying responses to the call. It will then consider the practical mechanics involved in obeying the command to write, and suggest why a *de facto* approval of visionary women writing accorded with the needs of the ecclesiastical authorities. It should at this point be established that in this paper, a visionary's 'writing' means both the visionary herself physically writing, and/or her dictating to a scribe. The important factor is the act of composition; the results of this act were recorded through either of the above means.[8]

The call-to-write vision was pivotal in the visionary experience. It was this divine command which thrust the visionary from the private space within her soul where she enjoyed ineffable communion with God, into confrontation with the world, into a public space in which all prophets were viewed with suspicion and women prophets were generally believed to be false until

<hr />

5   Ibid.

6   Bakhtin made a seminal distinction between the 'grotesque' body – corrupt, imperfect, fissured – and the 'classical' body, which was harmonious and sealed. These categories can be usefully applied to the medieval construction of, respectively, feminine and masculine. M.M. Bakhtin, *Rabelais and His World*, transl. H. Iswolsky (Cambridge, Mass., 1968), 19.

7   This is probably a heavily biased sample, since those women and works which did not conform to convention usually left no trace of their existence as either body or word.

8   For a discussion of women's writing/dictating, see Julia Boffey, 'Women Authors and Women's Literacy in Fourteenth- and Fifteenth-Century England', in *Women and Literature in Britain, 1150–1500*, ed. Carol M. Meale (Cambridge, 1993), 159–82. See also the account of Thomas Aquinas dictating to scribes in Mary Carruthers, *The Book of Memory: A Study of Memory in Medieval Culture* (Cambridge, 1990), 3.

proven otherwise. The call-to-write vision provided legitimation to the public for the communication of a woman's visions. Moreover, the call to write and the reaction of the visionary to that call provide valuable insight into the visionary's perception of her role, and of the consequences of her prophetic activity. The call-to-write visions fall into three main categories; in one category are those visions in which some divine figure explicitly commands the visionary to write her revelations; in another, the visionary represents her writing as inspired directly by God; in the third category, which could perhaps more accurately be labelled the call to publish, the visionary's completed writing is given the divine *imprimatur*. Some visionaries recounted experiencing more than one kind of call-to-write vision.

One of the most dramatic representations of the explicit divine command to write is that of Elisabeth of Schönau. Elisabeth was a nun at the Benedictine convent of Schönau in the middle of the twelfth century. When she first began to experience visions, she was compelled by the angel who served as her guide to reveal an apocalyptic prophecy to her Abbot, Hildelin. Elisabeth later wrote to Hildegard of Bingen, explaining her reluctance to comply and the consequences of that reluctance.

> In order that I might avoid arrogance, however, and that I might not be perceived as the author of novelties, I strove to hide these things [visions] as much as possible. Therefore . . . an angel of the Lord stood before me saying 'Why do you hide gold in mud?' . . . And having said this he lifted a scourge over me, which he struck me with most harshly five times . . . so that for three days I lay with my whole body shattered by this beating.[9]

She was then deprived of the power of speech until she handed over to her abbot, Hildelin, the book of revelations recorded by her brother Ekbert and some of the other nuns.

Hildelin was persuaded of the truth of her visions; during a public penitential preaching tour in Lent in 1155, his sermons incorporated Elisabeth's message, without direct attribution. However, some anonymous believer also sent letters in Hildelin's name, containing Elisabeth's prophecies, and these were read out in a public forum in Cologne. This uncontrolled publication of her vision led people to mock Elisabeth and characterize her visions as *muliebria figmenta* – womanish fictions. The public ridicule confirmed her worst fears of the consequences of revealing her visions.[10]

The fact that Elisabeth's angel resorted to physical violence to force her to publish her visions is a measure of Elisabeth's extreme reluctance, of her fear, and of the punishment which she associated with revealing the word of God.

---

[9] Kathryn Kerby-Fulton and Dyan Elliott, 'Self-Image and the Visionary Role in Two Letters from the Correspondance of Elizabeth of Schönau and Hildegard of Bingen', *Vox Benedictina* 2/3 (1985), 204–223 (215).

[10] This incident is recounted in full in Anne Clark, *Elisabeth of Schönau: A Twelfth-Century Visionary* (Philadelphia, 1992), 15.

It is significant not only that her body is subjugated, but also that her physical voice is silenced in favour of the written word. Representing herself as deprived of the power of speech is an indication that she understood that she was not to communicate her visions orally, but by writing only. She was a woman, so she kept silent; but she was also a prophet, divinely compelled to communicate; so she wrote. This account of her vision constructed her writing as both divinely authorized and beyond her control, independent of both physical body and voice.

While Elisabeth's experience of angelic assault is rather extreme, neither the reluctance to write nor the fact of coercion is unusual. Hildegard of Bingen (1098–1179) wrote that she 'refused to write for a long time through doubt and bad opinion and the diversity of human words,'[11] not with stubbornness but in the exercise of humility.'[12] She was then stricken with illness, which only lifted when she wrote her visions as commanded. 'O fragile human, ashes of ashes, and filth of filth! Say and write what you see and hear.'[13] Marguerite d'Oignt, a Carthusian visionary living toward the end of the thirteenth century, was so overwhelmed by her visionary experiences that she too became ill. She was cured only by writing down her visions.[14] Gertrude the Great of Helfta experienced another form of persuasion when God told her that she would not be allowed to die until she had finished writing her visions.

> Be assured that you will not be released from the prison of the flesh until you have paid the debt which still binds you.[15]

While 'Write your book and die' might not galvanize most authors to frantic scribbling, it served to motivate Gertrude.

These representations of reluctance and coercion are also evidence of fear of writing. In the Middle Ages great power and significance were attached to writing. Many writers employed modesty topoi, proclaiming their unworthiness to write; others disclaimed their authority as authors by attributing it to some superior who had either instructed them or given them permission to write; still others remained anonymous, preferring to attribute their work to some tried and true, well-established authority: Jerome, for example, or Dionysius. Visionary women shared this perception of the authority of writing, and their call-to-write visions portray their desire to refer authority and responsibility for their writing to the Supreme Power. In this self-construction their fear of writing coincided with their need as women visionaries and

---

11 Hildegard obviously recognized what we now call a 'communication problem'. Only God's words could ensure precise articulation and accurate understanding of the experience of the divine, and so she, like Gertrude the Great, was unable to write until God furnished her with the words to use.

12 Hildegard, 60.

13 Hildegard, 59.

14 Elizabeth Petroff, *Medieval Women's Visionary Literature* (Oxford, 1986), 278.

15 Petroff, 229.

prophets, to fashion themselves as essentially passive channels for God's words.[16]

One could argue that such formulations in the writing of women visionaries amount to no more than literary conventions. However, conventions, like clichés, develop and survive because they reflect a common reality, a shared perception of certain experiences or situations. The fact that virtually all women visionaries included in their writing some variation of the call-to-write vision should certainly not be taken to suggest that this was not, in fact, an important and vital part of their individual visionary experience.[17]

Not all commands to write were met with reluctance or accompanied by coercion. Margery Kempe calmly awaited the divinely appointed moment to begin her book: 'whan it plesyd ower Lord, he comawnded hyr & chargyd hir þat sche xuld don wryten hyr felyngs & reuelacyons & þe forme of her leuyng þat hys goodnesse myth be knowyn to alle þe world.'[18] She then set about doing it, though she did report feeling ill if she was not involved in the writing. As soon as she started again, 'sche was hei & hoole sodeynly.'[19] Angela of Foligno (1248–1309) simply recounted being commanded, after various revelations, that she should cause them to be written down. 'Then was an example showed me, and it was commanded me that I should cause it to be written down.'[20] Mechthild of Magdeburg did not dare keep silent after 'powerful love came, and provided me with these miracles,' and sought permission from her confessor to write as God had willed.[21]

These examples above represent one form of the call-to-write vision: the explicit divine command, often accompanied by some kind of coercion. The second variation of the call to write is inspired writing.

Inspired writing occurs when the words flow from the visionary without any conscious effort – from God's mouth to her pen. She is powerless to resist, she has absolutely no influence over the form or content of the final written product; she is just a channel, an instrument. Raymond of Capua, amanuensis to Catherine of Siena (1347–1380), described the circumstances of the writing of Catherine's major visionary work, *The Dialogue*.

---

[16] As well as incorporating call-to-write visions into their narratives, nearly all women visionaries describe being identified by God, or Christ, as a channel or vessel for his words. See e.g. Hildegard, 60, and, for Bridget of Sweden, Isak Collijn (ed.) *Acta et Processus Canonizacionis Beate Birgitte* (Uppsala, 1924–31), 80.

[17] See John Burrow's discussion of this issue, which he calls the 'conventional fallacy', in 'Autobiographical Poetry in the Middle Ages: The Case of Thomas Hoccleve', in *Middle English Literature: The British Academy Gollancz Lectures*, ed. John Burrow (Oxford, 1989), 223–46 (228–9).

[18] *The Book of Margery Kempe*, ed. Sanford Meech and Hope Emily Allen, EETS 212 (Oxford, 1940), 3–4.

[19] Margery Kempe, 219.

[20] *The Book of Divine Consolation of the Blessed Angela of Foligno*, transl. Mary Steegman (New York, 1966), 249.

[21] Mechthild von Magdeburg, *Flowing Light of the Divinity*, transl. Christiane Mesch Galvani (New York, 1991), 99–100.

About two years before her death, such a clarity of Truth was revealed to her from Heaven that Catherine was constrained to spread it abroad by means of writing, asking her secretaries to stand ready to take down whatever came from her mouth as soon as they noticed that she had gone into ecstasy.[22]

It reputedly took five days for the whole of *The Dialogue* to be written. Whether or not it actually happened this way, and there is some doubt that it was quite such a speedy composition, it is significant that the writing of *The Dialogue* is represented as inspired. The more Catherine – and other women visionaries – could minimize the focus on their own human agency, the more effective the portrayal of their writings as a result of divine will.

Gertrude the Great took advantage of all the divine assistance available. As mentioned above, she was finally motivated to write by the threat of not being allowed to die until she had finished her book. Although she conceded the necessity, when she sat down to do it she, like many authors, was unable to write. So God came to her assistance.

And for four days, at a convenient hour each morning, Thou didst suggest with so much clearness and sweetness what I composed, that I have been able to write it without difficulty and without reflection, even as if I had learned it by heart long before.[23]

Artistic representations of women visionaries often showed their subjects in the act of inspired writing as a way to indicate the source of their work and reinforce its divine authority. One of the illustrations in the original manu- script of Hildegard of Bingen's *Scivias* shows her, writing, with what look to be flames going into her head – evidently, the Living Light.[24] Bridget of Sweden appears in the woodcut in the 1492 printed edition of her *Liber Celestis* with a kind of cosmic lightning bolt linking her to the celestial choirs.[25]

Representations of inspired writing functioned in the same way as the ele- ment of coercion discussed in the first type of call-to-write vision. Inspired writing derived its authority from the highest level, permitting the visionary to disclaim any power of her own and to construct herself solely as a channel for the word of God.

The third type of call-to-write vision is the one which could be designated the 'call to publish'. These episodes occur when the visions and revelations have already been written down, often secretly, and the visionary is then divinely commanded to circulate her writing. When Mechthild of Hackeborn discovered that her visions had been written down without her knowledge by two of her fellow nuns, one of whom was Gertrude the Great, she was most

---

22 Catherine of Siena, *The Dialogue*, transl. Suzanne Noffke O.P. (New York, 1980), 12.
23 Petroff, 229.
24 A reproduction of this illustration can be found in *Illuminations of Hildegard of Bingen*, ed. Matthew Fox O.P. (Santa Fe, N. Mex., 1985), 26.
25 *Sancta Birgitta Revelationes*, ed. B. Ghotan (Lubeck, 1492), fol. 2v.

upset, and sought comfort from Christ. Christ told her that it was his will that the book be both written and read:

> I am þe vnderstondynge in the eere of þame þat hyeres of þe. . . . I am also in þe handde of þame þat writeth that booke, ande worcher with þame ande helpere in alle thynges.[26]

Mechthild then saw a sunbeam issue from Christ's heart into the hearts of the two women writing the book, which she took to be a sign of divine approbation of their writing. Later, Christ gave the book its title, the *Liber specialis gratiae*.

Gertrude the Great not only struggled with the writing of her book, she also prayed that its publication might be prevented, since she felt herself so unworthy to have written such a work. However, God persuaded her that it was his will. He 'graciously declared that he found both parts [of the book] welcome,'[27] and then conferred on the work its title, *Legatus divinae pietatis*. Margery Kempe, with a characteristic concreteness, told of a vision in which Christ, the Virgin Mary and several saints 'comyn in-to hir sowle & thankyd hir, seying þat þei wer wel plesyd wyth þe writyng of þis boke.'[28]

The call-to-write vision contributed significantly to the self-fashioning of medieval women visionaries as channels for the divine word, as instruments in God's almighty hand, as disembodied echoes of the disembodied Word. This self-fashioning arose from the need to divorce their bodies, culturally constructed as corrupt and corrupting, and their voices, instruments of deceit and seduction, from the prophetic message they felt impelled by God to deliver. The visions also served to locate the authority of their writing outside themselves, which both eased their fear of writing and protected them from accusations of teaching or being in authority over men.

However, being called to write is one thing; writing is quite another, particularly if you were a medieval woman who had little or no education, could not write and knew little Latin and less theology. The subtitle of this paper is 'Women Co-Writing the Book'. Medieval women visionaries really had two co-writers; the first was God (perhaps the original ghost writer); the second was an amanuensis, or scribe. Sometimes a whole editorial team would be created. Bridget of Sweden had two full-time scribe/translators as well as a very active editor.[29] Very few medieval women had the practical skills needed

---

26 *The Booke of Gostlye Grace of Mechthild of Hackeborn*, ed. Theresa Halligan, P.I.M.S. 46 (Toronto, 1979), 587. [I am the understanding in the ear of those who listen to you. . . . I am also in the hand of those who write this book, and I am a worker with them and a helper in all things.] [My transl.]

27 Gertrude the Great of Helfta, *The Herald of God's Loving Kindness: Books One and Two*, transl. Alexandra Barratt (Kalamazoo, Mich., 1991), 31.

28 Margery Kempe, 219. ['came into her soul, and thanked her, saying that they were well pleased with the writing of this book'.] [My transl.]

29 Birger Gregersson and Thomas Gascoigne, *The Life of Saint Birgitta*, transl. Julia Bolton Holloway (Toronto, 1991), 21, 25.

to write their own visions, and even fewer would have been able to translate them from the vernacular into Latin, a step which ensured both the greater credibility of the visions, and their wider distribution.[30] Catherine of Siena, for example, did not learn to write until three years before she died, and then she had divine assistance.[31] Bridget of Sweden was similarly aided in learning Latin when she was middle-aged. The chief exception to this general state of affairs occurred in some convents, such as Helfta, in the last half of the thirteenth century, where the nuns enjoyed a high standard of education.[32] The revelations of two of the three Helfta visionaries were physically written, in Latin, by the nuns. Gertrude the Great herself wrote part of her own *Legatus divinae pietatis* and part of Mechthild of Hackeborn's *Liber specialis gratiae*. She was assisted by another one of the sisters – an anonymous figure who will be designated 'the third nun'. However, in general, women's visions were written with the assistance of men, almost inevitably clerics. Clerics had the necessary education, skill and Latin literacy; they were also, most importantly, mainstays of ecclesiastical orthodoxy.[33]

Many women incorporated in the representations of their visions a divine call to the scribe. This vision served to validate the writing still more, as well as to authorize the scribe as one fitted to transmit the divine word from visionary to audience. One of the most graphic of these corroborating visions occurred in the *Liber specialis gratiae* of Mechthild of Hackeborn. The scribe herself, the shadowy 'third nun', had the vision in her sleep.[34] She dreamt that Mechthild offered her 'þe honye of heuenlye Ierusalem' from a honeycomb that she held. Mechthild then gave the scribe a piece of bread dipped in the honey; as the scribe held it in her hands

> wonderfullye þat gobette of breede with þe honye both togydders bygane to wexe owte into a loofe so þat the gobette of breede wexe owte in a hoole loofe ande the honycombe persede þe lofe withyn ande withowte, ande þorowe here handdis. Whilys sche helde þat loofe itt droppede in so

---

[30] Much has been written on this topic in recent years. For a good, brief survey of women's education and literacy in medieval England, see e.g. *Women's Writing in Middle English*, ed. Alexandra Barratt (New York, 1992) 1–23.

[31] Catherine of Siena, 6.

[32] For descriptions of life at Helfta see Mary Jeremy Finnegan O.P., *The Women of Helfta: Scholars and Mystics* (Athens, Ga., 1991), and Caroline Walker Bynum, 'Women Mystics in the Thirteenth Century: The Case of the Nuns of Helfta', in *Jesus as Mother: Studies in the Spirituality of the High Middle Ages* (Berkeley, 1982), 170–262.

[33] Lynn Staley Johnson succinctly outlines the role of the scribe: 'Ultimately the scribe can be described as a code that at once conferred authority and denied it, indicated scope and delimited it.' 'The Trope of the Scribe: The Question of Literary Authority in the Works of Julian of Norwich and Margery Kempe', *Speculum*, 66 (1991), 820–38 (838).

[34] The Middle English translations of the *Liber specialis gratiae*, that is, *The Booke of Gostlye Grace of Mechthild of Hackeborn*, use masculine pronouns to refer to the scribes. This is a mistranslation of the Latin which forcibly reflects the assumption that scribes were male. See Halligan, 106, n.585/18.

moche plenteuosnes ande habundaunce þat itt wette alle here lappe ande so ranne forth ande moystede alle the erth abowte þem.[35]

This vision was understood both as a sign of God's approval of the book and as an intimation of the effect of the book – that through the hands of this scribe God's words would saturate the earth with sweetness. There were many other examples of corroborating visions, or signs. Bridget of Sweden had a vision in which her scribe and translator, Peter of Alvastra, was given a message from Christ.

> Hear her, Brother Peter, and write down in Latin all the words that she will speak to you in my name. And for every letter, I will give to you, not gold or silver, but a treasure which will not grow old.[36]

Bridget also had a vision in which Christ confirmed her appointment of Alfonso of Jaen as her editor.[37] Margery Kempe's second scribe became convinced that his task was pleasing to God when he was miraculously enabled to read the handwriting of her original scribe.[38]

While corroborating visions bestowed divine authorization on the scribe, scribes participated in a process whereby ecclesiastical authorization was bestowed on the visionary. In addition to providing practical assistance with writing and translating, clerical scribes and editors functioned as a check on the orthodoxy of the women's revelations. This function accorded with the theological doctrine of *discretio spirituum*, the discernment of spirits, which was used to test whether visions were of divine or diabolical provenance.[39] The test was applied stringently to women, because of their reputation as daughters of Eve, easily deceived and eager to deceive. Jean Gerson, chancellor of the University of Paris, summed up the prevailing attitude in his 1423 treatise, *De examinatione doctrinarum*.

> Every teaching of women, especially that expressed in solemn word or writing, is to be held suspect, unless it has been diligently examined, and much more than the teaching of men. . . . Why? Because women are too

---

[35] Halligan, 590. [miraculously that lump of bread, together with the honey began to expand into a loaf, so that the lump of bread expanded into a whole loaf, and the honeycomb permeated the loaf inside and out, and through her hands. While she held the loaf it dripped in such plenty and abundance that it wet all her lap and ran forth and moistened all the earth about them.]

[36] Collijn, 510–11 [my transl.].

[37] Collijn, 512.

[38] Margery Kempe, 5.

[39] The role of *discretio spirituum* in influencing women's accounts of their visionary experiences is discussed in greater detail in my forthcoming article, 'Women's Words, Men's Language: *Discretio spirituum* as Discourse in the Writing of Medieval Women Visionaries', *The Medieval Translator* vol. v, ed. Roger Ellis (Exeter, Spring 1995).

easily seduced, because they are too obstinately seducers, because it is not
fitting that they should be knowers of divine wisdom.[40]

Probably the most important aspect of *discretio spirituum* as far as women
visionaries were concerned was the stipulation that they live in obedience to a
spiritual director, and should submit all visions to him immediately. Spiritual
directors were expected to establish that visions were orthodox and did not
conflict with Scripture or with traditional exegesis. In many cases the spiritual
director of a visionary was also involved in some capacity in the writing, and
so he was able to formulate the representations of the visions in such a way as
to satisfy the criteria established by ecclesiastical authorities.[41] Nearly all
women visionaries incorporated into their visionary works accounts of the
approval of their spiritual directors. Mechthild of Magdeburg consulted her
confessor after her divine call to write. He told her that of course she should do
so, but that she must 'be conscious of her great unworthiness that she, a
wretched woman, should have been commanded to write.'[42] Hildegard of
Bingen wrote of being encouraged to record her visions by Volmar of
Disibodenberg, her first amanuensis.[43] Margery Kempe cited several instances
when her spiritual director, or other eminent clerics, encouraged her to write
down her visions. Although she always replied to the effect that she was
waiting for God, rather than men, to tell her when to write, when that time
came she had impressive testimonials to recount.[44]

It was inevitable, surely, that the involvement of clerical scribes, editors and
translators would result in the filtering of women's visionary experience
through a mesh of masculine orthodoxy. Often there were several stages which
ensued between visionary utterance and final edition – first writing from
dictation, translation into Latin, editing and perhaps translation into another
vernacular language. At each of these stages the clerical co-writer had an
opportunity to test the orthodoxy, to query the formulation, to clarify the
doctrine. In the Middle English *Booke of Gostlye Grace of Mechthild of Hackeborn*,
for example, the translator interpolated into the text a warning about the
possible heterodoxy of Mechthild's teaching on infant baptism.

[40] Jean Gerson, *Oeuvres Complètes*, ed. P. Glorieux, 10 vols. (Paris, 1960–73), ix (1973), 467–8 [my transl.].
[41] For a discussion of shifts in the balance of power between holy women and their spiritual directors during the late Middle Ages, see Jo Ann McNamara, 'The Rhetoric of Orthodoxy: Clerical Authority and Female Innovation in the Struggle with Heresy', in *Maps of Flesh and Light: The Religious Experience of Medieval Women Mystics*, ed. Ulrike Wiethaus (Syracuse, 1993), 9–27; John Coakley, 'Friars as Confidants of Holy Women in Medieval Dominican Hagiography', in *Images of Sainthood in Medieval Europe*, ed. Renate Blumenfeld-Kosinski and Timea Szell (Ithaca, N.Y., 1991), 222–46.
[42] Galvani, 99–100.
[43] Hildegard, 60.
[44] See e.g. Margery Kempe, 3–4.

Offe þis ensaumple before beware, þat es to saye, þat a childe be the moderes vowe of cristiante schalle be savede þowe itt deye before, [baptism] for clerkes holdene þe contrarye opynoun.[45]

Clerical co-writers helped the ecclesiastical authorities maintain control of the communication of medieval women visionaries. Normally, they could not teach, they could not preach, and the above process ensured that their writing underwent intense scrutiny.[46]

The dilemma of the medieval visionary woman is best summed up by Julian of Norwich.

Botte god forbede that ȝe schulde saye or take it so that I am a techere, for I mene nouȝt soo, no I mente nevere so; for I am a womann, leued, febille and freylle. Botte I wate wele, this that I saye, I hafe it of the schewynge of hym that es souerayne techare. . . . . Botte for I am a womann, schulde I therfore leve that I schulde nouȝt telle ȝowe the goodenes of god, syne that I sawe in that same tyme that is his wille, that it be knawenn?[47]

The answer, for all medieval women visionaries, was 'Of course I should – and I must.' The solution was to write. Only in that way could the word of God be freed of its imprisonment in the physical body of a woman, be heard uncontaminated by the physical voice of a woman.[48] By representing themselves as divinely called to write, and by overcoming the considerable practical difficulties which writing involved, medieval women visionaries lay claim to the only avenue of communication available to them, and fulfilled their prophetic mandate.

---

[45] For a discussion of the translator's role in maintaining orthodox cultural standards see Ian Johnson, 'Prologue and Practice: Middle English Lives of Christ', in *The Medieval Translator: The Theory and Practice of Translation in the Middle Ages*, ed. Roger Ellis (Cambridge, 1989), 69–85. [Beware of this example above, that is to say, that a child shall be saved by the mother's vow of Christianity if it dies before baptism, for clerics hold the opposite opinion.] [My transl.]

[46] Women were permitted to teach children, and, sometimes, other women, in private, in certain circumstances.

[47] *A Book of Showings to the Anchoress Julian of Norwich* ed. Edmund Colledge O.S.A. and James Walsh S.J., 2 vols. P.I.M.S 35 (Toronto, 1978), i, 222. [But God forbid that you should say or understand that I am a teacher, for I do not mean that, and I never meant that; for I am a woman, ignorant, feeble and frail. But I know well, this that I say, for I have it from the revelation of He who is sovereign teacher. . . . Because I am a woman, should I therefore believe that I should not tell you of the goodness of God, since I saw at the same time that it is His will that it be known?] [My transl.]

[48] My concern in this paper is with the actual, physical voice or body of an actual physical woman. I am not attempting here to deal with the issue of whether or not visionary women's language is 'voiced' as female in some persistent, irreducible way; that is another paper – or a book. Elaine Scarry deals with the complex relationship of body and voice in *The Body in Pain: The Making and Unmaking of the World* (Oxford, 1985). Chapter 4, subtitled 'Body and Voice in the Judeo-Christian Scriptures and the Writings of Marx', is concerned in part with the relationship of the human body and God's voice, and has relevance for this paper.

'CRY OUT AND WRITE': MYSTICISM AND THE STRUGGLE FOR AUTHORITY

Grace Jantzen

'Cry out and write', came the voice of God to Hildegard of Bingen in the twelfth century,

> O human, who are fragile dust of the earth and ashes of ashes! Cry out and speak of the origin of pure salvation until those people are instructed, who, though they see the inmost contents of the scriptures, do not wish to tell them or preach them, because they are lukewarm or sluggish in serving God's justice . . . For you have received your profound insight not from humans, but from the lofty and tremendous Judge on high . . .[1]

With these words, Hildegard finds herself summoned to visionary experiences, and to an authoritative teaching position within the Church on the basis of them. It was a teaching position which she asserts should not have been necessary: if her male counterparts had been fulfilling their own calling, a woman would not have had to step in. But because they are 'lukewarm and sluggish in serving God's justice', God had to summon Hildegard, a 'poor little figure of a woman' (!). Since the men who should have been proclaiming the meaning of the scripture are lax, God has intervened directly to the lowest of the low, as had happened before when a woman was ready to bear Christ to the world.

Hildegard of Bingen stands as one of many visionary women in the High and Late Middle Ages who claimed spiritual authority on the basis of their visions: others include Gertrude the Great of Helfta, Catherine of Siena, Julian of Norwich, and Hadewijch of Antwerp, to name only a few. The ways in which these women received and passed on their visions, however, was far from uniform. Hildegard of Bingen, for instance, watched her own visions as one might watch a film, except that it was like a film that was directed personally toward her, and through her to the Church for whom she recorded it. She did not participate directly in what she saw; rather, she was a spectator receiving a specific message. By contrast, Catherine of Siena was not simply

---

1 Hildegard of Bingen, *Scivias* I.1, in Columba Hart and Jane Bishop, transl., Classics of Western Spirituality (New York, 1990).

watching something unfold in her visions, she was an active participant. When the newly circumcised Jesus gave her his foreskin to wear on her finger as a wedding ring, she was there to receive it and put it on: she was completely immersed in the action, not merely observing something which she then wrote down for other people. Julian of Norwich stands midway between the observer status of Hildegard and the complete immersion of Catherine. Unlike Catherine, she is not so taken up into the action that she forgets where she is: in fact, her awareness of herself severely ill in bed is a counterpoint to her vision of Jesus suffering on the cross. Yet neither is she a detached observer; she enters into conversation with God, raising questions, and persisting with them if she felt that she was not adequately answered. In the case of Gertrude the Great, a mixture of these ways of participating is found: sometimes she seems to be totally involved in the action, whereas at other times she is more of an observer, reporting what she sees.

The different levels of participation of these women in their visions should alert us to differences in the ways they wrote and claimed authority on the basis of them. Even calling them all 'visions' can be misleading unless we are aware of the rich variety among them. Yet what was common to them all was that they felt themselves called upon to make the content of the vision available to others through writing, and thereby they claimed authority which, because they were women, would be called into question by their readers, and usually by themselves as well.

The ways in which they claimed authority on the basis of their experiences, using an obligatory 'modesty formula' which likened them to Mary, the mother of Jesus, have been well documented. By means of the 'modesty formula' they could simultaneously affirm their humility and unworthiness, and claim the authority which had been given them directly by God in the visions which had been granted to them. In this way they could bypass the usual routes of authority: solid education in the writings of the Bible and the patristic writings, preferment and validation, and so on. It has often been suggested that the gender difference in visionary experience is related to the paths of authority open to women and men respectively: there are more accounts of female than of male visionaries, and there are numerous influential male writers who discount or discredit visionary experience. What I wish to do, therefore, is to look at the gendered struggle for authority which was going on during this period, focused in the question of visionary experience. It is interesting that contemporary writers made little distinction among the kinds of experience and relative degrees of participation in them which I have mentioned, and that present-day writers who discuss mystical or visionary experience usually follow them in ignoring these significant variations.

For all their variety, the writings of male mystics of the medieval period form a strong contrast to the writings of female visionaries. The men tend to be much more learned, often deeply immersed in scripture and scriptural language, and increasingly, through the twelfth and thirteenth century, using scholastic method and content as well. By taking representative figures approximately contemporary with the period when women visionaries were most prevalent, it is possible to trace the development of what is at first a benign tolerance of visionary experience into a deep mistrust and condemnatory attitude towards it. Although the men in question do not specifically condemn the women visionaries, nor link their prohibitions with discussion of gender, the overall effect was that women of spirit were marginalized, and 'true' mysticism was increasingly defined in male terms.

Bernard of Clairvaux was born in 1090, eight years before Hildegard of Bingen; and when she was abbess of the convent on the Rhine, he was abbot of Clairvaux, and the most dynamic leader the Cistercians had ever known. Hildegard wrote to him, asking in her most humble manner for his validation of her visions.

> I am very concerned about this vision which opens before me in spirit as a mystery . . . I am wretched and more than wretched in my existence as a woman . . . Gentle father, you are so secure, answer me in your goodness, me, your unworthy servant girl, who from childhood has never, not even for one single hour, lived in security . . .[2]

Bernard sent her a very brief and restrained reply, allowing that she has indeed received a gift from God, but stressing above all that she must be humble. The visionary experience that she had asked him about is not specifically mentioned, whereas the grace of God and its essential link to humility is emphasised.[3] As Jean Leclercq comments, 'She had asked him to judge. He replied with a brief bit of generally applicable advice, something which could have been written to anyone.'[4]

Shortly thereafter, Pope Eugene III examined Hildegard himself, reading her *Scivias* and having it read aloud in Trier when Bernard was present. The Pope decided that Hildegard's visions really were authentic; and from that time she was given widespread support and affirmation, and Bernard's stance toward her became much less reserved. From this incident it appears that in the mid-twelfth century there was an openness to the occurrence of genuine visionary experience on the part of the ecclesiastical hierarchy, but that its authority to pronounce upon the validity of such experience must be scrupulously maintained. As long as Hildegard was willing to abase herself and bow to the judgement of the Pope and his representatives, they could affirm her visions without undue threat.

---

[2] Hildegard of Bingen, letter 1 in her *Book of Divine Works with Letters and Songs*, ed. Matthew Fox (Santa Fe, N. Mex., 1987) 271. It is widely accepted that this translation leaves a good deal to be desired; but there is at present no other English edition of her letters.

[3] *The Letters of Saint Bernard of Clairvaux*, transl. Bruno Scott James (London, 1953) letter 390, p. 459. The traditional ordering places this letter at no. 366.

[4] Jean Leclercq, *Women and St Bernard of Clairvaux*, CSS104 (Kalamazoo, Mich, 1989), 62–7. Leclercq entirely fails to see how belittling this letter was, and how it reinforces all the stereotypes requiring women's self-abasement.

Nevertheless, Bernard himself, like most male writers of the twelfth century, would not put the accent on visions, though there can be no doubt that experience of a very different kind is central to his spirituality. According to his thinking, the whole aim of the Christian life is to come into union with God; and if this is the aim of the Christian life in general, all the more is it the aim of the Cistercian monk. The Cistercians adopted the Benedictine self-designation of a monastery as a 'school for the service of the Lord', a service that was fundamentally one of love.[5] Thus the motto of Clairvaux, the first of Bernard's many new foundations, was *In schola Christi sumus*: the main lesson to be learned was the lesson of how to live in charity.[6] This notion of charity, however, is not the watered-down idea we have of it today, such that 'living in charity' means little more than living in polite harmony. Charity (*caritas*), is in its primary designation for Bernard, none other than God: God is Charity. In its secondary designation charity is the gift of God, identified with the gift of the Holy Spirit and the presence of the Holy Spirit in the soul. To learn to live in charity, therefore, is nothing less than to learn to live in God, by virtue of God's indwelling and transforming spirit of charity. This is the goal of the Christian life.[7]

There is no doubt that experience is essential to Bernard's mysticism, since it has union with God as its goal, not as an abstract concept but as a felt reality. However, this is very different from the emphasis on visionary experience which we find in Hildegard: Bernard would never consider such visionary experience as the basis of mystical or spiritual authority.

Bernard does speak frequently about visions of God, as well as of hearing God's voice.[8] He cites prophets of the Hebrew Bible such as Jacob, Moses and Isaiah who saw God face to face, and mentions Paul who was 'rapt into Paradise, heard words that he could not explain, and saw his Lord Jesus Christ', though Bernard says that even in such cases their experience of God was not 'as he is but only in the form he thought fitting to assume'.[9] The unqualified experience of God is reserved for life after death, and is spoken of by such terms as Paradise, union with God, and the Beatific Vision – all, to some extent, metaphors for a reality which can be pointed to but not fully experienced in this life.

Far more important to Bernard than these external, quasi-sensory experiences of visual images or spoken words 'is another form of divine contemplation, very different from the former because it takes place in the interior, when God is pleased to visit the soul that seeks him'.[10] This is the deeply felt

---

5 See *The Rule of St Benedict*, transl. Anthony C. Meisel and M. L. de Mastro (New York, 1975), Prologue.
6 Etienne Gilson, *The Mystical Theology of St Bernard* (London, 1955), ch. 3.
7 Ibid., 24.
8 E.g. *Sermons*, 31–3.
9 *Sermon* 31. ii. 4.
10 Ibid.

sense of the presence of God, 'not in bodily form but by inward infusion', of which Bernard says,

> It is beyond question that the vision is all the more delightful the more inward it is, and not external. It is the Word, who penetrates without sound; who is effective though not pronounced, who wins the affections without striking on the ears. His face, though without form, is the source of form, it does not dazzle the eyes of the body but gladdens the watchful heart; its pleasure is in the gift of love and not in the colour of the lover.[11]

Nor are these experiences always the same; they are varied according to the needs of the recipient. Sometimes the divine Word comes 'like a physician with oil and ointments', healing hurts and correcting distortions; sometimes 'he joins up as a traveller . . . on the road', and by his presence makes hardship or drudgery easier to bear; perhaps he arrives like 'a magnificent and powerful king', bringing courage in time of stress or temptation. Bernard uses the imagery of the *Song of Songs*, and indeed of the Bible as a whole, to elucidate many such situations.[12] In each case the divine Word comes with love and helpfulness; but in each case, although there is an awareness of the divine presence, it would be stretching Bernard's meaning too far to suppose that there was an actual visionary experience. The one who truly yearns for God will find that 'his heart's desire will be given to him, even while still a pilgrim on earth, though not in its fullness and only for a time, a short time'.[13] The awareness fades, and though it may return again from time to time, for the most part this life must be lived by faith, not by continuous direct experience of God.

It is important to note how Bernard describes the one who comes: God is the 'divine Word'. Furthermore, in each of the ways the Word comes, as physician, traveller on the road, king and so on, the picture is drawn from one or another of the representations of Christ in the Gospels. What is happening here is that Bernard is speaking of encountering Christ by penetrating to the mystical meaning of Scripture. He is finding the divine Word in the words of the book, seeing Christ as the deepest meaning of the Bible, and in meditating on that meaning, encountering Christ in his own soul. And as we have already seen, this, which for Bernard is central to the development of spirituality, is not something that was widely available for women.

Bernard is quite clear that experiences of this sort, encounters with Christ through the mystical meaning of scripture, are to be sought and 'ardently desired'. By contrast, visionary experiences of the sort that Hildegard and other women mystics had were not to be sought. These could at best be 'corporeal images', and thus could never really represent God, whose reality

---

11 Ibid. 31. iii. 6.
12 Ibid. 31. iii. 7.
13 Sermon 32. i. 2.

must be spiritual.[14] Although Bernard does not actually condemn visionary experiences, and, at least after Hildegard's visions were ratified by the Pope, he was willing to support her, it is clear that in his view experiences such as hers are very much second-rate. Intentionally or not, Bernard reinforces the gender division in the Western mystical tradition: the *real* mystical experience will be largely a male prerogative.

Eckhart, born in 1260 and a younger contemporary of Hadewijch, took the matter considerably further. Much of Eckhart's preaching was in the vernacular, and his audiences often consisted of nuns, and probably also beguines. To them he preached sermons of very high quality, and showed thereby the extent of his respect for both their spirituality and their intellectual ability. The women did not have formal education, but he clearly did not consider them to be stupid; and when he was criticized for preaching as he did, his reply was, 'If we are not to teach people who have not been taught, no one will ever be taught, and no one will ever be able to teach or to write. For that is why we teach the untaught, so that they may be changed from uninstructed to instructed.'[15] He treated women as men's intellectual and spiritual equals: it may be that this was one of the reasons for the surge of criticism against him which eventually brought him to trial for heresy.[16]

There have been those who have been ready to treat Eckhart as a thirteenth-century feminist for this positive treatment of women.[17] However, as Frank Tobin points out in his excellent study, this is going much further than the evidence warrants. While it is true that Eckhart did indeed work hard for female audiences, it is also true that he often denigrated women, using the standard medieval clichés of women identified with the flesh or with mere matter, whereas man was identified with spirit or form or the higher principle.[18] Other scholars have gone even further, and have seen Eckhart as developing an uncompromisingly critical stance toward the spirituality of the women whom he was instructing, particularly toward its experiential base.[19]

Certainly with regard to visionary experiences Eckhart's attitude was uncompromisingly negative. He reserved his most scathing language for those who claimed or wished to have such experiences.

> Some people want to see God with their own eyes, as they see a cow, and they want to love God as they love a cow. You love a cow for her milk and her cheese and your own profit. That is what all those men do who love

---

14 Sermon 3. i. 1.

15 Eckhart, *The Book of Divine Consolation* iii, in *The Essential Sermons, Commentaries, Treatises and Defense*, transl. Edmund College, Classics of Western Spirituality (New York, 1981), 239.

16 See Frank Tobin, *Meister Eckhart: Thought and Language* (Philadelphia, 1986), 16–17.

17 E.g. Matthew Fox, *Breakthrough: Meister Eckhart's Creation Spirituality in New Translation* (New York, 1980), 35.

18 Tobin, 17, citing Eckhart's Latin commentaries on biblical books, *In Ex.* n. 207, *In Gen.* I n. 55.

19 For a full discussion, see Oliver Davies, *Meister Eckhart: Mystical Theologian* (London, 1991), ch. 3.

God for outward wealth or inward consolation – and they do not truly love God, they love their own profit.[20]

Eckhart did not single out women for this rebuke; but it is not hard to see that his scalding language could be used to reject any woman's pretension to spiritual authority on the basis of visionary experience. There is no room in his thinking for visionary experience based on higher motivation than personal profit, or for claiming of authority because of it: in his view all that can be said is that this would make the vision of God equivalent in value to the vision of a cow.

Indeed, Eckhart says that 'whoever seeks God by a special way gets the way and misses God'.[21] He does not seem to notice that few women had the opportunity to gain an education to study the scriptures, or to claim authority in any way other than through visionary experience. What he does say, in his typically dramatic manner, is that

> if a man thinks he will get more of God by meditation, by devotion, by ecstasies, or by special infusion of grace than by the fireside or in the stable – that is nothing but taking God, wrapping a cloak around his head, and shoving him under the bench.[22]

The same, of course, would be true of any who sought visions; and these might be mostly women. Once again, whether by intention or design, the spirituality typical of women was being marginalized in Western mysticism, with the effect that it came more fully under men's control and definition.

Jan van Ruusbroec, a Fleming born in 1293, is widely regarded as one of the most important of all the fourteenth-century mystics. He was strongly influenced by Hadewijch; and it might therefore be expected that he would be more sympathetic to visionary experience. This, however, is not the case. In his major work, *The Spiritual Espousals*, he describes the various stages a person may go through in spiritual progress. One such stage is a condition of great enthusiasm, where the individual is filled with jubilation and love. In Ruusbroec's view, this is a particularly dangerous state. To the individual in such high spirits may come dreams, visions and voices; but as likely as not these experiences come straight from the devil. Ruusbroec warns that 'they should be relied on only insofar as they are in accord with Holy Scripture and with truth, and no more than that', otherwise the person may be deceived.[23]

This much might be uncontentious; but he soon resumes the theme, likening

---

[20] Eckhart, *Sermons and Treatises* vols. i–iii, transl. M. O'C. Walshe (London, 1979–87), vol. i, 127.
[21] Walshe, vol. i, 117.
[22] Ibid.
[23] Jan van Ruusbroec, *The Spiritual Espousals and Other Works*, transl. James A. Wiseman, Classics of Western Spirituality (New York, 1985), 88.

such experiences to honeydew, a 'false sweetness' which occurs during
periods of heat and contaminates growing fruit.

> In the same way, some persons can be deprived of their external senses by
> means of a certain kind of light which is produced by the devil and which
> surrounds and envelops them. They sometimes have various kinds of
> images shown to them, both false ones and true ones, or they hear differ-
> ent kinds of locutions . . . Whoever makes much of this receives a great
> amount of it and in this way becomes easily contaminated.[24]

According to Ruusbroec, even the true images are from the devil. Visions are
to be entirely mistrusted: one should certainly not 'make much of them', as the
women did who used them as the grounding for their spiritual authority.
Again, Ruusbroec never explicitly mentions women visionaries; but again, the
implication for the gendered construction of mysticism is clear.

A frightening note is injected into all of this in a passage from another of
Ruusbroec's writings, *A Mirror of Eternal Blessedness*. His discussion is organized around groups of people who receive the Sacrament, saying what will
happen to them in accordance with how pure of heart they are. Some people
receive the Sacrament unworthily, being in a state of sin; and they will have to
suffer purgatory because of it. But by far the worst case is that of false mystics,
those who claim that they are in direct relationship with God and consequently are not bound by the rules of the Church. Ruusbroec is not talking
specifically about visionaries, but rather about those who 'say they live in a
formless way above all forms';[25] but it would not be a long extension to apply
his words to anyone who claimed authority on the basis of mystical
experience.

> This is the greatest error and the most perverse and foolish heresy that has
> ever been heard. No one should give the blessed Sacrament to such per-
> sons, neither during their lifetime nor at the time of their death, nor should
> they be given a Christian burial. Rather, they should rightly be burned at
> the stake, for in God's eyes they are damned and belong in the pit of hell,
> far beneath all the devils.[26]

These were not empty words. All across Europe the fires were being lit that
devoured 'heretics', a large proportion of them women. And in the succeeding
centuries those fires would become the huge conflagration of the witch-
burnings.

Having visionary experiences, and claiming authority on the basis of them,
became increasingly hazardous, especially for women. There were, of course,
men as well who had had visionary experiences: Francis of Assisi, for example,
and Richard Rolle. Interestingly, they were men who were also most accused

---

[24] Ibid. 89; cf. 137.
[25] Ibid. 231.
[26] Ibid.

of being 'feminine' in their dress, behaviour and activity: Richard Rolle, for example, clothed himself in his sister's cast-offs, and Francis of Assisi tended lepers, by tradition a woman's job. Neither of them placed much emphasis on formal education, nor did they undertake either the mystical exposition of scripture or the speculative mysticism of Eckhart and Ruusbroec.[27]

Although there were these exceptions, however, as the thirteenth century turned into the fourteenth many of the most influential male mystics rejected with increasing sharpness the validity, let alone the authority, of visionary experiences and of those who had them. The anonymous author of *The Cloud of Unknowing*, written in England in the late fourteenth century, had scathing denunciations for those who sought mystical experiences, whether visionary or of any other kind. He may actually have had Rolle in mind when he wrote,

> When they read or hear read or spoken how men should lift up their hearts to God, they look up to the stars as though they would reach above the moon, and cock their ears as though they could hear angels sing out of heaven. In their fantastic imagination they would pierce the planets or make a hole in the firmament to look through it. They would fashion a God according to their own fancy, and dress him in rich clothes, and set him on a throne . . . And so it is their habit to sit with their mouths open as though they were catching flies . . .[28]

His sarcastic lampoon of visionaries is relentless and without sympathy: they are 'like sheep with the brain disease'; they 'hold their heads on one side as though a worm were in their ears'; they squeak and splutter and waggle their heads and smile continuously 'as though they were girlish gossips or amateur jugglers unsure of their balance'.[29]

The stridency of his condemnation, coupled with the sexism never far beneath the surface, (and showing itself occasionally, as in the comment on the 'girlish gossips'), gives some indication of the extent to which authority was being reclaimed from visionaries. These visionaries were mostly (though not exclusively) women; and the repudiation of visions as a source of spiritual insight is a foretaste of what was to come. The author of the *Cloud* repeatedly links visionaries with heretics, and is quite sure that they will all 'go stark staring mad to the devil',[30] a devil with only one nostril which he will willingly turn upwards so that it is possible to see 'up it into his brain' which is 'nothing else than the fire of hell'.[31] It is the same constellation of ideas that was being used in standard descriptions of heretics, and was soon to re-emerge in the infamous *Malleus Maleficarum* and the destruction of thousands of women as

---

[27] For a fascinating study of affective experience and ecclesiastical authority in Richard Rolle, see Nicholas Watson, *Richard Rolle and the Invention of Authority* (Cambridge, 1991).
[28] *The Cloud of Unknowing*, ed. James Walsh, Classics of Western Spirituality (New York, 1981), 231.
[29] Ibid. 223.
[30] Ibid. 222.
[31] Ibid. 227.

witches. Of course, I am not saying that the author of the *Cloud* was responsible for the witch craze or that he would have approved of what happened. But his condemnation of visionaries and his lumping them together with heretics links up a set of ideas that consolidates a new social construction of who counts as a mystic, a construction that, once again, gives women very little place. These ideas would be ready to hand for those who sought spiritual justification for the atrocities that were to follow. Visionary women who had the audacity to obey the command to 'cry out and write' did so increasingly at their peril.

MECHTHILD VON MAGDEBURG:
HER CREATIVITY AND HER AUDIENCE

Elizabeth A. Andersen

As far as we know, Mechthild of Magdeburg's entire literary production is encompassed by a sole work, the *Fließende Licht der Gottheit* (*The Flowing Light of the Godhead*). This work is remarkable from a number of points of view. As a starting point, it is worth noting that in the German-speaking world it is the first mystical text to be written in the vernacular, and it was written by a woman.

Mechthild was born in the vicinity of Magdeburg in c.1207 and died in the Benedictine convent at Helfta near Eisleben in Saxony in c.1282.[1] It is thought that she wrote down the contents of the *Fließende Licht der Gottheit* from about 1250 to about 1275.[2] As one would expect from her geographical provenance, she wrote in a dialect that derived from Low German and Central German. Although some extant fragments testify to this, the only extant manuscript which contains the whole text is an Alemannic version from about 1345.[3] There is also a Latin version entitled the *Lux Divinitatis* which apparently was made shortly after Mechthild's death.[4] This translation is, however, not entirely faithful and the material has been edited quite differently.[5]

Virtually the only source of information about the life of Mechthild are some autobiographical statements which she makes in the *Fließende Licht der Gottheit*. Most of this information is concentrated in section 2 of Book iv. Here

---

[1] The convent followed the Cistercian Rule but was never accepted into the Cistercian Order.

[2] For a detailed reconstruction of the chronology of Mechthild's life see Hans Neumann, 'Beiträge zur Textgeschichte des *Fließenden Lichts der Gottheit* und zur Lebensgeschichte Mechthilds von Magdeburg', in *Altdeutsche und altniederländische Mystik*, ed. Kurt Ruh, Wege der Forschung 23 (Darmstadt, 1964), 175–239.

[3] Mechthild von Magdeburg, *Das Fließende Licht der Gottheit*, ed. Hans Neumann, besorgt von Gisela Vollmann-Profe, Münchener Texte und Untersuchungen zur deutschen Literatur des Mittelalters 100 and 101, 2 vols. (Munich, 1990 and 1993). The Alemannic dialect is spoken in the area that is today Baden-Württemberg and German speaking Switzerland. The Middle High German for subsequent quotations in English is given in the following notes and is taken from Neumann's edition.

[4] *Revelationes Gertrudianae ac Mechtildianae, vol.2: Sanctae Mechtildis virginis ordinis Sancti Benedicti Liber specialis gratiae accedit Sororis Mechtildis ejusdem ordinis Lux divinitatis* [. . .], ed. by the monks of Solesmes (Paris, 1877), 435–707.

[5] See Neumann, ' Beiträge', 176–7.

Mechthild gives us an account of her spiritual development as a mystic. She tells us that she received her first 'greeting' from the Holy Spirit at the age of twelve.[6] After this first 'greeting' Mechthild continued to have visions every day for the next thirty-one years, and reports that the experience was still growing in intensity.

Mechthild tells us that in her youth she left her parental home and went to Magdeburg. During her years there it would seem that she lived as a beguine, for in a short prologue in Latin which prefaces the *Fließende Licht der Gottheit*, Mechthild is described as a beguine who had chosen to suffer contempt and to devote herself to God in humility, poverty and contemplation, following the example of the Dominicans.[7] Although Mechthild herself does not draw particular attention to her identity as a beguine, Mechthild researchers, most notably Caroline Walker Bynum, have attached considerable importance to this biographical fact, regarding it as a key to understanding some of Mechthild's attitudes and opinions.[8] The historian Richard Southern describes the beguine movement as being:

> basically a women's movement. It had no definite rule of life; it claimed the authority of no saintly founder; it sought no authorization from the Holy See; it had no organization or constitution; it promised no benefits and sought no patrons; its vows were a statement of intention, not an irreversible commitment to a discipline enforced by authority; its adherents could continue their ordinary work in the world.[9]

Despite the amorphous nature of this movement, beguines did share certain features which gave them a particular religious profile (albeit one that has much in common with that of contemporary nuns): they practised chastity, poverty, humility, obedience and devotion to the Eucharist.[10] However, beguine women were poised between the secular world and the cloistered world, and their unregulated lives were a cause for suspicion and concern in

---

[6] Twelve is the only year in her life which Mechthild refers to specifically. Ulrike Wiethaus, 'The Reality of Mystical Experience: Self and World in the Work of Mechthild von Magdeburg' (unpubl. Ph.D. dissertation, Temple Univ., 1986), (*Dissertation Abstracts International*, A47/08 (1986), p. 3079), suggests (84–5) that 12 is to be understood symbolically and cites the biblical paradigm of Jesus beginning to reveal his true identity in the temple at the age of 12 (Luke 2: 42).

[7] 'Anno domini M CC L fere per annos XV liber iste fuit teutonice cuidam begine, que fuit virgo sancta corpore et spiritu . . .'

[8] Caroline Walker Bynum, *Jesus as Mother. Studies in the High Spirituality of the High Middle Ages* (Berkeley, Calif., 1982), 228–47. The only occasion on which Mechthild identifies herself as a beguine is in iii, 15, when she addresses a group of beguines: 'Ah, foolish Beguines! . . . Now I, who am the least of you all . . .'; 'O *ir* vil torehtigen beginen, . . . Nu ich bin die minste under uch . . .' (iii, 15, 1 ff.)

[9] Richard W. Southern, *Western Society and the Church in the Middle Ages* (London, 1970), 321.

[10] For a useful study of the origins and development of the Beguine movement see Ernest McDonnell, *The Beguines and Beghards in Medieval Culture* (New York, 1969).

clerical circles.[11] Towards the end of her life Mechthild entered the convent at Helfta. We can infer from what she tells us that during this period her health was failing.

Of Mechthild's family and social background we know almost nothing.[12] It is, however, generally assumed that Mechthild's references to courtly life and customs, her familiarity with the courtly love lyric and her obvious culture and refinement indicate that she was probably born into a wealthy family and she might even have been of the nobility. Mechthild informs us that she could read and write, but that she did not understand Latin.[13] Although she did not benefit from the formal education of the convent, she probably did receive some instruction and guidance from the Dominicans.

The *Fließende Licht der Gottheit* is divided into seven books, which are further sub-divided into 267 sections. Some of these sections only comprise a few lines; others extend to pages. As a literary work it defies categorization in terms of genre. It contains an assortment of mystical visions, prophecies, letters, parables, reflections, allegories, prayers, hymns, confessions, criticism and advice. As the narrator Mechthild casts herself in the role of visionary, lover, prophet, teacher, counsellor and mediator. She is boldly eclectic in her use of stylistic devices to convey her experiences and feelings, making use of prose, verse, monologue and dialogue, as well as lyrical, epic, dramatic and didactic elements.

A number of attempts have been made to discover some kind of cohesive logic in the arrangement of the material, but no satisfactory structural patterns have emerged which allow the *Fließende Licht der Gottheit* to be described as a coherent literary work.[14] In editing Mechthild's writings Hans Neumann came to the conclusion that the *Fließende Licht der Gottheit* is 'thoroughly feminine in its unsystematic nature'. In a more considered moment he commented that the various pieces were linked together by 'association rather than in a linear structure'.[15]

---

[11] See Southern, *Western Society*, 328–31, and McDonnell, *Beguines and Beghards*, 505–15.

[12] Mechthild refers to her parents once in a prayer for the welfare of their souls (vi, 37) and she addresses a letter on the nature of the will of God to her brother B. (vi, 42). Two annotations to this letter in the *Lux Divinitatis* (515: 25 ff.) inform us that this brother was called Baldwin and that he was well educated, that he entered the Dominican order, becoming a subprior at Halle, and that he singlehandedly made a copy of the Bible which was apparently read at table. See Neumann, 'Beiträge', 190–1.

[13] ii, 3; ii, 26; iii, 1; iv, 2; v, 22; vi, 41; vii, 36. Mechthild also makes reference to scribes who copied her writings (ii, 26). The following article was drawn to my attention too late to have influenced my argument, but would be worth reading in this context: Klaus Grubmüller, 'Sprechen und Schreiben. Das Beispiel Mechthild von Magdeburg', in *Festschrift Walter Haug und Burghart Wachinger*, ed. Johannes Janota et al., 2 vols. (Tübingen, 1992), i, 335–48.

[14] See e.g. Ruth A. Dick Abraham, 'Mechthild of Magdeburg's "Flowing Light of the Godhead"; An Autobiographical Realization of Spiritual Poverty' (unpublished Ph.D. dissertation, Stanford Univ., 1980), (*Dissertation Abstracts International*, A40/11 (1980), p. 5855).

[15] Neumann, 'Beiträge', 'ein sehr fraulich unsystematisches Werk' (226); 'die (Geschichte, Gebete und Betrachtungen) mehr assoziativ als konstruktiv miteinander verbunden sind' (206).

It would seem that a Dominican, possibly Heinrich von Halle, who was Lektor in Neuruppin from 1246 and who later became a member of the Dominican priory in Halle, helped Mechthild with the editing of her work; but there is also evidence to suggest that Mechthild edited some parts independently.[16] Mechthild certainly had a sense of the unity of her writings, for she regularly referred to them as a 'book'.[17] For her the individual pieces were all manifestations of the inspiration she received from God. In a dialogue between God and Mechthild's soul Mechthild uses the image of the book to describe their relationship. God says to the soul: 'Thou art a light before My eyes, a lyre to My ears, a voice for My words, a meaning for My joy.' And the soul replies: 'Thou hast written me in the book of Thy Godhead, Thou hast fashioned me after Thine own image.'[18] The *Fließende Licht der Gottheit* is unified by the person of the author and her biography, not by any literary structural principles.

In the autobiographical section in Book iv Mechthild tells us how she felt compelled by the 'mighty love of God' to write her experiences down after having kept silent about them for twenty years. None the less, she felt and continued to feel throughout her life unworthy to be the recipient of God's knowledge:

> Ah! merciful God! What hast Thou seen in me? Thou knowest I am a fool, a sinner, a poor creature both in body and soul. Such things as these Thou shouldst have shown to the wise.[19]

However, God leaves her in no doubt that He wants her to be His mouthpiece.[20] Mechthild then tells us how she went to her confessor for advice. He recognised the validity of her experiences and ordered her to write:

---

16 Neumann, 'Beiträge', 217.

17 E.g. iv, 2; vii, 3; vii, 48 and her Dominican editor refers to her writing as a 'book', e.g. vi, 43.

18 'Du bist ein lieht vor minen ovgen, du bist ein lire vor minen o r e n, du bist ein stimme miner worten, du bist ein meinunge miner v r o m e k e i t' and 'Du hast mich geschriben an din buoch der gotheit, du hast mich gemalet an diner *moenscheit*' (iii, 2, 10 ff. and 16 f.). Quotations in English are taken from the transl. by Lucy Menzies, *The Revelations of Mechthild of Magdeburg* (London, 1953). There is a more recent translation into English which came to my attention too late to be considered as the translation for passages quoted in this article: Christiane Mesch Galvani, *Mechthild von Magdeburg: Flowing Light of the Divinity*, Garland Library of Medieval Lit., 72 (New York, 1991). Both Menzies and Galvani work from the edition by Pater Gall Morel, *Offenbarungen der Schwester Mechthild von Magdeburg oder das fliessende Licht der Gottheit* (Regensburg, 1869). Morel separates Mechthild's writing clearly into prose and verse. Menzies follows his pattern. However, the distinction between prose and verse in her work is not as clear as Morel would have it. Neumann attempts to reflect the fluidity in Mechthild's style more accurately by highlighting through expanded spacing rhyme words embedded in stretches of prose.

19 'Eya milte got, was hast du an mir g e s e h e n? Joch weistu wol, das ich ein tore, ein súndig und ein arm mensche bin an libe und an s e l e. Dis ding soltestu wisen lúten g e b e n, so moehtest du sin gelobet w e s e n.' (iv, 2, 118 ff.)

20 This sense of being a medium for God is a common feature in medieval women's visionary writing. Hildegard of Bingen, for example, describes herself as God's trumpet.

Then He commanded me to do that for which I often weep for shame when my unworthiness stands clear before my eyes, namely: that I, a poor despised little woman, should write this book out of God's heart and mouth. This book has come lovingly from God and is not drawn from human senses.[21]

These passages illustrate the parameters within which Mechthild would have her writing understood; that is, the divine nature of her impulse to write, the authority which she receives from God and the sanction she has received from her Dominican confessor. For Mechthild the writing of the *Fließende Licht der Gottheit* was an act of religious obedience.[22]

Mechthild's claim that she was a channel of communication for God inevitably caused unrest among others, and Mechthild refers on a number of occasions to how her writings have been received and the criticism she has been subjected to.[23] Unfortunately, all our evidence of this criticism is internal to the *Fließende Licht der Gottheit*, but from what Mechthild tells us it would seem that this criticism could be severe. For example, in Book ii, section 26 she says:

I was warned about this book and told by many that it should not be preserved but rather thrown to the flames.[24]

Her response, as always in the face of such criticism, is to appeal to God who leaves her in no doubt about the nature of her task:

'Beloved! Fret not thyself too sore!
The Truth may no man burn. . . .
    Now see in all these words
How praisefully they proclaim My holiness
And doubt not thyself!'[25]

Mechthild's frequent expressions of her unworthiness may, of course, be interpreted as a means of pre-empting criticism from others. She is very conscious of her own vulnerability in a number of respects. For example, she draws attention to her lack of education; and on a number of occasions she

---

21 'Do hies er mich das, des ich mich dikke weinende schemme, wan minú grossú u n w i r d e k e i t vor minen ovgen offen s t a t, das was, das er eim snoeden wibe hies us gottes herzen und munt dis buoch s c h r i b e n. Alsust ist dis buoch minnenklich von gotte har k o m e n und ist us mensclichen sinnen nit g e n o m e n.' (iv, 2, 130 ff.).

22 See Marianne Heimbach, *'Der ungelehrte Mund' als Autorität. Mystische Erfahrung als Quelle kirchlich-prophetischer Rede im Werk Mechthilds von Magdeburg*, Mystik in Geschichte und Gegenwart, 6 (Stuttgart-Bad Cannstatt, 1989), 151.

23 E.g. iii, 1; iii, 5; v, 17; vi, 31; vi, 37; vi, 38; vii, 7.

24 'Ich wart *vor* disem buoche g e w a r n e t, und wart von menschen also g e s a g e t: *Woelte* man es nit b e w a r e n, da moehte ein brant über varen.' (ii, 26, 1 f.).

25 'Lieb minú, betruebe dich nit ze v e r r e, die warheit mag nieman v e r b r e n n e n. . . . Nu sich in allú disú wort, wie loblich si mine heimlichheit m e l d e n t, und zwivel nit an dir s e l b e n!' (ii, 26, 9 ff.).

expresses her incomprehension about why God should have chosen her and not someone who was better-educated.[26] But again God reassures her:

> One finds many a wise writer of books
> Who in himself, to My sight, is a fool.
> And I tell thee further, it greatly honours Me
> And strenghtens mightily Holy Church
> That unlearned lips should teach
> The learned tongues of My Holy Spirit. (ii, 26)[27]

This reassurance places Mechthild beyond criticism. It also draws strength from a topos frequently found in medieval hagiography, that is, that the holy person's lack of formal education and their reliance on the Holy Spirit was a way of authenticating their experiences and disarming potential opponents.[28]

Although Mechthild insists on the authority and, indeed, authorship of God, she is nonetheless the producer of texts which seek to translate her experiences of Him. It is in the lyrical recording of her love relationship with God that Mechthild's creativity is most apparent. In her attempts to express and shape in words what is, in essence, ineffable, Mechthild draws on a variety of religious and secular literary forms known to her. She is not constrained by these forms but rather makes use of them eclectically as need demands. As Kurt Ruh has commented, in Mechthild's work one has a very real sense of what quintessentially poetry is, of the need it meets and how poetic forms arise.[29] The succession of striking images, clustering in particular around the imagery of water and light, to convey her emotions, is witness to the creative energy released in Mechthild by her experiential knowledge of God.

In Book v, section 12 Mechthild addresses one 'Master Heinrich', who may or may not be Heinrich of Halle.[30] It would seem that Heinrich had expressed surprise, and perhaps some criticism to judge from Mechthild's response, about the style of her writing. Mechthild says:

---

[26] E.g. ii, 3; ii, 26; iv, 2.

[27] 'Man vindet manigen wisen meister an der s c h r i f t, der an im selber vor minen ovgen ein tore i s t. Und ich sage dir noch me: Das ist mir vor inen ein gros e r e und sterket die heligen cristanheit an in vil s e r e, das der ungelerte munt die gelerte zungen von minem heligen geiste l e r e t.' (ii, 26, 29 ff.).

[28] See John Margetts, 'Latein und Volkssprache bei Mechthild von Magdeburg', *Amsterdamer Beiträge zur älteren Germanistik*, 12 (1977), 119–136, and Nigel F. Palmer, 'Das Buch als Bedeutungsträger bei Mechthild von Magdeburg', in *Bildhafte Rede im Mittelalter und früher Neuzeit*, ed. Wolfgang Harms and Klaus Speckenbach (Tübingen, 1992), 217–35 (224).

[29] Kurt Ruh, 'Beginenmystik: Hadewijch, Mechthild von Magdeburg, Marguerite Porete', *Zeitschrift für deutsches Altertum*, 106 (1977), 265–77 (276).

[30] See Neumann, 'Beiträge', 189.

Master Heinrich! You are surprised at the masculine [31] way in which this book is written? I wonder why that surprises you? But it grieves me to the heart that I, a sinful woman, had so to write. Yet I cannot otherwise describe to anyone the true knowledge and holy, glorious revelations save in these words alone, which seem to me all too poor as against the Eternal Truth.[32]

Mechthild is sensitive to Heinrich's criticism, anxious, perhaps, that as a woman she was particularly vulnerable. She asserts that there was no other option open to her and deflects attention from the criticism by emphasizing the inadequacy of language to express the inexpressible. Again she appeals to God, who responds thus:

Ask Master Heinrich how it came to pass that the Apostles who first showed such weakness, became strong and fearless after they had received the Holy Ghost? And ask further where Moses was when he saw nothing but God? And ask yet further how it was that Daniel was able to speak (so wisely)[33] in his youth?[34]

In the *Fließende Licht der Gottheit* Mechthild is not only concerned with the mystical aspect of her life. She accepts a responsibility towards the spiritual community.[35] In the preface to her book Mechthild reports God as saying:

This book I now send forth as a messenger to all spiritual people both good and bad – for if the pillars fall, the building cannot stand.[36]

Her work is directed primarily at 'spiritual people', all those concerned with

---

[31] Morel (n. 19) has 'menlicher' (i.e. 'masculine') at this point, but Hans Neumann convincingly rejects this reading and proposes 'sumenlicher' (i.e. 'some'). See vol. 2 of his edition (n. 3), 89.

[32] 'Meister Heinrich, úch wundert *sumenlicher* worten, die in disem buoche gescriben sint. Mich wundert, wie úch des wundern mag. Mer: mich jamert des von herzen sere sid dem male, das ich súndig wip schriben muos, das ich die ware bekantnisse und die heligen erlichen anschowunge nieman mag geschriben sunder disú wort a l l e i n e: si dunken mich gegen der ewigen warheit alze k l e i n e.' (v, 12, 1 ff.).

[33] Lucy Menzies indicates through her brackets round 'so wisely' that this phrase is not there in Morel's edition (nor indeed in Neumann's).

[34] 'Vrage in, wie das geschach, das die aposteln kamen in also grosse k u o n h e i t nach also grosser b l o e d e k e i t, do si enpfiengen den heligen g e i s t. Vrage me, wa Moyses do w a s, do er niht wan got a n s a c h. Vrage noch me, wa von das w a s, das Daniel in siner kintheit sprach.' (v, 12, 9 ff.).

[35] See Heimbach, *Der ungelehrte Mund*, 129.

[36] 'Dis buoch das sende ich nu ze b o t t e n allen geistlichen lúten beidú boesen und guoten, wand wenne die súle vallent, so mag das werk nút gestan . . .' (Prologue). On the question of whether this passage is to be understood as Mechthild or God speaking through her, see Alois Haas, 'Mechthild von Magdeburg – Dichtung und Mystik', *Amsterdamer Beiträge zur älteren Germanistik*, 2 (1972), 105–56 (107), Palmer, 'Buch als Bedeutungsträger', 217–35, and Eberhard Nellmann, '*Dis buoch . . . bezeichent alleine mich*. Zum Prolog von Mechthilds 'Fließendem Licht der Gottheit', in *Gotes und der werlde hulde. Literatur im Mittelalter und Neuzeit*, ed. Rüdiger Schnell (Stuttgart, 1989), 200–5.

the religious life. Mechthild tells us that until her first vision she had been 'one of the simplest people' and knew 'nothing of the devil's wickedness, of the frailty of the world and of the falseness of spiritual people' (iv, 2). Mechthild is thus careful to point out that her insight into corruption is divine in inspiration. And indeed, she frequently invokes the authority of God when castigating spiritual people for their shortcomings.[37] The bulk of her criticism is directed towards the clergy. Although Mechthild supports and reinforces the authority of the Church, she is nonetheless acutely aware of the temptations and hazards of power. As many scholars have pointed out, Mechthild displays 'an agonized awareness of the corruption of the Church'.[38] In Book vi, section 21 she launches a bitter attack on the depraved priesthood:

> Thy gold is dimmed in the filth of evil desire; thou art become poor, thou hast no true love, thy purity is burned up in the consuming fire of greed; thy humility is sunk in the swamp of thy flesh; thy truth is brought to nought by the lies of this world; the flowers of all the virtues have fallen from thee. Alas! for the fallen crown of the priesthood![39]

And in Book v, section 14 she paints a horrific picture of the purgatory which bad priests must endure.

The targets of Mechthild's criticism are usually referred to in general terms, but on occasion she can be more specific. In Book vi, section 2 Mechthild tells us how she was asked by a canon called Dietrich to pray for him. He had been appointed deacon to the cathedral of Magdeburg and was uncertain of how to conduct himself. Mechthild reports the advice God has given her for this man in some detail, for example in matters of faith:

> When he is tempted he must call Me powerfully and I will hasten to help him.

And in practical matters:

> He shall sleep on a straw pallet between two woollen blankets and shall have two pillows under his head.[40]

In the section that follows Mechthild reveals why God has chosen Dietrich; he is to rescue and reform the clergy of the cathedral. Words are not minced in Mechthild's report of God's opinion of the cathedral clergy:

---

[37] E.g. ii, 26; iii, 1; iii, 8; vi, 2; vi, 3; vi, 21; vii, 13.

[38] Bynum, *Jesus as Mother*, 231.

[39] '... din golt das ist verfúlet in dem pfuole der *unkúscheit*, wan du bist v e r a r m e t und hast der waren minne nit; din kúscheit ist verbrant in dem girigen fúre des f r a s s e s; din diemuot ist versunken in dem sumpfe dines vleisches; din warheit ist ze nihte worden in der lugine dirre welte; din bluomen aller tugenden sint dir abgevallen.

Owe crone der heligen pfafheit...' (vi, 21, 5 ff.).

[40] 'Swenne er bekoret ist, so sol er mich crefteklich anrueffen, so wil ich im snelleklichen helfen.' and 'Er sol ovch sclaffen uf dem s t r o v u w e zwúschent zwein wullinen tuochen, und zwoei kússin sol er haben under sinem h o v b e t e...' (vi, 2, 16 f. and 23 f.).

That God calls the Cathedral clergy goats is because they reek of impurity regarding Eternal Truth, before His Holy Trinity . . . Our Lord was asked how these goats should become lambs. He spoke thus: 'If they will eat the fodder which Master Dietrich has laid in the manger for them, that is holy penitence and faithful counsel in confession, they may become lambs, that is lambs with horns.'[41]

Where Mechthild is virulent in her comments about the clergy, she is fulsome in her praise of the Dominican Order, and of its founding Saint, Dominic, in particular.[42] Despite her praise, the Dominicans are not, however, immune from her critical eye, and in Book iii, section 1 she chides them for their lack of preaching activity and their reluctance to hear confessions. In a prophetic passage (iv, 27) God tells Mechthild of how a new order of preachers will emerge which will instruct the Dominicans to be wiser, less concerned with material needs and more aflame with the Holy Ghost.[43]

There was a natural affinity between the mendicant orders and the beguine way of life in their espousal of apostolic poverty. The Church had also given these orders special responsibility for coping with the surge of female piety which occurred in the twelfth and thirteenth centuries.[44] The preface to the *Fließende Licht der Gottheit* states that Mechthild:

followed the light and teaching of the Preaching Order steadfastly and absolutely, advancing steadily and improving herself from day to day.[45]

Clearly Mechthild had the blessing of the Dominicans. Her praise of St Dominic and his followers indicates where her sympathies lay, and no doubt her comments about the order could have been interpreted by the clergy as a further reproach to them, given the tension that existed between the clergy and the preaching orders over the matter of priestly office and the administering of sacraments.[46]

Interestingly enough there is little criticism directed towards religious

---

[41] 'Das got die tuomeherren heisset boeke, das tuot er darumbe, das ir vleisch stinket von der unk ú sc h e i t in der ewigen w a r h e i t vor siner heligen d r i v a l t e k e i t. . . . Und únser herre got wart gevraget, wa mitte dise boekke lambere moehten werden. Do sprach únser herre alsus: ''Wellent si das vuoter essen, das in her Dietrich in die kripfen leit, das ist die helige buosse und der getrúwe rat in der bihte, so soent *si* einer hande lamber werden, die man heisset wider, lamber mit hornen.' (vi, 3, 4 ff.).

[42] E.g. iii, 1; iv, 20; iv. 21; iv, 22; iv, 27.

[43] A number of scholars have seen the influence of Joachim of Fiore in Mechthild's description of this order of preachers who will witness the end of the world. See Heimbach, *Der ungelehrte Mund,* 160, n. 303.

[44] See Herbert Grundmann, 'Zur Geschichte der Beginen im 13. Jahrhundert', in *Monumenta Germaniae Historica Schriften*, 15/1 (Stuttgart, 1976), 201–21.

[45] '. . . und nachvolgete vesteklich und vollekommenlich dem liehte und *der* lere *des* predier orden und *kam* vúr von tage ze tage und besserte sich tegelich.' (Preface, 37 ff.).

[46] See William A. Hinnebusch, *The Early English Friars Preachers* (Rome, 1951), 318–28.

women.[47] In Book iii, section 24 Mechthild reports a conversation between a spiritual sister (presumably a nun) and a beguine:

> Now I will write of a truly spiritual sister and a worldly Beguine who conversed together. The sister spoke from the true light of the Holy Spirit without sorrow, but the Beguine spoke materially in the spirit of Lucifer, in a complaining way.[48]

Thus, Mechthild draws a comparison between these two women; the spiritual sister is pure while the beguine is tainted with this world. Perhaps Mechthild wished to draw attention here to the difficulties inherent in living the life of a beguine. Mechthild never criticizes the convents. On the contrary, she eulogizes the life of the convent in an allegory entitled 'Of a Spiritual Convent' (vii, 36) written when she had entered the convent at Helfta.

Increasingly in the *Fließende Licht der Gottheit* there is a refrain about the suffering inflicted by her critics and adversaries which Mechthild has to bear, for example in Book vi, section 38:

> Ah Lord! How long must I stay here on earth in this mortal body like a post or target at which people throw stones or shoot, those who have long assailed my honour with their evil cunning?[49]

There is evidence in her work that some of Mechthild's writings were circulated before they were gathered together as a volume, for she responds to criticism on occasion and defends them. For example, in Book ii, section 4 Mechthild tells of a vision she had in which John the Baptist celebrated Mass and gave her, 'a poor maid', Communion. This vision seems to have aroused great controversy to which Mechthild replies in Book vi, section 36. She puts up a spirited defence and does not allow herself to be intimidated by her critics. From what Mechthild says it would seem that her critics felt that her vision implied that a layman could say Mass and administer Communion. Mechthild argues in reply that the vision must be understood in a spiritual sense, and that in this sense John the Baptist is not a layman because he touched God as priests do. She finishes by saying:

> No Pope nor Bishop nor Priest could speak the Word of God as John the Baptist spoke it, save in our supernatural Christian Faith which cannot be

---

[47] In her vision of Hell the only women that Mechthild sees are women of the nobility (iii, 21).
[48] 'Nu wil ich *úch* schriben von einer waren geistlichen swester und von einer weltlichen beginen; die *widersprechent* sich alsust: Dú geistliche swester sprichet usser dem waren liehte des heligen geistes sunder h e r z e l e i t, aber dú weltlich begine sprichet us von irem fleische mit Lutzifers geiste in grúwelicher a r b e i t.' (iii, 24, 1 ff.).
[49] 'Eya lieber herre, almehtiger got, wie lange sol ich hie stan in der erden mines v l e i s c h e s glich eime stekken oder einem m a l e, da die lúte zuo lovffent, werfent und s c h i e s s e n t und lange miner eren hant g e r a m e t mit geswinder argheit?' (vi, 38, 1 ff.).

grasped by the senses. Was he then a layman? Instruct me ye blind! Your lies and your hatred will not be forgiven without suffering![50]

What appears to have triggered this controversy off is a fear amongst the clergy of anticlericalism. Mechthild's response indicates that she was sensitive to this issue, for her defence rests not on a justification of John the Baptist as an extraordinary layman, but rather in claiming for him priestly status in a metaphorical sense.[51]

There is further evidence in the *Fließende Licht der Gottheit* of Mechthild's sensitivity towards the opinions of the clergy. Mechthild's writings explicitly reinforce the authority of the Church and the clergy rather than undermining it. Thus, for example, in Book ii, section 24 Mechthild distinguishes clearly between her position and the power of the clergy. She cites an example of where a devil tempted her to exercise powers beyond her. She replies as follows:

> Thou hast an eternal sickness. If thou wouldst be healed thou must go and show thyself to a Priest or Archbishop or the Pope. For I myself have no power save to sin.[52]

Herbert Grundmann has drawn attention to a synod held in Magdeburg in 1261 which gives us an interesting context in which to set this statement.[53] The synod ordered that the beguines of Magdeburg must obey their parish priests. Failure to do so was to be punished by excommunication. In this decree the clergy of Magdeburg were following the example of other synods. The underlying problem was the beguines' attempt to choose exclusively Dominicans as confessors and spiritual advisors, thereby evading the control and supervision of the Church.

A more telling example of Mechthild's attitude towards the ecclesiastical hierarchy comes in Book v, section 5. Mechthild tells of the death of a beguine and how this virtuous woman had to spend some time in Purgatory before ascending to Heaven:

> She was on the ascent and longed to hasten, but the dark night was ever before her. It was self-will without guidance which so sorely hindered this otherwise good woman.[54]

---

[50] 'Das Johannes Baptista gottes wort sprach, alsus verre mag es niemer babest noch bischof noch priester vollebringen denne alleine mit *únsrem* unsinnelichem cristanem gelovben. Was dis ein leie? Berihtent mich, ir blinden; úwer luginen und úwer has wirt úch niemer vergeben ane pine!' (vi, 36, 19 ff.).

[51] See Walker Bynum, *Jesus as Mother*, 237.

[52] 'Du hast ein ewig siechi: wiltu gnesen, so var hin und zoege dich einem priester oder einem bischof oder einem ertzbischof oder dem babest. Ich enhan enheinen gewalt denne alleine, das ich súndegen mag.' (ii, 24, 58 ff.).

[53] Neumann, 'Beiträge', 228.

[54] 'Si was bevangen mit einer grossen vinsternisse und begerte vil sere zuo dem ewigen liehte.

Mechthild's comment that it was 'self-will without guidance' which hindered this woman's assumption into Heaven must have won approval in clerical circles and clearly indicates her awareness of the potential risks involved in adopting the beguine way of life.[55] Mechthild asks the beguine what she can do for her. The beguine, however, knows her own failings and why prayer cannot assist her:

> 'On earth I did not wish to follow human advice according to Christian ordinance, therefore no human prayer or longing can help me.[56]

Mechthild appeals to Christ on the beguine's behalf. Christ's reply reinforces the need for obedience to the authority of the Church:

> Virtues exercised without obedience are less valuable to Me. I myself came to earth under obedience and I served on earth in utter submission to My father and all men . . .[57]

From the writings contained in the *Fließende Licht der Gottheit* a complex, passionate and spirited personality emerges. The freshness and individuality of Mechthild's mystical revelations are as startling as is her absolute certainty of her own salvation. In order to have her work properly in focus it is essential to bear in mind on the one hand the interface between Mechthild as author and God as inspiration, and on the other the interface between Mechthild and her contemporary audience.

So si was in eim ufzuge, so was ie dú vinster naht da vor, das was der eigen wille ane r a t, der disen vollekomenen menschen also sere gehindert h a t.' (v, 5, 12 ff.).

55 Heimbach, *Der ungelehrte Mund* , identifies 'falseness' and 'self-will' (143–7) as being the two key vices which preoccupy Mechthild. Kurt Ruh, 'Beginenmystik', illustrates the risks which the beguine way of life could incur, 267–8.

56 'Ich wolte in ertriche keines menschen rat volgen nach cristanlicher ordenunge. Darumbe mag mir keines menschen gebet noch gerunge helfen.' (v, 5, 16 ff.).

57 'Alle tugende sint mir u n m e r e, die ane rat g e s c h e h e n t, wan ich kam in ertrich mit rate und ich diente uf dem ertrich mit grosser u n d e r t e n e k e i t minem vatter und allen menschen . . .' (v, 5, 20 ff.).

CATHERINE OF SIENA:
REWRITING FEMALE HOLY AUTHORITY

Thomas Luongo

It is by now a commonplace to observe that in the Middle Ages women were associated with bodiliness or fleshliness, and to argue that women could thus be considered to offer men a special avenue to *imitatio Christi*, by experiencing through affection and suffering Christ's 'femininity'.[1] As Carolyn Walker Bynum has argued, for men the feminine could become a source of liminality, the means by which men could call into question their own exalted, 'spiritual' status and join Christ on the cross in fleshly humility.[2] Indeed, Vauchez and others have identified in the later Middle Ages a model of sanctity which associated femininity with an affective, as opposed to an intellectual, spirituality. Raymond of Capua, biographer and confessor of Catherine of Siena, concerned to justify Catherine's outspokenness and active life, argued for Catherine's sanctity in precisely these terms; he interpreted Catherine's authority to speak as deriving from her position on a margin co-defined by her female virginity and her direct access to divine gifts through prophecy and participation in the suffering of Christ.[3]

While Bynum's model of female liminality is confirmed by the hagiography of Raymond and others, modern scholars have generally not looked past the hagiographic packaging in order to understand the process of negotiation whereby someone like Catherine acquired her authority.[4] Despite the fact that her letters show her engagement in pressing social and political concerns (particularly the crisis of public authority in Italy), Catherine is consistently

---

[1] See e.g. Carolyn Walker Bynum, 'The Female Body and Religious Practice in the Later Middle Ages', in *Fragmentation and Redemption* (New York, 1991), 181–238; and Karma Lochrie, 'The Language of Transgression: Body, Flesh, and Word in Mystical Discourse', in *Speaking Two Languages. Traditional Disciplines and Contemporary Theory in Medieval Studies*, ed. Allen J. Frantzen (Albany, NY, 1991), 115–40.

[2] For Bynum's appropriation and adaptation of Victor Turner's terminology, see esp. 'Women's Stories, Women's Symbols: A Critique of Victor Turner's Theory of Liminality' in *Fragmentation and Redemption*, 27–51.

[3] Raymond of Capua, 'Vita S. Catherinae Senensis', in *Acta Sanctorum*, April, v.3 (Paris, 1866), 862–967.

[4] A notable exception to this generalization is Aviad Kleinberg, *Prophets in Their Own Country. Living Saints and the Making of Sainthood in the Later Middle Ages* (Chicago, 1992).

89

read as addressing these concerns from a position that is always already marginal and liminal. By accepting as natural the terms in which Catherine was represented, such scholarship cannot appreciate how her authority was constructed, nor can it account for Catherine's own participation – whether by complicity or subversion – in the establishment of her authority.

In order to appreciate how Catherine communicated and negotiated her authority, I will suggest in this paper a reading of one of Catherine's most famous letters within its historical and rhetorical contexts and against the context provided by her hagiography. Writing to Raymond of Capua, Catherine describes how she accompanied to the scaffold and accomplished the conversion of a young man named Niccolò di Toldo, who was accused of a crime against the Sienese state.[5] In this letter, her rhetoric appeals to the association between femininity and fleshliness as well as to a variety of gendered cultural images in order to construct her own gender and authority. Not only does this letter show Catherine actively establishing the margins from which she can speak, it shows her doing this in ways which manipulate, but which are not identical to the terms of the hagiographic reception of her authority.

Although the Niccolò di Toldo letter has played a disproportionate part in Catherine's reputation as an author (at least in Italian literary history), it was not easily or completely absorbed into her hagiography. Most notably, although the letter is addressed to Raymond, the event she describes is not included in Raymond's *Legenda maior* of Catherine, which was and is the standard (though far from exclusive) source for her life. The letter is not dated, and Catherine does not mention the name of the young man who is executed. What external evidence we have for the details of this letter derives mainly from accounts of Catherine's life written after the *Legenda maior* by Tomasso d'Antonio 'Caffarini', a Sienese Dominican disciple of Catherine who led the campaign for her canonization in the years after Raymond's death. In the *Legenda minor* of Catherine, an adaptation for popular dissemination of Raymond's prolix *vita*, Caffarini added a number of details not mentioned by Raymond, including the Niccolò di Toldo affair. Caffarini cites the case of Niccolò di Toldo as one of a series of examples of miracles Catherine performed for the spiritual well-being of criminals:

A similar case, at which I was personally present, occurred in Siena, and concerned a certain noble Perugian by the name of Niccolaus Tuldi. He had incurred the capital sentence for certain rash words he had spoken against the Sienese state. As a result of this he fell into desperation, and so the virgin visited him and comforted him, and he proceeded to death like

[5] All references are to E. Dupré Theseider, *Epistolario di S. Caterina da Siena*, i (Rome, 1940), 126–32. This is letter 31 in Dupré Theseider's incomplete ed. of Catherine's letters, and number 273 in the Tommaseo/Misciatelli ed. A translation in English of Dupré Theseider's ed. can be found in Suzanne Noffke (ed.), *The Letters of Catherine of Siena*, i, Medieval and Renaissance Texts and Studies 52 (Binghamton, NY, 1988), 107–11. I have used Noffke as a reference throughout.

a happy lamb. And by the merits and prayers of the virgin his soul ascended visibly into heaven. Concerning this event we have a beautiful letter.[6]

In the manuscripts of the letters themselves, 7 out of the 11 copies have an unusually prolix rubric, describing the letter as concerning 'a singular grace performed for a young Perugian, who had his head cut off in Siena, and [Catherine] received it into her hands'.[7] And in one of the Sienese manuscripts (which does not contain this rubric), Caffarini himself has added a marginal note identifying the condemned man and referring the reader to the *Legenda minor* for more details.[8]

Although the hagiography only hints at the political nature of Niccolò's crime, and casts Catherine's intervention in conventional, 'saintly' terms, Catherine's appearance at Niccolò's execution might very well have been seen by the Sienese authorities as a political act.[9] There is only sparse evidence for the identity and crime of the Perugian, but references to the case in the Sienese archives suggest strongly that he was connected in some way to papal interests in the battle between the papacy and the Florentine league – the 'War of Eight Saints' – at a time when Siena had reason to be especially wary of compromising Florentine support.[10] Catherine spent nearly all of 1375 in Pisa with

---

6   E. Franceschini (ed.), *Sanctae Catharinae Senensis Legenda minor*, (Fontes Vitae S. Catharinae Senensis Historici x; Siena, 1942), 92: 'Quasi similis casus accidit adhuc in ipsa civitate Senarum, personaliter ibi me presente, de quodam nobili Perusino nomine Nicolaus Tuldi; qui, cum ex quibusdam verbis statum civitatis concernentibus incaute prolatis ab eo, capitalem sententiam incurrisset, et ex hoc per carcerem uti deperatus incederet, ex quo virgo visitavit eum atque confortavit, velut agnus corde letissimo processit ad mortem; cuius anima meritis et orationibus eiusdmen virginis visibiliter ipso tunc evolavit ad celum. Super qua materia pulcram habemus epistolam.'

7   E.g. London, British Library, Harley MS 3480, f.53r: 'Questa lettera mando essa katerina al padre dell anima sua maestro Raymondo notificandoli una singolare grata inpetrata per uno giovane perugino al quale in siena fu tagliata la testa et ella la ricolse in mano.' See also Dupré Theseider, *Epistolario*, 126.

8   Siena, Biblioteca Comunale T.II.2, f.119v (Caffarini's marginalia): 'Hic fuit mentio de quodam nobili de Perusio, qui fuit decapitatus in Senis, et dictus est Niccolaus Tuldi, de quo habetur in Legenda minori et in contestationibus, et qui in desperatione constitutus, per istam virginem ad Dominum est reductus et miro modo salvatus.' See also Dupré Theseider, *Epistolario*, 127n.

9   The Sienese government clearly worried from time to time about Catherine's possible intervention in politics; e.g. in a letter of 1377 she responds to suspicions concerning her activities while staying at Rocca d'Orcia, the stronghold of the Salimbeni family, erstwhile rebels against the Sienese government (letter 123 in the Tomasseo/Misciattelli edn).

10   Gérard du Puy, papal legate in Perugia, intervened for Niccolò with the Sienese magistracy at least twice, and on the second occasion pleaded for Niccolò's release on the grounds that he was 'an ecclesiastical person', a likely indication that Niccolò was engaged in some business for the legate and thus for the church. The spring of 1375 was a time of heightening tension in relations between Florence and the papacy, which left Siena in a precarious position between stronger Italian powers. Indeed, letters around this time from the Florentine government and from Sienese ambassadors informed the Sienese magistracy of a pact between the papacy and the Milanese tyrant Bernabo Visconti, a threatening development for the Tuscan city-states.

Raymond, preaching the crusade and urging civic leaders not to rebel against the papacy. In fact, she was in Pisa shortly before and after the supposed date of Niccolò's execution, suggesting that she might have returned specifically for this event. Indeed, to suppose that Catherine knew of Niccolò and involved herself in his case because of his connection to the papal party would be in keeping with the political and institutional nature of her relationship with Raymond, who was assigned to Catherine as director in August 1374 and who brought her immediately into the ambit of ecclesiastical politics in Tuscany.[11] That Raymond was assigned to Catherine largely for political and institutional reasons is suggested by his previous offices and by his diplomatic activities after being assigned to her (which kept them apart more often than they were together). Indeed, a papal privilege of 17 August 1376 confirmed Raymond in his capacity as director of Catherine for the purpose of their work for the crusade and for 'other business of the Holy Roman Church'.[12]

This letter can be read not only in the context of the political nature of Catherine's relationship with Raymond, but also as an artifact of their early personal relationship. It is presumed to have been written in late June or early July 1375, which would make it the earliest extant letter from Catherine to Raymond. However much Raymond had known of Catherine before, at the time of this letter he had been her director for less than a year. Thus Catherine wrote this letter at a time when one would expect that she still needed to articulate her authority to Raymond, her older and more experienced superior. From the perspective of Catherine's reader, therefore, this letter can be read as claiming both an authoritative perspective on political events and some spiritual authority over Raymond. To support each claim, Catherine employs images of female alterity.

Catherine's letter moves from an exhortation to Raymond to a description of her encounter with Niccolò as a romance culminating in marriage on the scaffold. The letter concludes with Catherine gesturing to an exemplary purpose of her story for Raymond. The thematic link between the sections is signalled not only by her final comment, but more obviously by the

Moreover, the Florentines had just given essential aid in helping the Sienese put down a rebellion by the Salimbeni, the most powerful and volatile of the Sienese magnate families: an act of friendship of which the Florentine priors during this time continually reminded the Sienese. Further, according to the 17th-cent. historian Tomassi, Gérard du Puy was encouraging the Salimbeni to stay in revolt in order to weaken Siena and keep it out of the league with Florence. Whatever Niccolò's precise offence, it is clear how threats to the government on the domestic and international fronts combined to make Siena at this time especially apprehensive of danger from agents of the papacy.

For a fuller, although sometimes speculative, treatment of Niccolò di Toldo from evidence of the Perugian archives, see Anna Imelde Galletti, ' "Uno capo nelle mani mie": Niccolò di Toldo, perugino', in *Simposio Internazionale Cateriniano-Bernardiniano*, 121–7.

[11] See A.W. Van Ree, 'Raymond de Capoue, éléments biographiques', *Archivum fratrum praedicatorum*, 33 (1963), 159–241.

[12] See Van Ree, 168n; and M.H. Laurent (ed.), *Documenti*, Fontes vitae S. Catharinae Senensis Historici 1 (Florence, 1936), n.38.

reappearance of an image which exercises a controlling influence on the letter as a whole: the fragrant and bloody open wound of Christ. As it figures in the hortatory section of the letter, the open wound presages the visual and olfactory impact of Niccolò's bloody apotheosis, infusing Catherine's language from the start with the odour of blood, and establishing the passionate and erotic register of her account of Niccolò's death. On the thematic level, the exemplarity of his death for Raymond depends on the parallels between Catherine's exhortation to Raymond to enter into the open side of Christ, and Niccolò's penetration of the wound in Catherine's vision. Thus the full meaning of Catherine's 'marriage' to Niccolò and the meaning of the letter as a whole depend on how one understands the space Catherine opens for her reader within the wound in Christ's side.

'Affogato e anegato nel sangue dolce del Figliuolo di Dio'

In the opening section of the letter, Catherine exhorts Raymond by invoking her own desire to see him 'enflamed and drowned in the sweet blood of the Son of God, which blood is blended with the fire of his most burning charity'.[13] She goes on to explain that it is to gain humility that Raymond must bathe himself in the blood, since experiencing the love of God engenders humility by inspiring hatred of self. In the course of this explanation, the emotional pitch heightens as Catherine pointedly changes the terms, moving from contemplation of the virtue of charity to the more affective 'love': the 'fire of most burning charity' (*fuoco dell'ardentissima carità*) of Christ's blood becomes the 'most burning love' (*ardentissimo amore*) with which the lamb was slain. It is *amore*, not *carità*, that teaches the soul hatred of self.

Catherine concludes her excursus on the theme of love and humility by concretion. Extending the sensory imagery of fire and heat, she writes that the soul engulfed in blood will emerge purged, 'as the iron issues purified from the furnace'. She then directs Raymond to the source of the affection necessary for purification:

> Enter into the open side of the Son of God, which is an open shop, so full of fragrance that sin [itself] becomes fragrant. Therein the sweet bride reclines on a bed of fire and blood, therein is seen and made manifest the secret of the heart of the Son of God.[14]

---

[13] 'scrivo a voi e racomandomivi nel pretioso sangue del figliuolo di Dio, con desiderio di vedervi affogato e anegato nel sangue dolce del Figliuolo di Dio, el quale sangue è intriso col fuoco dell'ardentissima carità sua' (*Epistolario*, 126–7).

[14] 'E così l'anima nesce con perfettissima purità, sì come el ferro esce purificato della fornace. Così voglio che vi serriate nel costato uperto del Figliuolo di Dio, el quale è una bottiga aperta, piena d'odore, in tanto che 'l peccato diventa odorifero. Ine la dolce sposa si riposa nel letto del fuoco e del sangue, ine vede ed è manifestato el segreto del cuore del Figliuolo di Dio'(*Epistolario*, 127).

Typically, Catherine does not develop images in a logical or linear way, but rather invokes them in patterns or constellations around her theme as her ideas become more complex. Thus the energetic and industrial mood established by the image of the furnace, modified by the commercial tenor of the 'open shop' (*bottiga aperta*), is altered radically by the allure of the 'sweet bride' (*dolce sposa*).

Catherine adds another image to the constellation, proclaiming in an ecstatic apostrophe:

> O tapped cask (*O botte spillata*), which gives to every enamored desire drink unto drunkenness, and gives happiness and illuminates every understanding, and fills every memory so that therein one is so exhausted that one cannot hold nor understand nor love anything other than this sweet and good Jesus, blood and fire, ineffable love![15]

Catherine insists that Raymond, having drunk from this source of 'immeasurable desire', must persevere 'even when things seem most cold' up to the time when 'we see spilled the blood of sweet and amorous desire'.[16] Thus the themes of love and desire mix with the pervasive influence of blood in this letter, culminating in the sweet fragrance of the open wound of Christ, and anticipating the bloodiness and the amplified eroticism of the narrative of Niccolò's death which follows.

The 'costato uperto del figliuolo di Dio'

It is worth pausing for a moment to consider Catherine's vision of the wound, an image to which she returns throughout her letters in a number of crucial contexts. Her language here appears to be appropriated (directly or indirectly) from the meditation on the passion of Christ in the pseudo-Bonaventuran *Stimulus amoris*. The Franciscan text endows the image of the 'open shop' with more obvious meaning by relating it to the traditional notions of Christ as physician/apothecary, and the wound in Christ's side as the special source of his saving medicine:[17]

---

[15] 'O botte spillata, la quale dà bere e inebbrii ogni inamorato desiderio, e dài letitia e illumini ogni intendimento, e riempi ogni memoria che ie s'affadiga, in tanto che altro non può ritenere, né altro amare se non questo dolce e buono Gesù, sangue e fuoco, ineffabile amore!' (*Epistolario*, 127–8).

[16] 'E guardate che per illusioni di dimonio, le quali so che v'ànno dato impaccio e daranno, o per detto di che vedeste la cosa più fredda, infine che vediamo spargere el sangue con dolci e amorosi desiderii' (*Epistolario*, 128).

[17] An intriguing miniature illustrating the theme of Christ as apothecary exists in the early 16th-cent. *Chants royaux du Puy de Rouen* (Paris, Bibliothèque Nationale Fr. 1537, f.82v). A smiling Christ is shown behind the counter of a realistic and fully stocked pharmacy, writing out a prescription for a naked – and apparently uncomfortable – Adam and Eve; see *La médicine médiévale à travers les manuscrits de la Bibliothèque Nationale* (Paris, 1982), 19.

> Behold, it is an open shop full of all fragrances, and rich in medicines. Enter therefore through the windows of the wounds, and receive the medicine which heals, restores, preserves, and conserves.[18]

It is easy to see how the social resonance of the language of the *Stimulus amoris* might have appealed to Catherine. This image evokes mundane experience to convey a sense of the welcome expansiveness of the wound, which opens into a chamber in which the interior is larger than the exterior. The streets of a Tuscan city were (and often are) so narrow as to grant only a slight glimpse of sky. To walk into a Sienese or Florentine shop or workshop was to move from the outside to the inside, yet from a smaller to a larger space. It is to this sensation that Catherine appeals in her use of this image, plotted in a way which anticipates the social drama – the execution – which she is about to describe.

The domestic tenor of this vision of Christ's pharmacy is disturbed and transformed, however, by the alluring figure of the 'sweet bride'. This image evokes the erotic spousal language of the Song of Songs, particularly according to its dominant late medieval interpretations, in which focus on the poem as a model for the soul's experience of love of Christ supplanted traditional allegorical interpretations. The poem was thus assimilated to devotion for the Sacred Heart.[19] In this tradition, the transfixion of Christ could be understood as an act of love, and his wound seen as the point of entry to the heart: 'You have wounded my heart, my sister, my spouse' (Song of Songs 4:9). For the author of the *Stimulus amoris*, the open wound allows the joining of a human heart with Christ's.[20] The 'spouse' could represent the soul in its longing for Christ, the bridegroom. At the same time, it could represent the anthropomorphized virtue of *caritas*, in connection to a representational topos of Christ crucified by the virtues (a theme based on Bernard's commentary on Ephesians).[21] And the 'spouse' could also evoke the Virgin Mary, Christ's heavenly bride, whose 'wounding' by the sword of compassion could be represented as parallel to Christ's wounding with the lance.[22]

Catherine's 'sweet bride' reclining 'on a bed of fire and blood' can be seen

---

[18] 'Ecce aperta est apotheca omnibus aromatibus plena, et medicinalibus opulenta. Per vulnerum ergo fenestras intra, et accipe medicinam sanitivam, restauritivam praeservativam et conservativam' (*Stimulus amoris* in *S. Bonaventura Opera Omnia* xii, A.C. Peltier (ed.), Paris, 1868, 634).

[19] For an excellent discussion of the late medieval history of this topos, see Jeffrey Hamburger, *The Rothschild Canticles. Art and Mysticism in Flanders and the Rhineland circa 1300* (New Haven, Conn. 1990), 70–87.

[20] 'Quid mirabilius, quam quod mors vivificet, vulnera sanent, sanguis album faciat, et mundet intima, nimius dolor nimium dulcorem inducat, apertio lateris cor cordi conjungat?' (*Stimulus amoris*, 633).

[21] Hamburger (75–6) discusses this theme and its representation in the Heisterbach miniatures, in which *caritas* stands to Christ's right and thrusts the lance into his side, as well as a parallel representation in the Rothschild Canticles.

[22] Hamburger, 76.

most obviously as a personification of *carità*, consistent with her earlier exhortation to Raymond to immerse himself in Christ's blood, 'blended with the fire of his most burning charity'. Extending this image, and keeping in mind the rhetorical importance of the wound as the site of Raymond's access to union with Christ, the 'sweet bride' also serves by metonymy as a feminized Christ. In this way, Catherine's pastiche of spousal images reverses the positions of the bride and bridegroom by evoking Song of Songs 3:1, 'In my bed by night I sought him whom my soul loves'. This reversal of Christ's gender makes sense in the context of the affective experience that entry into the open wound is meant to provide Raymond. He is to be stirred to an emotional engagement by which, through love of Christ, he will comprehend his own sinfulness and thus achieve humility. Catherine represents the wound here as a physical threshold into a liminal space – a site of precisely the kind of transgression made possible by the logic of the male/female, spirit/flesh binaries. Having configured Christ's wound as the site of Raymond's fleshly and passionate engagement in Christ's humanity, Catherine feminizes Christ, which accords well with what Bynum and others have written on the representation of Jesus as mother in the Middle Ages. There too the wound figures as a kind of breast.[23]

Here, however, although Catherine's use of the image does convey an idea of feeding – the blood from the *costato* is to be Raymond's drink – the image possesses an erotic force beyond any merely nutritional meaning. More than feminizing Jesus by representing him as a nursing mother, Catherine feminizes him by configuring the wound like a woman's vulva. A rounded or arched opening, rather than a horizontal slit, is suggested by the parallel and homonymous images of the *bottega* and the *botte*. Moreover, the emphasis here is on entering in rather than flowing out. Phallic images prevail: the soul is purified in the blood as an iron is purified in the furnace; Raymond is to enter in to the open side just as sin enters and is made fragrant; and the *botte spillata* (the 'tapped cask') is opened with a *spillo* or *spilla*, an instrument for puncturing the seal with a metal spike.[24] The blood which flows from the open wound, as from a punctured cask, is 'the blood of sweet and amorous desire', suggesting the blood of the marriage bed, a reading implied as well by the image of the 'dolce sposa' reclining on a bed of fire within the open wound.

This reading of Catherine's imagery is reinforced by a brief look at the description of the act of union of the soul with the crucified Christ in the *Stimulus Amoris*. That text exhibits a similar fluctuation of gender, and registers an erotic pitch even more heightened than Catherine's.[25] The *Stimulus-*

---

[23] E.g. see Carolyn Walker Bynum, 'The Female Body and Religious Practice in the Later Middle Ages', in *Fragmentation and Redemption*, 181–238.

[24] Niccolò Tommaseo, *Dizionario della lingua italiana* (Turin: 1872), 1109, s.v. 'Spillo'.

[25] The eroticization of Christ's wound in the *Stimulus amoris* is discussed by Wolfgang Riehle, who sees 'a quite consciously intended analogy between this wound of Christ and the female pudenda' in the pseudo-Bonaventuran text as characteristic of Franciscan mysticism: Wolfgang Riehle, *The Middle English Mystics* (London, 1981), 46.

author identifies his own emotional engagement in the Passion with that of the Virgin Mary, 'whose soul the sword of her Son's Passion pierced', and then conflates the wounded Virgin with her wounded Son: 'For if He has given birth to me, He must then, like a mother, feed me with His breasts, lift me up with His hands, hold me in His arms, kiss me with His lips, and cherish me in His lap . . .'[26] The author describes the entry of the soul into Christ's wound in physical and sexual terms, and clearly shifts the bodily geography of the wound:

> O most loving wounds of our Lord Jesus Christ! For when on a certain time I entered into them with my eyes open, my eyes were so filled with blood that they could see nothing else; and so, attempting to enter further in, I groped the way all along with my hand, until I came unto the most inward bowels of His charity, from which, being encompassed on all sides, I could not go back again. And so I now dwell there, and eat the food he He eats, and am made drunk with His drink.[27]

Like Catherine, the *Stimulus*-author evokes vividly the language of the Song of Songs: 'My beloved put his hand through the opening, and my insides trembled at his touch' (5:4), and its association of affection and wounding: 'You have wounded my heart, my sister, my spouse' (4:9).

To describe the *Stimulus amoris* as Catherine's 'source' might imply a kind of authorial practice foreign to a semi-literate person like Catherine. But her use of this imagery of a female Christ has an erotic meaning which parallels the *Stimulus*-author's conception of union with Christ as sexual union with a woman. That Catherine consciously employs this gendered image is borne out in the way she describes her encounter with Niccolò.

'Uno capo nelle mani mie'

In her letter, Catherine introduces the story of Niccolò's execution in a way that provides internal evidence for the political meaning of the situation and of Catherine's relationship with Raymond. Having proposed to Raymond the stimulation of the blood in Christ's wound, Catherine calls him to action:

> 'Up, up my most sweet father, and let us no longer sleep, for I am hearing news which makes me want neither bed nor pillow. I have begun already by receiving a head in my hands, which was to me of such sweetness that the heart cannot conceive, nor tongue speak, nor eyes see, nor ears hear.

---

[26] 'Sed certe, etsi me peperit, debebit sicut mater me lactare uberibus, levare manibus, portare brachiis, osculari labiis, foveri gremiis' (*Stimulus amoris*, 634).

[27] 'O amatissima vulnera Domini nostri Jesu Christi! Nam cum in ea quadam vice oculis subintrarem apertis, ipsi oculi sanguine sunt repleti, sicque nihil aliud videns coepi ingredi manu palpans, donec perveni ad intima viscera charitatis suae, quibus post undique circumplexus reverti nequivi. Ideoque ibi inhabito, et quibus vescitur cibis, vescor, ac inebrior suo potu' (*Stimulus amoris*, 634).

The desire of God progresses through the other mysteries accomplished already, of which I do not tell because it would take too long.[28]

Catherine's apparent excitement is reflected in the confusion of this passage. It is not clear what Catherine has 'begun already', or how 'receiving a head into my hands' begins the action to which Catherine is calling Raymond. The 'news' is apparently Niccoló's death and the visionary experience which accompanied it, which, according to the paradoxical logic of the mystic, makes sense in relation to Catherine's description of the event as beyond sense perception: for, having heard what cannot be heard and seen what cannot be seen, Catherine is about to tell what cannot be told. Catherine's excited language of imminent action here resembles the language she uses elsewhere to introduce news about the crusade or the return of the pope to Rome. By referring to Niccolò's execution and her own part in it, Catherine is calling to Raymond to join her in a social movement, which she links to the theme of desire ('The desire of God progresses . . .') – a movement either of God's desire or desire for God. The sense that Catherine is speaking of a plan to which both she and Raymond are party is strengthened in a subsequent conspiratorial reference to Niccolò as 'one whom you know'.[29]

Catherine writes that she went to visit Niccolò, comforted him and brought him to confess his sins, and promised to be with him at the time of execution. The next day she visited him and led him to holy communion which, she writes, 'he had never before received'. In language redolent of blood and desire – immediately suggesting the terms of the opening section of the letter – Catherine tells Raymond how Niccolò's fear of death is conquered by his love and desire for her:

> But God's measureless and burning goodness tricked him, creating in him such an affection and love in the desire of me in God, that he did not know how to abide without God, and he said: 'Stay with me and do not leave me. Like this I cannot but be alright, and I will die content!' and he had his head resting on my breast. I sensed an intense joy, a fragrance of his blood, and it was not without the fragrance of my own, which I wait to shed for the sweet husband Jesus.[30]

---

[28] 'Su su, padre mio dolcissimo, e non dormiamo più, ché io odo novelle che io non voglio più né letto né testi. O cominciato già a ricevere uno capo nelle mani mie, el quale mi fu di tanta dolcezza, che 'l cuore no 'l può pensare, né la lingua parlare, né l'occhio vedere, né orecchie udire. Andò el desiderio di Dio, tra gli altri misterii fatti inanzi, e quali non dico, ché troppo sarebbe longo.' (*Epistolario*, 128–9).

[29] 'Andai a visitare colui che vi sapete' (*Epistolario*, 129).

[30] 'ma la smisurata e affocata bontà di Dio lo ingannò, creandoli tanto affetto e amore nel desiderio di me in Dio, che non sapeva stare senza lui, dicendo: Stà meco e non m'abandonare, e così non starò altro che bene, e morrò contento! e teneva el capo suo in sul petto mio. Io sentivo uno giubilo, uno odore del sangue suo, e non era senza l'odore del mio, el quale io aspeto di spandere per lo dolce sposo Gesù' (*Epistolario*, 129).

The odour of blood conveys an erotic charge reminiscent of the fragrance of the wound. Given medieval medical understanding of semen as blood, the mixing of Catherine's and Niccolò's blood reads as a technical description of sexual intercourse.[31]

Just as Catherine acts as God's proxy in this divine trick, her language suggests that Niccolò stands in for Jesus as the husband for whom Catherine waits. With 'desire in [her] soul growing', she transfers her own aspiration and longings to Niccolò, extending to him an understanding of his approaching execution as marriage: 'Be comforted my sweet brother, because soon we shall reach the wedding'.[32] Catherine recounts to Raymond Niccolò's transition from fear to joy, reporting his exultant anticipation of their coming tryst:

> Whence comes such grace, that my soul's sweetness will wait for me at the holy place of justice. . . . I will go all joyous and strong, and when I think that you will be there it will seem to me a thousand years until I arrive.[33]

And Catherine comments: 'He spoke such sweet words as to make me burst at the goodness of God'.[34]

Before Niccolò arrives, Catherine awaits him 'in continual prayer and in the presence of Mary and Catherine virgin and martyr'. Catherine then places her own head on the block, praying for her own martyrdom. Although martyrdom is not granted her, Catherine pleads with Mary that at the moment of death she grant Niccolò peace of heart, and then allow Catherine to 'see him attain his goal'. Believing that Mary has made her a 'sweet promise', and now in ecstasy, Catherine reports that her soul was so full that, despite the multitude of people who had assembled for the execution, she could see no-one.[35]

Niccolò arrives, humble 'like a gentle lamb' and laughing, and asks Catherine to bless him with the sign of the cross. After blessing him, Catherine instructs him to prepare for the wedding: 'Down for the wedding, my sweet brother, for soon you will be in everlasting life!' She then places his neck on the block and reminds him of the blood of the lamb. Niccolò's final words gesture to the role Catherine is playing in this marriage as proxy for Christ: 'his mouth

---

[31] See Danielle Jacquart and Claude Thomasset, *Sexuality and Medicine in the Middle Ages*, tr. Matthew Adamson (Princeton, NJ, 1988), 52.

[32] 'Confortati, fratello mio dolce, ché tosto giognaremo alle nozze' (*Epistolario*, 129).

[33] 'Unde mi viene tanta gratia che la dolcezza dell'anima mia m'aspettarà al luogo santo della giustitia? . . . Io andarò tutto gioioso e forte, a parammi mille anii che io ne venga, pensando che voi m'aspettarete ine' (*Epistolario*, 130).

[34] 'e diceva parole tanto dolci che è da scoppiare della bontà di Dio!' (*Epistolario*, 130).

[35] 'Aspettàlo al luogo della giustita, e aspettai ine con continua oratione e presentia di Maria e di Caterina vergine e martire. Prima che giognesse elli, posimi giù, e distesi el collo in sul ceppo; ma non mi venne fatto che io avessi l'effetto pieno di me ine su. Pregai e constrini Maria che io volevo questa gratia, che in su quello punto gli desse uno lume e pace di cuore, e poi el vedesse tornare al fine suo. Empisi tanto l'anima mia che, essendo la moltitudine del popolo, non potevo vedere creatura, per la dolce promessa fatta a me' (*Epistolario*, 130).

said nothing but 'Jesus" and 'Catherine", and in this way I received his head into my hands, closing my eyes in divine goodness, and saying, "I will"!'[36]

As if in response to her declaration of desire and assent, Catherine then sees in a vision Niccolò's soul ascend to heaven. Consistent with the fleshly consummation of her encounter with Niccolò, Catherine sees Jesus, 'God and Man', receiving first Niccolò's blood into His own blood, 'a flame of holy desire ... into the fire of His own divine charity', and then placing Niccolò's soul in the 'open shop of his side', bringing him into union with the crucified Christ:

> O how sweet and inestimable to see the goodness of God, with what sweetness and love he awaited that soul departed from the body – turning the eyes of mercy towards him – when he came to enter into the side, bathed in his blood, which availed through the blood of the Son of God. Thus received by God (through the power God was powerful enough to do), the Son, wisdom and incarnate word, gave him and made him share in the crucified love, with which he received the painful and shameful death, through the obedience which he showed to the Father, for the good of the human race.[37]

As in the hortatory section of her letter, Catherine represents union with Christ as entering the wound in his side. By being joined to Christ's crucified and wounded flesh – earlier represented as 'female' – Niccolò's gender is transformed:

> [Niccolò] made a sweet gesture which would charm a thousand hearts. ... He turned as does a bride when, having reached her husband's threshold, she turns her head and looks back, nods to those who have attended her, and so expresses her thanks.[38]

---

36 'Poi gli gionse, come uno agnello mansueto, e, vedendomi, cominciò a ridare, e volse che io gli facesse el segno della croce; e, ricevuto el segno, dissi: Giuso alle nozze, fratello mio dolce, ché testé sarai all vita durabile! Posesi giù con grande mansuetudine, e io gli distesi el collo, e chinàmi giù ramentàli el sangue dell'agnello: la bocca sua non diceva, se non 'Gesù' e 'Caterina', e così dicendo recevetti el capo nelle mani mie, fermando l'occhio nella divina bontà, dicendo: Io voglio!' (*Epistolario*, 130).

37 'Allora si vedeva Dio e Uomo, come si vedesse la chiarità del sole, e stava aperto e riceveva sangue nel sangue suo: uno fuoco di desiderio santo, dato e nascosto nell'anima sua per gratia, riceveva nel fuoco della divina sua carità. Poi che ebbe ricevuto el sangue e 'l desiderio suo, ed egli ricevette l'anima sua e la misse nella bottiga aperta del costatom suo, piena di misericordia, manifestando la prima verità che per sola gratia e misericordia egli el riceveva, e non per veruna altra operatione. O, quanto era dolce e inestimabile a vedere la bontà di Dio, con quanta dolcezza e amore aspettava quella anima partita dal corpo, – vòlto l'occhio della misericordia verso di lui, – quando venne a 'ntrare dentro nel costato, bagnato nel sangue suo, che valeva per lo sangue del Figliuolo di Dio! Così ricevuto da Dio, – per potentia fu potente a poterlo fare, – el Figliuolo, sapientia verbo incarnato, gli donò e feceli participare el crociato amore, col qualle elli ricevette la penosa e obrobriosa morte, per l'obedientia che elli osservò del Padre in utilità dell'umana natura e generatione' (*Epistolario*, 131).

38 'Ma elli faceva uno atto dolce, da trari mille cuori (non me ne maraviglio, però che già gustava la divina dolcezza): volsesi come fa la sposa quando è gionta all'uscio dello sposo, che

After seeing Niccolò enter into Christ's side, Catherine concludes by describing her state of happy calm after the ecstasy of her vision, confirming her active role in the consummation of this marriage: 'My soul rested in peace and quiet in such a fragrance of blood that I could not bear to wash away the blood which had splashed on me from him.'[39]

Finally, words failing her, Catherine returns to earth, commenting to Raymond that 'the first stone is already laid', an image which Catherine uses in connection with the martyrs – the stones on which the church is built. Catherine concludes the letter by reminding Raymond of her earlier exhortation, and gesturing to the link between the exhortation and Niccolò's execution: 'So do not be surprised if I impose on you only my desire to see you drowned in the blood and fire which pours out of the side of Christ'.[40]

Having introduced the story of Niccolò's death by evoking the open side of Jesus, a border to direct experience of the divine, within the narrative of the execution Catherine conjures a vision of the wound. This vision is prompted by her 'I will', and is, in a sense, under her control. Catherine portrays herself acting in the middle of a political drama and on a social stage; indeed, up to a point Catherine's activities conform to the social function fulfilled by members of *confortiere* confraternities, who accompanied prisoners to the scaffold in hopes of bringing them to remorse and to a good death.[41] But Catherine represents her engagement in the political and social scene by transforming it. Her vision in the midst of this political drama allows her a privileged understanding of the meaning of Niccolò's death, as that of a martyr, which both comments on the political and at the same time transcends it.

A level of unreality is established, among other elements, by the solitude within which Catherine casts her encounter with Niccolò. She conspicuously excludes onlookers from her story; no gaoler or other prisoners are mentioned, nor does she acknowledge any companions either in her visit to Niccolò in prison or as she attends him at the place of execution. Catherine makes reference to the crowd only to dismiss them, despite the fact that, in reality, there must have been a great many people there from the start (including, by his account, Caffarini himself); thus she sets herself apart and distances her own view of the event from the view of others. This solitude also emphasizes the sudden and surprising appearance of the Virgin Mary and Catherine of

---

volle l'occhio e 'l capo adietro, inchinando chi l'à acompagnata, e con l'atto dimostra segni di ringratiamento' (*Epistolario*, 131).

39 'L'anima mia si riposò in pace e in quiete, in tanto odore di sangue che io non potei sostenere di levarmi el sangue, che m'era venuto adosso, da lui' (*Epistolario*, 132).

40 'Parmi che la prima pietra sia già posta, e però non vi maravigliate se io non v'impongo che 'l desiderio di vedervi altro che anegati nel sangue e nel fuoco che versa el costato del Figliuolo di Dio' (*Epistolario*, 132).

41 Kathleen Falvey, 'Early Italian Dramatic Traditions and Comforting Rituals: Some Initial Considerations', in *Crossing the Bounderies. Christian Piety and the Arts in Italian Medieval and Renaissance Confraternities*, ed., Konrad Eisenbichler (Kalamazoo, Mich., 1991), 33–55.

Alexandria, who are not shown acting in any way in the drama, but are invoked so that the ensuing action takes place in their presence; the two saintly virgins serve as silent, but conspicuous, witnesses to the execution. But the importance of these two figures in this scene is suggested by Catherine's treatment of Niccolò's execution as a marriage, to which she signals her assent by saying 'I will' and receives as a token Niccolò's head. Although Catherine describes in several places how Christ married humankind by granting the token of the ring of his circumcised flesh, by having Catherine of Alexandria and the Virgin Mary as witnesses, she here appears to invoke both the pictorial tradition of the mystical marriage of Catherine of Alexandria, in which the Virgin Mary is often placed between Christ and Catherine as both celebrant and witness, and the popular theme of the marriage of the Virgin Mary. This reference operates on several levels at once, necessitating fluctuating gender identities which transform the romantic element of the story into something much more fantastic. Catherine scripts herself as Catherine of Alexandria both in her desire for martyrdom and in her mystical marriage to Niccolò/Christ; she also acts as the Virgin Mary in her marriage, and by standing over Niccolò whose marriage to Christ/Catherine is consummated in his execution; and she stands in for Christ as Niccolò's prospective husband.

The multiple identities which Catherine assumes in this 'marriage' parallel the polysemous image of the 'sweet bride' in the first part of the letter, and the vision in which Catherine sees Niccolò enter into the open side of Christ evokes immediately the earlier reference to the wound. Having called on Raymond to seek his bride in the wound of Christ, Niccolò achieves his apotheosis by becoming a bride and crossing her husband's threshold, beyond which (one imagines) the bridegroom awaits on the marriage bed. Not only do both images employ spousal and erotic language, but they are also consistently and intentionally heterosexual: Raymond as a man goes to meet his bride, while Niccolò – very much a man in his romance with Catherine – is feminized in his union with the bridegroom Christ. Apart from maintaining erotic engagement on a heterosexual matrix, by portraying Niccolò's union with Christ as a transformation in gender Catherine represents union with Christ in terms of the abjection and transgression to be found in the female body. The exemplary nature of her story suggests that Raymond too in some sense must be feminized, and thus Catherine appeals to the notion of *imitatio Christi* which introduced this paper. Catherine extends to her male reader the opportunity for conversion by experiencing, through suffering and affection, Christ's 'femininity'.

Although Catherine might appeal here to familiar and orthodox spiritual models, the way she represents her own part in this process of conversion is provocative. Having presented Raymond with a feminized and eroticized body of Christ as the source of the reversal necessary for the male to experience the love of Christ on the cross, Catherine then scripts herself in the role of a female *alter Christus* as the agent of Niccolò's conversion, achieved through love of Catherine. Indeed, as the marriage with Niccolò suggests,

Catherine represents herself as both the bride and the bridegroom, a direct parallel to her earlier spousal image; the 'sweet bride' awaiting Raymond inside the open wound is both a female Christ and Catherine herself. To obey Catherine's command, Raymond must enter into the side of Christ as Niccolò does – through female flesh – and thus Catherine offers herself to Raymond in the position of the lover, a site of affection through which he can experience the liminality necessary to salvation.

Both Catherine's privileged view of the political scene, and the exemplary meaning of her account of Niccolò's execution, reveal her establishing her own liminality, plotting the borders from which she can speak authoritatively, in ways that are related to, but not identical with, the received notion of the marginal female. It is worth remembering that Catherine wrote this letter early in her relationship with Raymond, when (by Raymond's own account) he was not entirely convinced of her sanctity, and thus at a time when she might have needed to establish her authority with her new spiritual director. If this letter is at all shocking to the modern reader, it is not unlikely that Raymond also did not know precisely what to make of it. We do know that the Niccolò Toldo affair, so appealing to later hagiographers as evidence of Catherine's solicitude for her neighbour's spiritual salvation, does not appear in Raymond's account of Catherine's life. This is perhaps because of Catherine's representation of her own participation in a political affair and her potentially inflammatory interpretation of Niccolò's death as martyrdom, but probably also because of the way Catherine realized the metaphor of the female body of Christ – an aspect of the letter unnoticed or ignored by her fifteenth-century hagiographers. Indeed, it is ironic to juxtapose Catherine's self-authorizing representation of an eroticized female body of Christ in this letter with Raymond's most explicit evidence of Catherine's status as *alter Christus*: a vision in which Catherine's face takes on the features, briefly, of Jesus – a bearded man.

In conclusion, while both the hagiographers and most modern scholars have conspired to domesticate the alterity of a figure like Catherine, this letter shows Catherine claiming authority precisely by destabilizing the terms in which her biographer understood her. Whether or not such appropriation and manipulation of cultural norms could provide liberation for her, it is possible that Catherine's appeal to others derived precisely from the trouble or excitement her language caused. It is hoped that this paper has suggested advantages in reading past the hagiography to understand the discourse within which the authority of a holy woman might have been negotiated

'TO MY DEAREST SISTER':
BEDE AND THE EDUCATED WOMAN

Benedicta Ward S.L.G.

Some time before AD 735, Bede received a request from a nun for a book: would he provide her and her sisters with some way of understanding as prayer the more than opaque words which they sang at the Office of Lauds every ferial Friday in the Canticle of Habakkuk? Bede was delighted to respond and wrote for them his most deeply mystical treatise, *In Canticum Abacuc Cantica.*[1]

Who was this nun? There is no reason to suppose that this form of address was a literary artifice by Bede, writing in the genre of letters of spiritual counsel, since his other commentaries on scripture are also addressed to correspondents, mostly well-known friends and colleagues. Bede addressed her as 'my dearest sister', a monastic endearment underlining love and kinship in Christ rather than a natural blood relationship. She was part, presumably the head, of a monastery in the first part of the eighth century, that period of which Bede was so searingly critical in his letter to Egbert:

> There are innumerable places, as we all know, allowed the name of monasteries by a most foolish manner of speaking but having nothing at all of a monastic way of life, some of which I would wish to be transformed by synodal authority from wanton living to chastity, from vanity to truth, from over-indulgence of the belly and from gluttony to continence and piety of heart.[2]

In the familiar Anglo-Saxon pattern of double monasteries, this condemnation included nuns, and in fact Bede specifically says that some of these lax monasteries were in the control of the wives of thanes. Even in the golden days of monastic life recorded in the *Ecclesiastical History of the English People*, all had not been perfect in the monasteries: he had had to recount not only the

---

[1] Bede *In Cantica Habacuc Allegorica Expositio* ed. J. E. Hudson, CCSL 119B (Turnhout, 1983), 381–409.
[2] Bede, *Letter to Egbert*, transl. D. Whitelock in *English Historical Documents 1: 500–1042*, 170 (London, 1955).

105

impenitent death of a brother blacksmith of his own monastery,[3] but the heed-less gaiety of the naughty nuns of Coldingham, who spent their time making themselves new clothes and going to parties.[4] Alert to such problems, Bede would have been all the more enthusiastic to receive this request for instruc-tion coming from nuns not at all of this kind, but as seriously concerned with their way of life as he was himself. The sisters who asked for his help belonged to a serious convent, liturgically up to date, with sisters well able to under-stand Latin and inclined to think deeply about what they read. It sounds very like the convent of the nun Edburga at Minster, where the sisters were serious copyists of texts for the use of Boniface in his German mission including among their efforts a copy of the letters of St Peter in gold; they may have been among the nuns who previously attended his lectures and, if prevented from doing so by distance, had taken correspondence courses from him and 'learned the scriptures daily page by page'.[5] Or perhaps it was Wimbourne under the abbess Tetta, where Lioba, most learned of nuns, was educated, a sister who, they said,

> read with attention all the books of the Old and New Testaments and learned by heart the commandments of God. To these she added by way of completion the writings of the church fathers, the decrees of the councils and the whole of ecclesiastical law.[6]

Any convent is a mixed bag, of course, and Wimbourne was no exception; there were the bookworms, but there were also young nuns who went and danced with rage on the grave of a specially severe nun.[7] It may be that Lioba as abbess of Bischofsheim remembered the problems at Wimbourne and made sure that her sisters did not behave badly; she constructed a timetable which allowed them enough sleep in order to be alert for study, and when the young nuns read aloud to her during her afternoon siesta, they found their mistakes corrected by their abbess even in her sleep.[8] Bede himself seems to have had no contact with Minster or Wimbourne but the scholarship of these nuns is an indication that not all monasteries were as deplorable as the Letter to Egbert suggests; it was from this tradition that the request came. Moreover there was contact between the world of Boniface and the world of Bede, for although Bede did not refer to Boniface at all, Boniface knew his writings and prized them highly.

If the commmunity asking for the commentary was not one of these houses,

---

[3] Bede, *Ecclesiastical History of the English People*, ed. and transl. B. Colgrave and R. A. B. Mynors (Oxford, 1962), v, 14, 503–505.

[4] Ibid. iv, 25, 425–7.

[5] Willibald, 'Life of St Boniface', transl. C. H. Talbot, *Anglo-Saxon Missionaries in Germany* (London, 1954), 31.

[6] Rudolf 'Life of St Leoba', in *Anglo-Saxon Missionaries*, 215.

[7] Ibid. 208–9.

[8] Ibid. 215.

perhaps the choice should be made within Bede's circle of acquaintance, among communities who knew Bede well enough for them to send him a message and ask for his personal attention. He had contact with the convents of Ely, Barking, Coldingham and Whitby when he received information from them about their histories. The choice can be limited further by the fact that it must have been a community which used the canticle of Habakkuk as a liturgical text. A general suggestion in the Rule of St Benedict indicates the use of Scripture canticles in the morning Office[9] and this particular canticle was also used on Good Friday in the Roman rite. These two facts perhaps suggest a convent aware of the recommendations about the Office in the Rule of St Benedict and also up to date in Roman liturgical practice; this suggests connection with either Wearmouth and Jarrow after the visit of John the archchanter had updated their liturgical practice in the Roman style, or with Ripon and the Romanizing tradition of Wilfrid. This would, however, rule out the obvious candidate, Whitby, since its Celtic ethos may still have affected the liturgy there, and also Barking, where the learned recipients of Aldhelm's *De Virginitate* were also influenced by Irish liturgical patterns. The request came from a convent where religious life was taken seriously, where the meaning of words was both known and questioned, where the sisters had enough Latin to wonder very much what it was all about and knew enough about Bede to ask his help; it is not possible to be more specific.

How was this commentary different from Bede's others? The request of the unknown nun gave Bede a unique chance to respond with fundamental spiritual exposition of a short but difficult text. In one way, the fact that it was for nuns did not enter into Bede's consideration, in the sense that he did not in any way condescend to the sisters as if they were weak or unintelligent women. The commentary on Habakkuk was in Bede's immaculate Latin, and it was as appropriate to men as to women, but another fact gave him a freeedom to write for the sisters rather especially from his own depth of understanding. Bede's other commentaries on the scriptures had been intended for the use of clerics less well equipped than himself with books to enable them to understand the scriptures about which they were preaching; or else they were his contribution to the study undertaken by his equals, such as Bishop Acca, the abbot Hwatberht or his brothers at Jarrow. They were for preachers and teachers and therefore contained a good deal about the literal and grammatical sense of the text and about its orthodox interpretation. Even on the traditionally mystical text of the Song of Songs, Bede was aware of his audience and had matters relating to heresy to consider. In this case it was different. He was not instructing preachers who were responsible for teaching the truth of the texts but speaking to co-workers in the art of arts, prayer; he was not therefore constrained to spend too much time on literal explanation.

---

[9] Rule of St Benedict, cap.13.

Moreover, he was breaking new ground. He had one predecessor, Jerome, but Jerome had written for a bishop and in a very different ethos.[10] The difference between their commentaries underlines the way in which the kind of audience expected affects a text. Commenting on the same text, and with Jerome under his hand, Bede chose to do something essentially different in approach and in content.

What was there, on the other hand, about this commentary that is in line with Bede's usual approach to women? It was yet another instance, this time a personal one, of a theme that ran through all Bede's work, that of the enabling role of women. They were the life-givers: among the pagan Anglo-Saxons more specifically they were the breakers of bread and givers of life, just as men were the sharers of gold and glory. In the case of Christian Anglo-Saxon women, they were the ones who broke the bread of the Scriptures and gave life to souls. The 'double' monastery system in England meant that the head of the house would be a woman and Bede saw those abbesses, and indeed on a smaller scale, the mothers of families, as breaking the word of God for others:

> It is not only bishops, presbyters, deacons or even those who govern monasteries who are to be understood as pastors, but all the faithful who keep watch over the little ones of their house are also properly called pastors, insofar as they preside with solicitous watchfulness over their own household.[11]

Bede saw women at the centre of education in the vital role of nurturing. The education of Wilfrid at Lindisfarne and later his plan to study in Rome, for instance, were both secured and arranged by Queen Eanflaed:

> He (Wilfrid) went at once to Queen Eanflaed because she knew him and it was through her counsel and at her request that he had been admitted to the monastery. She was delighted with the youth's excellent plan and sent him to King Eorcenberht of Kent who was her cousin asking him to send Wilfrid honourably to Rome.[12]

The saintly abbess Hilda at Whitby was another such woman:

> She compelled those under her direction to devote so much time to the study of the holy scriptures and so much time to the performance of good works that there might be no difficulty in finding many there who were fitted for holy orders, that is, for the service of the altar.[13]

Bede did not suggest that the great secular or monastic ladies were necessarily themselves teachers, but rather that they assumed responsibility for the education of others. It was within this context that Bede received without

[10] Cf. my discussion of this in *Studia Patristica*, vol. xxv (Leuven, 1993), 189–193.
[11] Bede, *Opera Homilectica*, ed. D. Hurst, CCSL 122 (Turnhout, 1955), i, 7, 49.
[12] Bede, *Ecclesiastical History of the English People*, v, xix, 519.
[13] Ibid. iv. 23, 409.

surprise this request from the sisters, and in this instance he himself became one of those who were encouraged by them. They caused him to undertake a commentary which he made into a compendium of the whole of Christian theology. It begins with the widest possible programme for thought and prayer:

> Beloved sister in Christ, the Canticle of the prophet Habakkuk which you have asked me to explain to you, sets out above all the mystery of the Lord's Passion . . . it describes mystically the events of his incarnation, resurrection, ascension into heaven and both the faith of the gentiles and the unbelief of the Jews.[14]

Bede provided the sisters with a thoroughgoing course in theology, based upon words they would recite each week; but it was no cold or distant intellectual exercise. At the end he took up the word 'Habakkuk' and accepting Jerome's interpretation of it as meaning in Hebrew 'embraced' or 'embracing' applied it with warmth to the affection between himself and 'my very dear sister and virgin of Christ', both being 'embraced' together with Christ in the embrace of the Trinity of love:

> If we strive with all our heart, all our mind, all our strength to embrace him, he deigns to enfold us in the heart of his love. I remember the promise of him who said 'if any man loves me, he will be loved of my father and I will love him and manifest myself unto him'; thus we will deserve to be members of the bride who in heaven will sing with joy 'his left hand is under my head and his right hand doth embrace me'.[15]

Bede was a severe and exacting teacher but he never wanted a proud academic learning for its own sake for any of his Anglo-Saxon pupils or readers. Bertha, first of the Christian queens, and her daughter Ethelburgh were 'literati', educated women, who received letters from Popes, but their learning held no central role as such in the account Bede gave of them; that was reserved for their prayer. Latin learning mattered to Bede but it was not an end in itself; indeed in his letter to Egbert he did not make it a priority for everyone, even priests, to learn Latin, which had been to him the treasured way into wider and fuller worlds; if they cannot learn Latin, he said, let them have translations into English; it was the central matter of redemption and life in Christ which was the true learning. The exercise of the mind to its capacity was essential but it was a tool only as part of the total life of each person in Christ. The reading and writing of books opened the person to wide realms of past and future, but that was not the end. From the first Bede had been cautious about learning for its own sake:

> Better is a stupid and unlettered brother who working the good things he knows, merits life in heaven than one who though being distinguished for

14 Bede, *In Cantica Habacuc Allegorica Expositio*, 381.
15 Ibid. 409.

his learning in the scriptures or even holding the place of a doctor, lacks the bread of love.[16]

It was the personal contact which reading afforded with the living God through the sacred page which mattered. Pagan writers therefore who did not have this other dimension to their words he considered should be read with great prudence, and replaced by the scriptures wherever possible:

> With much more caution must the rose be plucked from among sharp thorns than the lily from soft leaves; much more securely is sound advice sought in apostolic than in Platonic pages.[17]

Though Bede insisted that teachers and preachers must be sincerely learned, this was only a preparation for insight, for real vision was an uncovenanted gift of God. Drythelm, the visionary who journeyed through heaven and hell, was a simple married man in Northumbria; Caedmon, the first Anglo-Saxon poet, was a cowherd who could not read, write or sing; and there was Owine, an East Anglian thane of Queen Etheldreda who, when he went to join the monastery of Chad at Lastingham, carried with him an axe and an adze to show that he wanted no part in the discipline of book-learning, yet it was he who saw and heard angels who came to take the soul of Chad into heaven, not the more bookish brothers.[18]

Education is surely never a matter of accumulating information which will give the person possessing it more status. The word itself is, after all, derived from *educare*, 'to draw out' the full potential of a person. In the Crewian oration in 1993, Seamus Heaney referred to the understanding Robert Frost had of education as not being about getting to a higher class by achieving another level of knowledge but allowing perspectives to be so re-aligned that it becomes possible to establish a critical angle on whatever determines ideas of high and low in the first place. It is this expanding of the mind by discipline in order to know what matters that lies behind Bede's view of education. In the constant effort of the converters of the Anglo-Saxons to tranform and transfigure their polished, sophisticated pagan society into a Christian *koinonia*, this very change had to take place. This was especially true among the nuns of the royal abbeys of England. Great ladies might become abbesses of their own estates and households and continue their great position unchanged at the centre of things; but attention to brightness, glory, nobility, generosity that shows one's own position, needed re-aligning in the new way of the Cross,

> Where the way up is the way down
> The way forward is the way back
> And where you are is where you are not.[19]

---

[16] Bede, *In Proverbia Salomonis*, ed. D. Hurst, CCSL 119B (Turnhout, 1983), xii, 9, 76.

[17] Bede, *In Apocalypsin sancti Johannis*, PL 93, 133, preface.

[18] Bede, *Ecclesiastical History of the English People*, v, 12, 488–498; iv, 24, 414–420; iv, 3, 338–342

[19] T. S. Eliot, *Four Quartets*.

Given the chance to write for the nuns of what was most probably a noble house, Bede at once showed what should be the sisters' concern now: a conviction that the things worth working for were centred on Christ, and not on themselves or their kin. He took for granted a capacity of mind, which included a power of streamlined concentration upon God and his revelation in Christ. Of course he was aware that the sisters needed to understand the Latin of the text, but it was not *grammatica* in itself which was the aim of their schooling; their education was meant to ensure that they could, for the whole of life, continue to go as deeply as possible into learning about Christ. They were permanently *famulae Christi*, slaves of Christ, Bede's own name for himself. In his commentary on Proverbs he had urged this approach to learning in relation to the verse 'Get wisdom, get understanding, forget it not neither decline from the words of my mouth. Forsake her not and she shall preserve thee, love her and she shall keep thee. Wisdom is the principle thing, therefore get wisdom and with all thy getting get understanding' (Proverbs 4:5,6,7).

> In all the goods you get, keep in mind 'in all your getting, get understanding', despising all that you possess on earth when you see the way of wisdom. That is what Solomon himself did when given a choice he preferred the love of wisdom to all things, and in the gospel he who was seeking a precious pearl sold all that he had that he might find it.

In the next phrase, Bede used the same word that he used at the end of his commentary on Habakkuk, 'embrace' (*amplectus*) to conclude with a promise:

> If we embrace wisdom so much more will spiritual grace increase our heads, that is the centre of awareness (*principali mentis*), that they will be given a crown of life in future.[20]

It was not the head swelled with learning that Bede coveted for his dearest sister but a complete person crowned with the glory of wisdom.

[20] Bede, *In Proverbia Salomonis*, 19.

'SHARPEN YOUR MIND WITH THE WHETSTONE OF BOOKS': THE FEMALE RECLUSE AS READER IN GOSCELIN'S *LIBER CONFORTATORIUS*, AELRED OF RIEVAULX'S *DE INSTITUTIONE INCLUSARUM* AND THE *ANCRENE WISSE*

Gopa Roy

'Sharpen your mind with the whetstone of books', wrote Goscelin to the recluse Eve in his *Liber Confortatorius*.[1] Reading, together with prayer, meditation and psalm-singing, had long been enjoined on those who had withdrawn from the world to seek God, whether in communities or as solitaries.[2] The three works I shall discuss form part of a long tradition of guidance written by men for ascetic women. Early examples include works by Tertullian and Cyprian in the second and third centuries, Jerome and Ambrose in the fourth, and Augustine in the fifth.[3] My assessments of 'the female recluse as reader' of Goscelin, Aelred, and the *Ancrene Wisse* author, will be based principally on what the texts reveal of the authors' expectations of their readers. During the 140 years or so spanned by these works, changes took place which affected the female recluse as reader: changes in spirituality, in attitudes towards women and in opportunities for them in study and the religious life.

The *Liber Confortatorius* was written (in Latin) by the monk Goscelin. Goscelin came to England in 1058 from the abbey of St Bertin in Flanders.[4] He

---

[1] 'The *Liber Confortatorius* of Goscelin of Saint Bertin', ed. C. H. Talbot, *Analectica Monastica*, ser. 3, 37 (1955), 1–117 (80). Further quotations from this work are followed by page references in the text [my translations]. I am grateful to Geoffrey Needham for his help with these.

[2] See e.g. the *Rule of St Benedict*, ch. 48 (ed. and transl. by Justin McCann, London, 1952); H. Mayr-Harting, 'Functions of a Twelfth-Century Recluse', *History*, 60 (1975), 337–52 (350).

[3] Tertullian, 'De Cultu Feminarum', in *Tertulliani Opera*, ed. Ae. Kroymann, CCSL 1 (Turnhout, 1954), 341–70; Cyprian, 'De Habitu Virginum', in *Thasci Caecili Cypriani: De Habitu Virginum*, ed. and transl. by Sister Angela Elizabeth Keenan, Patristic Studies 34 (Washington, 1932); Jerome's letters to Paula, Eustochium, and others, especially Letter 22 to Eustochium, PL 22: 394–425; Ambrose, 'De Virginibus ad Marcellinam', PL 16: 198–244; Augustine, Letter 211, PL 33: 958–65.

[4] Talbot, 'The *Liber Confortatorius*', 4–5.

was – and is – best known in his capacity as a professional biographer of English saints who were associated with the various monasteries he visited.[5]

Goscelin became closely associated with Wilton Abbey in Wiltshire, where he may have served as chaplain.[6] In 1065, Eve, then a girl of seven, was given to Wilton by her parents. Goscelin acted as her friend and spiritual adviser, and he regarded her as his spiritual daughter. In about 1080, aged around twenty-two, Eve left Wilton without telling Goscelin, to live as a recluse in an eight-foot cell at Saint-Laurent in Angers. Later, in about 1102, she moved to an enclosure at St-Eutrope, where she lived near a monk, Hervé (with whom, according to contemporary accounts, she shared an irreproachable friendship and love), until her death in about 1125. Goscelin wrote his 'Book of Comfort' for Eve in about 1082 or 1083, while Eve was at Angers, to comfort and guide her in her chosen way of life.[7] Unlike his hagiographical works, this book is a private work, written in the form of a letter to Eve. Goscelin was deeply distressed that Eve should have left without telling him, and this is evident throughout his book. A close personal engagement between writer and reader is in fact characteristic of works in this tradition; but even so, the depth of feeling found here is unusual. The work is the only one of its kind extant from this date in England. It survives in one twelfth-century copy.[8] St Bertin had a reputation for scholarship; and it appears that in the second half of the eleventh century Wilton Abbey was capable of providing a nun with an excellent education.[9] Goscelin makes it clear that he thinks highly of Eve's intellectual ability and spiritual capacity, although he also reminds her that she is striving for perfection, but has not yet attained it.

Goscelin's book is allusive and discursive, and it is not set out as a *Rule*. His examples and allusions draw on a wide range of writings both sacred and secular. Goscelin recommends that Eve should divide her time between reading and prayer, and that she should read to nourish her spiritual life. While prayer is the more important (82), Eve should 'sharpen her blunted mind' after prayer 'with the whetstone of books' and 'the fire of divine love should always burn on the altar of her heart and she should feed it with the fuel of the examples of the saints and their works' (80). The windows of her cell, her tongue and her ears should be shut against idle talk, and even more, against slander (here he is repeating the advice given by Jerome to

---

[5]   D. W. Rollason, 'The Translation and Miracles of St Mildrith', *Mediaeval Studies*, 48 (1986), 139–210 (141).

[6]   *The Life of King Edward*, ed. and transl. by Frank Barlow (London, 1962), 98.

[7]   André Wilmart, 'Eve et Goscelin (I.)', *Revue Bénédictine*, 46 (1934), 414–38, and 'Eve et Goscelin (II.)', *Revue Bénédictine*, 50 (1938), 42–83; Talbot, 'The *Liber Confortatorius*', 22–3; Sharon Kay Elkins, *Holy Women of Twelfth-Century England* (Chapel Hill, NC, 1988), 22–7.

[8]   BL Sloane 3103.

[9]   On Wilton in this period, see Elkins, 6–13, 21.

Eustochium) (ibid.).[10] She should not keep any animals, no cat, no poultry[11] and no pet animals. Let her be alone with God.

> I pray, I beseech, and I implore you to consume the holy food of sacred volumes with eager appetite [. . . and] to hunger and thirst for it [the holy food] as for the bread of life [and] as for the water of life; so that it may sharpen your slender intellect (*ingeniolum*) [. . .], fill your lamp with oil, and cause it to burn more and more with celestial love. (ibid.)

She should attempt to understand the mysteries of the Scriptures, 'with the help of Jerome, Augustine, Gregory and other excellent doctors' (ibid.). She should also read the lives of the (desert) fathers, and especially the life of St Antony. He recommends Augustine's *Confessions*. Eusebius's *Ecclesiastical History*, Augustine's *City of God*, Orosius's *De Ormesta Mundi* and Boethius's *Consolation of Philosophy* will pass the time and her solitude will delight her. He would like the window of her cell to be large enough to admit such a large collection of books[12] (ibid.). Among the Fathers Goscelin quotes apart from those already mentioned are Ambrose (63, 80, 98), Cyprian (90) and Tertullian (95). The list of secular authors to whom he refers is also considerable; it includes Virgil (e.g. 36, 47, 49. 70), Horace (48, 70), Cicero (70), and Seneca (79). Goscelin assumes her familiarity with at least some of them.

Books, and a sense of their importance, had always been something Goscelin and Eve had shared. When he is recalling their early relationship he mentions that she had given him books which he had wished for (28). They had also written to one another on the subject of religion (29).

There is one passage which raises an interesting question:

> How often have I sighed for a little lodging like yours [but with a little door into the church . . .], where I might pray, read, and write, where I might escape the crowd that ravages my heart, where I might lay down the law for my stomach at my own little table, where, as in a place of pasture, I might devote myself to books instead of a banquet, and revive the dying spark of my slender intellect (*ingenioli*) [. . .]. But the Lord has cast me off and destroyed me, and my days are vanished like smoke. (34)[13]

Is this only what he longed for for himself, living, as he did, much more in the world, subject to external discipline? Or is it also, possibly, how he sees Eve living in her little dwelling?

Goscelin clearly has a high regard for Eve's abilities, and shows no conde-

---

10 Letter 22.29, PL 22: 415–16.
11 *altilia*: perhaps 'fat stock cattle' (as in Matthew 22: 4).
12 'Ipsa quoque ut possit admittere bibliotecam tam capacem, in longum esse uelim huius celle fenestram, aut per fenestram te legere posse a foris apposita'. The last clause may mean 'or that you could read it through the window [if it was] placed outside'.
13 He quotes from Psalms 22: 2, 59: 3 (or 88: 39) and 101: 4.

scension to her as a woman. This is further borne out by his treatment – and significant omissions – of familiar stories and themes. He does not, as might have been expected, play on the name 'Eve' in order to bring the Eve he is addressing into any particular relationship with the first (and usually sinful) Eve.[14] She does not bear an extra burden of guilt and punishment because she is a woman. This is in marked contrast to the attitude of writers in the tradition of Tertullian and Jerome – writers nevertheless whose works were among those which Goscelin advised her to read.

Goscelin's treatment of virginity is also interesting. It occupies a relatively small proportion of the work, whereas it was a prominent concern in other works in this tradition; his readings of the familiar stories of virgin martyrs are in some ways unexpected. First, the theme of virginity is subordinated to wider concerns: the examples of virgin saints are found in a chapter on pride and humility (97). Secondly, while these virgins were prepared to suffer and die for their faith, there is a story of a virgin threatened with a brothel, which Goscelin takes from Ambrose, but to which he adds some dramatically heightening elaborations.[15] The virgin is prepared to lose her virginity if this is God's will, and Goscelin has her crying out to God (as Ambrose does not), saying: 'If I deserve to be neither your spouse nor your martyr, I shall, constant in belief in you, be your whore' (98). On a more personal level, the relationship between Goscelin and Eve continues to make its presence felt in his reading of this story. He places great emphasis on the part of the young man who exchanged his clothes with the virgin in order to protect her, and on the eternal companionship they can look forward to in heaven, an idea not found in Ambrose (99).

Goscelin's distress at Eve's departure, which is expressed throughout the book – and is, indeed, its *raison d'être* – does not detract from the fact that it is nevertheless a work of genuine spiritual instruction, and one which does not assume that women are intellectually or morally inferior to men, more sexually dangerous, or that a woman's struggle towards spiritual perfection is very different from a man's. Just a few examples have been given here from what is a long, dense, wide-ranging and highly literary work. Goscelin clearly considered that Eve would be a worthy reader of it – although at times it must have made painful reading for her.

With Aelred's *De Institutione Inclusarum*, we move into the realms of Cistercian spirituality, and a very directed kind of reading.[16] Aelred was abbot of the Cistercian house of Rievaulx in North Yorkshire from 1147 until his death in 1167. He wrote the work in 1162 or 1163 at the request of his older

---

[14] The poet Hilarius, writing in Angers c.1125, after Eve's death, cannot resist the opportunity: the first Eve is the one who gave the seed of sin to the world, and this Eve had been chosen for himself by God. The passage is quoted by Wilmart, 'Eve et Goscelin (I.)', 422.

[15] See Ambrose, 'De Virginibus', PL 16: 224–8.

[16] *De Institutione Inclusarum*, in *Aelredi Rievallensis: Opera Omnia*, ed. A. Hoste and C. H. Talbot, CCCM 1 (Turnhout, 1971), 636–82. Refs. to this work will be given by chapter in the text.

sister. She had been living as a recluse for some years (it is not known where), and had repeatedly asked him to provide her with a rule adapted for her way of life (ch. 1). Her request may reflect the difficulties and lack of support women were encountering by this time if they wished to lead a religious life.[17] The work is a treatise in the form of a letter on how a recluse should regulate her exterior and interior life. It was popular and influential. It was quoted, copied, translated and incorporated into other rules for recluses – not only for women.[18]

Aelred always claimed he was not a scholar.[19] It is true that we do not find the range of allusion in this work that we do in Goscelin's. For his instructions on external discipline Aelred drew largely on the *Rule of St Benedict*, the foundation of Cistercian observance. To this – both for this section and the whole of the treatise – he added material from the Letters of Jerome, Cassian's *Institutes* and *Conferences*, the *De Virginibus* of Ambrose, works by Augustine (the *Confessions* are a particular influence) and Gregory, and also Isidore and Sulpicius Severus.[20] The sections on the interior life are a fine example of Cistercian spirituality, the fruit of Aelred's own experience, of his reflection on the Scriptures, shaped for the needs of his sister in her life as a recluse. Aelred does not tell his sister what she should read, so much as describe what her reading should lead her to. The focus is not on the breadth of reading, but its depth; on a movement from reading the texts, especially, of course, the Scriptures, to meditation on them, and towards contemplation.[21]

The prelude, however, the prerequisite for growth in the spiritual life, was the practice of ascetic discipline. The first section of the work (chs. 1–13) is concerned with the practical ordering of the recluse's exterior life. The hours of her day were regulated according to the *Rule of St Benedict*. Her time should be divided between prayer, reading and manual work. With regard to her reading, Aelred follows St Benedict: after Vespers, in the time set aside for reading, she may read the lives, Institutes and miracles of the Desert Fathers. What Aelred adds to the Rule here is to specify that the purpose of her reading is to arouse compunction, so that she may say Compline with an ardent spirit and retire to rest with a heart filled with devotion (ch. 9).

Instruction on domestic and other matters is adapted for the female recluse. Aelred gives his sister guidance on fasting, and on food and clothing. He advises her against keeping animals (ch. 3), giving alms, teaching children,

---

[17] C. H. Talbot, 'The *De Institutis Inclusarum* of Aelred of Rievaulx', *Analecta Ordinis Cisterciensis*, 7 (1951), 167–231 (172–3); Sally Thompson, 'Why English Nunneries Had No History', in *Medieval Religious Women 1: Distant Echoes*, ed. John A. Nichols and Lillian Thomas Shank, CSS 71 (Kalamazoo, Mich., 1984), 131–49 (134–6).

[18] Talbot, 'The *De Institutis Inclusarum*', 169–71.

[19] Amédée Hallier, *The Monastic Theology of Aelred of Rievaulx*, transl. Columban Heaney, CSS 2 (Shannon, 1969), 79.

[20] Talbot, 'The *De Institutis Inclusarum*', 171–2.

[21] On this mode of reading, see Michael Clanchy, *From Memory to Written Record*, 2nd edn (Oxford, 1993), 195.

exchanging gifts, and receiving guests, for all this would distract her from her chosen life of prayer and meditation (ch. 4). He also warns about the effects on her way of life of listening to 'gossiping old women or scandal-mongering women' at her window. As a consequence of having listened to their stories, the recluse, filled with laughter and pleasures, would 'stagger in her psalms as if she were drunk, grope blindly in her reading, waiver in her prayers' (ch. 2).[22] Aelred also warned the recluse that it would be dangerous for her to spend time in the company of a man. By the time Aelred was writing, and particularly in the Cistercian milieu, contact between men and women had come to be regarded as fraught with peril: the voice of the same man, warns Aelred, could upset the recluse's quietness of heart (ch. 7). However, she should not spend much time with women either; no more than was required for her practical needs (ch. 4). He pointed out that his sister did not need to be told these things, but that he included them because he was also writing for the guidance of other younger women who wished to follow this way of life (ch. 7).

In the second section (chs. 14–28) Aelred turned to the inner life of the recluse, and here we begin to see something more of his approach to reading. The guiding theme of the section is virginity. The recluse's aspiration is towards God, and Aelred wrote that she should continually consider 'how precious a treasure she bears in how frail a vessel'. With this treasure she will win the love of Christ. 'The spikenard of your virginity sends forth its fragrance even to heaven and causes the king, who is the Lord your God, to desire your beauty.' Here she meditates on her virginity through the words of the Song of Songs and the words of the Psalms (which she would have by heart), and by these means she is led towards God (ch. 14).[23]

Her reading, we are shown, is meditative, reflective. Aelred writes not *lege*, 'read', but *cogite*, 'ponder', and *revolve*, 'reflect upon' (chs. 15 and 16). This reading, closely allied to prayer, will bear its fruit. If the enemy troubles the calmness of her chastity with hostile thoughts: 'Reflect upon the most blessed Agnes [. . .]; the material fire was unable to burn the blessed Agnes, in whom the flame of the flesh had cooled, and whom the fire of love inflamed' (ch. 16). Aelred assumes her familiarity with Ambrose's story; he describes how she may use her knowledge of the text in her need.[24]

He turns again to the Scriptures. He wishes the recluse to be fearful always, to visit streams of water like the timid dove, to discern, as in a mirror, the shape of the hawk flying above her; and to be wary. The streams of water are the precepts of the Scriptures, which, flowing from the purest springs of wisdom, reveal to her the shape of the devil's suggestions, and enlighten the understanding. Nothing drives out unprofitable thoughts, nor curbs wanton ones, more than meditation on the word of God, to which the virgin should so

---

22 My translations.
23 Canticle 1: 11; Psalm 44: 12.
24 Ambrose, 'De Virginibus', 1.2, PL 16: 189–91.

accustom her spirit that even if she wishes to meditate on something else, she cannot, in all her waking thoughts and in her dreams (ch. 20).

As Aelred's treatise progresses, its spirituality deepens, and the sex of its recipient becomes less and less important. In the final section (chs. 29–32) he turns to how the love of God may be aroused and nourished in the recluse by meditation on things past, present and future (ch. 29).

Among the subjects he lists for meditation are events from the Gospels: for example, in Bethany, with Martha, Mary and Lazarus, she should meditate on how Mary broke an alabaster box of precious ointment and poured it on Christ's head. This should be what the recluse also should do: 'Break, therefore, the alabaster box of your heart, and whatever you have of devotion, of love, of desire, of affection, pour it all over the head of your Spouse, worshipping man in God, and God in man'. She should meditate on Christ's humanity, and on his suffering. She should approach the cross and weep with the virgin mother and virgin disciple (ch. 31).

Aelred reminds his sister that Christ has been with her in her present life:

> How often, when you were singing psalms or reading, has he illuminated you with the light of spiritual understanding; how often, while you were praying, has he ravished you with an ineffable longing for him; how often has he transported your mind (or 'heart': *mentem*) away from earthly things to the joys of heaven and the delights of paradise'. (ch. 32)

Aelred was allowing his sister access to a spirituality which might otherwise not have been easily available to her. Central to twelfth-century spirituality was the yearning of the soul for the love of God, and Aelred shared with his sister his experience of how this aspiration might be fulfilled.

Finally, we turn to the early thirteenth-century English 'Guide for Anchoresses', the *Ancrene Wisse*. It has been argued that the anonymous author was a priest and a member of an Augustinian community;[25] but the case for Dominican authorship has recently been reopened.[26] The work was originally written at their request for an audience of three well-born sisters who had renounced the world to become anchoresses.[27] The author appears to have been their spiritual director, and, perhaps, confessor. He later produced a revised text for a community of anchoresses which had grown to twenty or more.[28] The English in which it is written is that of the West Midlands. The work achieved early and lasting popularity and influence; it was translated into French and Latin, and was copied and adapted throughout the Middle Ages.[29]

Aelred's letter to his sister greatly influenced the *Ancrene Wisse*, particularly

---

[25] E. J. Dobson, *The Origins of 'Ancrene Wisse'* (Oxford, 1976).

[26] Bella Millett, 'The Origins of *Ancrene Wisse*: New Answers, New Questions', *Medium Aevum*, 61 (1992), 206–28.

[27] *The Ancrene Riwle*, transl. M. B. Salu (London, 1955), 84.

[28] Salu, 112.

[29] *Ancrene Wisse: Parts Six and Seven*, ed. Geoffrey Shepherd (London, 1959), pp. ix–xii.

in its discussion of the ordering of the exterior life; but the *Ancrene Wisse* is very different in tone, content and method. It does not attempt to approach the depth of spirituality of Aelred's work, and while it is serious and affectionate in its attitude to the anchoresses, and in its efforts to provide guidance for them, it expresses more of the prejudices concerning women which were characteristic of its day.

The author himself is clearly a scholarly man. He is learned in the Scriptures and commentaries; he is familiar with writings in the ascetic tradition; and his work is imbued with many of the devotional concerns of his own and the preceding period. He is in touch with the activities of scholars and theologians of the twelfth century.[30] He is also a writer of considerable literary skill. He is well-equipped, indeed, for providing a work of guidance for an audience of recluses who are not so learned themselves, probably because they have not had the opportunity to acquire much learning.

The *Ancrene Wisse*, first of all, is written not in Latin but in English. The sisters knew some Latin, because the first section, the detailed guidance on their devotions, shows that they were able to recite the Psalms by heart, and they would be familiar with the words of the Mass and the Office.[31] But, throughout, the author translates for them the Latin he quotes, usually quite freely, interpreting or allegorizing as he goes, so that one feels they are rather at the mercy of his interpretations.[32] The author does not expect the anchoresses to be familiar enough with certain authorities to recognize them, and thus he often tells them whom he is quoting.

The sisters could read English and French, and they are permitted to read devotions in these languages during any spare time they have, although the author expects that some of the audience of his revised version would be able to read, some not: '[she who cannot read] must do more work of other kinds, and say her prayers without books'.[33] The sisters are to read the last part of the author's Guide to their women once a week until they know it, which suggests that reading aloud to one another may have been a common practice for them (191). It appears that the sisters could write: 'Each is to say her hours in the way that she has written them down' (8–9). But they were not to send or receive letters or write anything without their director's permission (188). Benedict had said much the same thing in his *Rule*, in fact, although Goscelin appears to have envisaged more flexibility for Eve.

---

[30] Shepherd, pp. xxv–xxix; *Medieval English Prose for Women*, ed. Bella Millett and Jocelyn Wogan-Browne, rev. edn (Oxford, 1992), pp. xxx–xxxi.

[31] Barbara Raw, 'The Prayers and Devotions in the *Ancrene Wisse*', in *Chaucer and Middle English Studies in Honour of Rossell Hope Robbins*, ed. Beryl Rowland (London, 1974), 260–71; Roger Dahood, 'Design in Part I of *Ancrene Riwle*', *Medium Aevum*, 56 (1987), 1–11.

[32] Santha Bhattacharji has kindly pointed out to me that the 'Little Office of the Virgin' used by the anchoresses did not allow for the number of readings from the Scriptures or from the Fathers that the longer monastic Office did. See John Harper, *The Forms and Orders of Western Liturgy from the Tenth to the Eighteenth Century* (Oxford, 1991).

[33] Salu, 2–3. Further refs. are to this edition.

The author does recommend reading, though in a rather general way. He comments, in the midst of his guidance on their devotions, 'Take great care, I beg of you, never to be idle, but work or read, or be at your prayers, and so always be doing something from which good may come' (19). Reading is but one of many in a long list of weapons against temptations: 'prayers, faith, reading, fasting, vigils, bodily exertions, humility, generosity of heart, and the constancy of love above all the rest' (106).

More specifically, he advises that reading can help provide a remedy for Sloth, and writes:

> Often, dear sisters, you ought to say fewer fixed prayers so that you may do more reading. Reading is good prayer. Reading teaches us how to pray and what to pray for, and then prayer achieves it. In the course of reading, when the heart is pleased, there arises a spirit of devotion which is worth many prayers. For this reason St Jerome says: 'Always keep some holy reading in your hand.' (127)[34]

This reminds one of the *lectio divina* described by Aelred, but the *Ancrene Wisse* author does not take this instruction further; as has been pointed out by others, he does not provide guidance for a mystical life, for contemplative prayer. It is possible that he leaves such advice, or more detailed guidance about books, to be given in person. We know of the other English works associated with the *Ancrene Wisse*: the works of the Katherine Group and the Wooing Group – the kind of reading which would have been approved and available. Nevertheless, reading is clearly not given the prominence in the guidance provided for the *Ancrene Wisse* recluses that it had in Goscelin's work, or in Aelred's, in their different ways.

The anchoresses he addresses, however, are reading his work; indeed, the only work he mentions specifically (as far as I can see) as one they should read daily is his own:

> Read something, much or little, of this book every day when you are free. I hope that by God's great grace it will be very helpful to you if you read it often, else I have spent much of my time to little purpose. God knows, I would rather undertake the journey to Rome than begin the writing of it again. (192)

Since he hopes that his own book will play such a large role in shaping the anchoresses, the view which he presents to them of themselves is significant. It is dangerous for them to look out of their windows: 'My dear sisters, be as little fond of your windows as possible. Let them all be small, those of the parlour smallest and narrowest' (21). Eve is held up as a warning, for her sin first entered through her eyes: 'The apple, my dear sister, symbolizes all those

---

[34] Jerome, Letter 22.17, PL 22: 404.

things towards which desire and sinful delight turn. When you look upon a man, you are in Eve's case; you are looking on the apple' (23).

The author elsewhere recommends silence – as Benedict had, and as Aelred had. But again, the *Ancrene Wisse*'s guidance has a particular flavour. If the recluse finds that she has to talk to someone at the parlour window (a priest, for example), she should listen, and speak as little as possible:

> Some anchoresses are so learned or can talk with such wisdom that they would like their visitors to know it. . . . In this way a woman who ought to be an anchoress sometimes sets up as a scholar, teaching those who have come to teach her. . . . She is looking for esteem and instead she incurs blame; at the very least, when he has gone he will say, 'This anchoress talks a great deal'. In Paradise Eve talked a great deal to the serpent.   (28–29)

Finally, it is worth comparing the different ways in which Aelred and the *Ancrene Wisse* author expect the reader to think of Christ's passion. Aelred had written about meditation on Christ's suffering as a means to arouse compassion and love; and although the *Ancrene Wisse* author devotes a whole section of his work to love, and says that 'love is the rule which rules the heart' (181), he is frequently more earthbound. Whenever the recluse is tempted in any way, she should remember Christ's suffering. For example, in warning against the dangers of touching: '[He] was made to suffer grievously in all his five senses. . . . God's hands were nailed to the cross. By those nails I adjure you anchoresses . . . : keep your hands inside your windows' (51).

These windows can be seen as symbolic of the attitudes of the three authors. Goscelin, we remember, had hoped that Eve's window should be large enough to admit all the books he suggested she read. Aelred had warned his sister about the distractions they offered from her life of prayer. In the *Ancrene Wisse*, the warnings form part of the *Ancrene Wisse*'s inner rule, and they are founded on a belief in feminine weakness, stemming from Eve.

The recluse was enclosed in her cell; but as the world outside her window changed, so too, inevitably, did hers. 'Dead to the world', she was nevertheless dependent on it. Between the late eleventh and the early thirteenth centuries, opportunities for women in the religious life, and in the learning that might have come with it, had declined. The flexibility which had characterized the life of a female recluse in the earlier period had given way to a much more highly structured existence, with male authority over female religious very firmly established. The thirteenth-century recluse was presented with a book – and a view of herself – very different from those offered to her sisters of earlier generations.

PATRONAGE ENGENDERED:
HOW GOSCELIN ALLAYED THE CONCERNS
OF NUNS' DISCRIMINATORY PUBLICS

Georges Whalen

Patronage involves the use of power to favour others. It requires advertising, though the best promotion is effectiveness. Prospective beneficiaries and clients must know where to apply for protection, and what protection is available. Medieval patrons were not all equally powerful; those with enough clout or connections used literary specialists to flaunt their merits, and, unsurprisingly, we find records of far fewer female than male patrons. Authorial reputations become visible through the literary patronage afforded, sought or required by the author of a given text, when an author's identity is recoverable for that text. Many medieval authors' reputations are lost to the greater glory of the patron. This is particularly true of writing which historians now term hagiographic. Yet in late eleventh-century England a large identifiable corpus exists in the hagiographic production of the Flemish monk Goscelin, who probably ended his peripatetic monastic career at St Augustine's, Canterbury, at around the turn of the twelfth century. Goscelin wrote about their heavenly patrons for several commissioning monastic patrons,[1] which allows us a contextualized consideration of women's communities' monastic patronage; and a comparison between the perceived (rarely-defined) larger audiences and the immediate monastic ones, permits us to understand the social context in which he wrote. This comes closest to being spelled out in prefatory passages where the audiences' reasons for approaching the text are addressed. The unusually large number of *vitae* penned by Goscelin give evidence for this in many examples of varying combinations of primary sponsors, according to the gender of both the saint (the heavenly patron) and the commissioning community (the author's patron). Thus there exist broadly similar expressions of audience motivation and tolerances, and by viewing them side by side we can discern how gender affected the politics of the commissioning of hagiographic writing.

---

[1] For a full survey and reconstruction see ch. 2 of T. J. Hamilton, *Goscelin of Canterbury: A Critical Study of his Life, Works and Accomplishments*, Ph.D., Univ. of Virginia (1973), 49–129, esp. 76–124, where a corpus of *vitae* is established.

The dedication of one of the earliest *vitae* written by Goscelin, the *Vita Sanctae Edithae*,[2] was probably composed soon after the 1078 death of the monk's first patron in England. The Lotharingian bishop Herman of Sherborne had brought him to England when returning from a three-year self-imposed exile in the Flemish monastery of St-Bertin at St Omer. Goscelin's need for a different source of patronage seems a clear impetus for his sudden literary flowering. He found little welcome in the household of Herman's successor, Osmund (1078–1099), and increased his production of hagiography, possibly turning energies away from musical and poetic functions, in which he is known to have been proficient.[3] This poetic reputation helps explain a good and generous welcome in Wilton's famed poetic and literary circle, whence came his first known commission, and which he very fondly recalled in writing to Eve a few years later once she had left the nunnery of her childhood for an Anjou hermitage.[4]

At Sherborne, Goscelin had observed the Old Wessex fringes of England's ecclesiastical hierarchy, since the time of Alfred increasingly removed from the principal centres of power.[5] Herman tried in many ways, amongst which we should include perhaps his bringing Goscelin to England, to introduce Continental norms of episcopal conduct and authority to the ancient Anglo-Saxon sees he occupied. His involvement in various late eleventh-century moves of the West Country sees witnesses a desire to bring sees' locales in line with proper (i.e. more urban) standards. Herman hoped to enhance his ability to function effectively as bishop by moving his episcopal seat: his failed take-over attempt in 1055, aimed at Malmesbury Abbey, led him to resign the see of Ramsbury and retire to St-Bertin; and, recalled to the see of Sherborne in 1058,

---

2 Goscelin, 'La légende de Ste Edith en prose et vers par le moine Goscelin', ed. André Wilmart, *Analecta Bollandiana*, 56 (1938) 5–101, 265–307.
3 William of Malmesbury, in *De Gestis Regum Anglorum*, ed. William Stubbs, Rolls ser. vol. xc (London, 1887, 1889) ss. 342, vol. ii, 389 calls him 'post Bedam secundus'; and Reginald of Canterbury in F. Liebermann (ed.), 'Raginald von Cantebury', *Neues Archiv der Gesellschaft für ältere deutsche Geschichtskunde*, 13 (1888), 517–56, poem xv 'Gozelino monacho suo suus, amico amicus Raginaldus', ll. 542–4, makes him 'musarum dulcis amicis'. William and Reginald are the two standard references to his good reputation which appear in Goscelin, *La légende de Ste Edith*, 5–7; and Goscelin 'Texts of Jocelyn of Canterbury which Relate to the History of Barking Abbey', ed. Marvin L. Colker, *Studia Monastica*, 7 (1965), 383–460, at p. 385. They first apear together in André Wilmart, 'Eve et Goscelin (I.)', *Revue Bénédictine*, 46 (1934), 414–38, and are associated by many others in his wake.
4 Wilton's Norman reputation for harbouring poets is discussed in J. S. P. Tatlock, 'Muriel: the Earliest English Poetess', *PMLA*, 48 (1933), 317–21 (317–8).
5 A similarly unusually high concentration of mints in Wessex centres mirrors the concentration of sees there, emphasizing the Wessex origins and ties of Egbert's royal descendants still evident in Domesday Book. Pauline Stafford, 'The 'Farm of One Night' and the Organization of King Edward's Estates in Domesday', *Economic History Review*, 33 (1980), 491–502. See also Janet Nelson, 'Debate: Trade, Industry and the Wealth of King Alfred', *Past and Present*, 135 (May 1992), 151–63.

with a new Continental retinue including Goscelin, by 1075 he had success-
fully moved from that monastic site to the borough of Old Sarum.[6]

The St-Bertin-trained monk's move to Wilton was probably, for Goscelin, an
improvement in his social milieu. The poor foreign-staffed see would not have
had the social prestige of a nunnery like that of Wilton, which was closely
associated with the royal court through the many kinship and other connections of every resident (though an actual period of residence cannot be proved,
it does seem to fit a pattern evident in his later composition of *vitae*, where he
lived with the community to collect information necessary for his compositon,
and it seems to extend a pattern of visits to Wilton begun with the diocesan
bishop, Herman, which he reveals in his *Liber confortatorius*). Wilton had also
been linked to the court of bishop Herman's original patron, Edward the
Confessor,[7] through his wife, Edith Godwinsdaughter. His previous associ-
ations with this monastery – a fairly important one in Herman's diocese –
made Goscelin an ideal reporter of the traditions governing the sanctity of
Edith's patronal namesake. He wrote in accordance with the widespread,
Continentally-inspired, eleventh-century desire for Latin *vitae*, which seems to
have been greatly encouraged by the Norman clergy and authorities in
England after the conquest of 1066.[8] Herman's travels had exemplified the
extent to which proper episcopal conduct was felt to require significant material resources, which one could expect to obtain through the vigorous development of one or more saints' cults. Goscelin's attachment to Herman's
household could thus owe much to the sought-after expertise with which
St-Bertin certainly equipped all the monks it trained, that is to say the documentary skills necessary for the translation and documentation of saints' cults;
as both had been first perfected there early in the tenth century.[9]

Anglo-Saxon or Anglo-Norman monastic women with material aspirations
would have looked towards Wilton. The richest women's house in eleventh-

---

6 See André Wilmart's n. 4 in Goscelin, *La légende de Ste Edith*, 37.

7 Herman had been a royal chaplain like the other foreign bishops, Giso and Leofric; see
Antonia Gransden, 'Traditionalism and Continuity in the Last Century of Anglo-Saxon Monasticism', *Journal of Ecclesiastical History*, 40 (1989), 159–207 (187).

8 As part of the wider literary interests mentioned in Nicholas Brooks, *The Early History of the
Church of Canterbury. Christ Church from 597 to 1066* (Leicester, 1984), 276–7; Susan J. Ridyard,
The Royal Saints of Anglo-Saxon England: A Study of West Saxon and East Anglian Cults (Cam-
bridge, 1988), 173–5; and esp. Ridyard's 'Condigna Veneratio: Post-Conquest Attitudes to the
Saints of the Anglo-Saxons', *Anglo-Norman Studies*, 9 (1986), 179–206. She notes with regard to
Bury St Edmunds (ibid. 187) that Edward the Confessor's appointment of Continental clerics
may to some extent have prepared the ground for such tastes, for which there is, however, little
evidence in England under his rule.

9 Monks in the Flemish monastery were probably better informed about England than many,
since Anglo-Saxon travellers used St-Bertin's as a principal cross-Channel first stop on continental journeys. As a result St-Bertin's was one of the top four foreign ecclesiastical institutions holding land in Kent in the 11th century even after the Conquest, as Domesday Book
testifies: Andrew Ayton and Virginia Davis, 'Ecclesiastical Wealth in England in 1086', *Studies
in Church History*, 24 (1987), 47–60 (56).

century England, it had a long association with the house of Wessex, dating back to its foundress;[10] and this had been greatly strengthened by the presence of St Edith and her mother Wulfthryth in the nunnery in the late tenth century. Their residence had made Wilton the female focus of the Benedictine reform movement's royal patron, Edith's father, King Edgar (in so far as there was a female focus at all to the reform – several refounded houses of monks had previously been double monasteries headed by abbesses).[11] The royal connection was maintained by Edith's half-brother Æthelred II and his Danish conqueror, Cnut.[12] In 1065, Edward the Confessor's wife, Edith, completed the construction of a stone church in the monastery for her own burial and future retirement which rivalled her husband's building at Westminster.[13] Stone was an uncommon building material in the eleventh-century Anglo-Saxon monasteries remaining in the possession of women.[14] In Domesday Book's valuation, Wilton, the wealthiest of the women's religious houses, comes thirteenth among monastic wealth rankings, when men's houses are included in the reckoning.[15] Such prominence may explain the rapid decision to use Goscelin's pen in providing the textual support the Normans expected of an established saint's cult. Without Latin texts the new clergy were at some loss in determining how to respect Anglo-Saxon traditions; and the liturgy they followed

[10] St Ealburga, sister to King Egbert. For an account of Wilton's origins see William Dugdale, *Monasticon Anglicanum*, ed. John Caley, Henry Ellis and Bulkeley Bandinel (London, 1817–1830), ii, 315; though the nunnery's royal links intensified in the 10th century: Sharon R. Elkins, *Holy Women of Twelfth Century England* (Chapel Hill, 1988), 1, 6–8, and Mark Meyer, 'Patronage of the West Saxon Royal Nunneries in Late Anglo-Saxon England', *Revue Bénédictine*, 91 (1981), 332–58 (334–5).

[11] For instance, the former double monastery at Ely was given to monks: Edward Miller, *The Abbey and the Bishopric of Ely*, Cambridge Studies in Medieval Life and Thought, n.s., vol. ii (Cambridge, 1951), 8–15; and Gransden, *Traditionalism and Continuity* (1989), 169; see also Meyer, *West Saxon Royal Nunneries* (1981), 332 n. 1.

[12] For Cnut's generosity towards the nuns, with respect shown to Edith's shrine and trust in her power, see Goscelin, *La Légende de Ste Edith* (1938) ch. 12, 278–9; Michael Kenneth Lawson, *Cnut: The Danes in England in the Early Eleventh Century* (London, 1993), 135, 157.

[13] As in André Wilmart, 'Eve et Goscelin. II', *Revue Bénédictine*, 50 (1938), 42–83, (58 n. 5). See also the text stylistically not quite similar enough to be attributed to Goscelin, ed. Frank Barlow, *The life of King Edward who rests at Westminster attributed to a monk of Saint-Bertin* (London, 1992), 70–2, on the stone church of Queen Edith describing the rivalry; and Emma Mason, ' "The Site of King-making and Consecration": Westminster Abbey and the Crown in the Eleventh and Twelfth Centuries', in *The Church and Sovereignty c.590–1918: Essays in Honour of Michael Wilks*, ed. Diana Wood, Studies in Church History, Subsidia, vol. ix (Oxford, 1991), 57–76, (60–1).

[14] The wooden chapel built to St Denis by St Edith described in Goscelin's *La légende de Ste Edith* (1938), 265, 269, is cited in Richard D. H. Gem, 'Tenth-Century Architecture in England', in *Il Secolo de Ferro: Mito e realtà del Secolo X: Settimane di Studi sull'alto medioevo* (Spoleto, 1990), 803–36 (831–2), where he also notes Bradford-on-Avon's stone minster, given to the Shaftesbury nuns in 1001 as a temporary refuge, which he would date as just pre-Conquest, though Harold M. Taylor and Joan Taylor, *Anglo-Saxon Architecture* (Cambridge, 1965), i, 86–9, make the building early 10th century and therefore constructed for canons prior to this gift.

[15] See David Knowles and R. Neville Hadcock, *Medieval Religious Houses: England and Wales* (London, 1971), 136, 702; cited in Elkins, *Holy Women* (1988), 2 n. 3, which gives a 15th position rather than the 13th place Knowles accords Wilton in the 1940 edn.

required a more consistent textual basis than was available in Anglo-Saxon monastic houses.[16] Wilton's resident authority on Norman tastes from 1066 to her death in 1075, the former queen, Edith Godwinsdaughter, would have ensured the foundation she fostered knew how to remain in favour.[17]

The independent-minded and exemplarily ascetic leadership which Goscelin shows St Edith to have exerted (as had the majority of his female hagiographic subjects),[18] while appealing to English tradition, was not an attitude with which Normans would have had much experience. The nunneries of Normandy were generally under strict episcopal control, a model Professor Sharon Elkins has shown to have appealed to Anglo-Norman bishops.[19] Thus Goscelin proposed a model which would not find an Anglo-Norman resonance and would certainly not be imitated in the twelfth-century spate of religious foundations for women in England. The eleventh century had seen the relative place of monasteries decline in Anglo-Saxon society, possibly more so for women's houses than for men's given the greater limitations restricting women's communities; and they would be less well-placed than men's houses to fight the introduction of a Norman-style monastic subservience to episcopal authority.[20]

In the preface to the life of Edith a passage shows Goscelin's awareness of societal limitations and expectations placed upon women. He specifically tries

---

[16] This is a significant point central to the much discussed Anselm-Lanfranc quarrel over the validity of English cults discussed in Eadmer, *The Life of St Anselm, Archbishop of Canterbury*, ed. Richard W. Southern (Oxford, 1972), 51–4, as well as by Michael T. Clanchy, *England and its rulers, 1066–1272: Foreign Lordship and National Identity* (Oxford, 1983), 95–8, who emphasizes the loss of a vernacular prayer tradition where Anselm would introduce new styles and attitudes as well as language; cf. Thomas H. Bestul, 'St Anselm and the Continuity of Anglo-Saxon Devotional Traditions', *Annuale Medievale*, 18 (1977), 20–41. See also Gransden, *Traditionalism and Continuity* (1989), 198–9. Recent discussions emphasize the adaptability of Normans to the new cults, e.g. David Rollason's 'Goscelin of Canterbury's Account of the Translation and Miracles of St Mildrith (BHL 5961/4). An Edition with Notes', *Medieval Studies*, 48 (1986), 139–210 (145).

[17] Barlow, *Life of King Edward* (1992), pp. lxxii–lxxiii, shows Edward the Confessor's cult as originating among his foreign courtiers and given further prominence by Queen Edith's commission of his biography, hastily refocused on his religious life in mid-composition after Edith's brother Harold II died at Hastings (pp. xx–xxi). This work verifies that her cultural horizons reflected those of her husband's cosmopolitan court, allowing for her to do more for Wilton than simply provide the extension of an Anglo-Saxon twilight, as suggested in Meyer, *West Saxon Royal Nunneries* (1981), 357.

[18] Elkins, *Holy Women* (1988), 7–10, presents the typical examples of Edith, Werburga and Wulfhilda.

[19] Though principally focusing on the 12th century, she sees the seeds of the tendency in the 11th-century situation; Elkins, *Holy Women* (1988), 17–18.

[20] Championed by both Lanfranc and Anselm who had ironically fought this authority tooth and nail while in positions of monastic authority at Bec. Yet both, in Canterbury, fought St Augustine's monks' attempts to maintain particular status: Sally Vaughn, *Anselm of Bec and Robert of Meulan. The Innocence of the Dove and the Wisdom of the Serpent* (Berkeley, 1987), 322–8, and Marjorie Chibnall, 'From Bec to Canterbury: Anselm and Monastic Privilege', *Anselm Studies: An Occasional Journal*, 1 (1983), 23–44.

to counter the social difficulties under which his patrons laboured, realizing
that they were such that they needed to be addressed and countered to assure
an effective promotion of the cult of their saintly and royal patron. The preface
appeals for protection for the nunnery in its dedication to archbishop
Lanfranc.[21] For Wilton to reach beyond the see to Canterbury for protection
underlines the nunnery's national prominence, and points out the limited
scope of the local bishop's authority. The connection the dedication makes to
Canterbury is Edith's supposed Kentish birth, though the locality was in fact
in the diocese of Rochester.[22] The great influence of England's premier archbishop was desired for the land's premier nunnery.

In his preface, Goscelin mentions that his witnesses are mainly women.
Their reliability is exemplified by New Testament passages. Mary's crucial role
as mother of Christ is mentioned and two passages which stress feminine
testimony follow. Gender roles in Jewish funerary custom put women first at
the tomb to see the announcement of the Resurrection (Matt. 28: 10 and John
20: 18; though Goscelin does not remind his audience that even then the male
apostles had trouble believing their word and sought and demanded further
verification). The other instance of female witnesses shows women alongside
men inspired by the gift of the Holy Spirit to speak in tongues (Acts 1: 34, 2: 2,
2: 18).[23] At the end of his prologue, Goscelin claims to put forward only a little
of the information of faithful witnesses as good as that found in the books of
the fathers,[24] a standard formula which does not apply directly to this *vita*.
This relatively recent saint, about whom few texts existed, could not *prima facie*
sustain a rote reference to male authority grouped under the heading of
church fathers which was seldom directly useful in Anglo-Saxon cults, though
more so in this case, where even Bede predates possible witnesses.[25] The

---

[21] A choice of dedicatee which may also underline the author's problems with bishop Osmund
of Old Sarum, the successor to his much-loved patron Herman. See previously, p. 124 and
references in nn. 3–4 for Goscelin's activity at this time.

[22] There was a church of St Edith at Kemsing, the spot Wilmart identifies in two notes to the
first chapters of Goscelin, *La Légende de Ste Edith* (1938); 38 n. 2 and 41 n. 2. It only appears in
later documents, so how early it existed is difficult to ascertain.

[23] Goscelin, *La Légende de Ste Edith* (1938), 36–7: 'Illustrissima uero monasterii sui primiceria
domna Godyua, que ab eius digne memorie genitrice nu<n>c habetur quinta, cetereque
presentes matres, tam fideles quam generose, inter reliqua que ipse oculis conspexere, affir-
mant confidenter cum aliis idoneis testibus ea que ab his uenerabilibus matribus audiere, que
ipsam sanctam uirginem et uidere, et deuotissime sunt obsequute; quarum et parentele et
religiose vite non minorem fidem quam libris noscuntur habere. Neque uero is sexus a testimonio ueritatis refellendus erit, qui Domini uerbum portauit, qui sua fide apostolorum incre-
dulitatem arguit et angelica legatione dominica<m> resurectionem predicauit. Postremo tam
ancille Domini prophetant quam serui, et linguis loquuntur in eadem gratia Spiritus sancti.'

[24] Ibid. 39: 'Pauca autem de multis que fidelium testimonio uel patriis libris didicimus tam
fiducialiter exponimus, ut pro hystorie notitia pocius epithalamium odizare gestiamus.

Illa modo candida columba que de Christi pectore in hac sancta anima requieuit im spiritu
ueritatis dictatrix assit, et exclusis fastidiosis, aspiret affectuosis.'

[25] Bede's authority was considerable; however, his misogyny was recently underscored by
David Pelteret, 'Bede's Women', International Society for Anglo-Saxonists' conference paper,

unusual decision to use this term when the sources are not directly appealed to seeks to add the weight of tradition in favour of testimony it might also be used to oppose. His introduction of the strong-willed patron of Wilton, Edith, shows Goscelin's awareness of antipathy to such a model, and therefore bolsters the reputation of feminine witnesses to faith with reminders of their theological equality in Christ, as well as equating oral with written testimony. A century before, just after the material peak of women's monasticism in later Anglo-Saxon England,[26] Goscelin's predecessor, Ælfric, the abbot of Eynsham, similarly reminds his audiences of this theological gender equality in his Old English *Saints' Lives and Homilies*.[27]

On one occasion Goscelin issues similar warnings, referring, in fact, to the same biblical texts in the life of another late tenth-century woman, Wulfhild. She attracted the attention of King Edgar (as would Edith's mother, Wulfthryth, at a later date) and was, in Goscelin's narrative, assiduously pursued, despite signs of an obvious vocation, on account of her eminent beauty. One can suspect that the attraction stemmed in part from Wulfhild's impeccable family credentials: her successor in the royal chase, Wulfthryth, was in fact her cousin.[28] Unlike Wulfthryth, Wulfhild did manage to escape the king's marital and sexual desires and pursue her vocation at Barking, where she was abbess for a time, until removed by Edgar's last wife, Ælfthryth.[29]

After the Conquest the inmates of this women's house engaged Goscelin to write a whole series of lives of their saintly abbesses. The *Vita Vulfildae* is addressed to Maurice, bishop of London, who had recently been involved in a translation of the saints (and whose see had long links with the ancient nunnery at Barking), and is no doubt designed to help focus some attention on the

---

Oxford, August 1–6 1993, who recommended Stephanie Hollis' *Anglo-Saxon Women and the Church. Sharing a Common Fate* (Woodbridge, Suffolk, 1992), 243–52. Pelteret provides an intriguing psychological link of child oblate development to the disassociation of women and learning Hollis amply demonstrates to be part of Bede's authorial agenda. However, even for early Anglo-Saxon saintly abbesses and queens, where Bede avoids details of the female saint's lives and first-person speech, Goscelin creates fuller portraits of human saints.

[26] Meyer, in *West Saxon Royal Nunneries* (1981), shows the decline of feminine foundations as part of a general trend in all foundations, starting with the AD 990 Danish invasions, 355–8.

[27] This is the topic of Georges Whalen, 'Ælfric and the Anglo-Saxon Feminine Experience', Society for Canadian Medievalists' Conference paper, Carleton Univ., June 2–4, 1993, discussing among other examples showing the use of the word *wif* in theological discussions of salvation, the *ge weras ge wifmenn* who will attend Christ in heaven, closing a homily on the Final Judgement from *Homilies of Aelfric: A Supplementary Collection*, ed. J. C. Pope, EETS 259, 260 (London, 1967–68), 19, ll.435–9, 609: 'Soðlice þa halgan siðiað mid Criste, / to heofonan rice mid hys halgum englum, / ge weras ge wifmenn, swa swa hi on worulde lyfodon / and siððan wuniað gesælige mid him / on unasecgendlicre blisse á butan ende, Amen.'

[28] Goscelin, 'La Vie de Sainte Vulfhilde par Goscelin de Cantorbéry', ed. Mario Esposito, *Analecta Bollandiana*, 32 (1913) ch. 4, p. 17, states she was her paternal uncle's daughter. Edgar's lustful reputation was widespread. His son Edward's hagiographer emphasized the martyr's chastity, a virtue which could not be included in the praise of the father in *The Life of Edward, King and Martyr*, ed. Christine E. Fell, Leeds Texts and Monographs, n.s. (Leeds, 1971), 1–2.

[29] She held three abbacies at one point. See Meyer, *West Saxon Royal Nunneries* (1981), 343–5.

holy patrons of Barking.[30] His protection against the gnashing teeth, *ferocium dentes*, of disbelievers, is invoked immediately after a shorter version of the justification of women's testimony given in the *Vita Eadithae*. In the Wulfhild life's preface the New Testament references follow the identification of the chief witness, Judith (who had once been named Wulfrun),[31] an ancient nun who had met Wulfhild as a young novice.[32] Those raging toothily against the recognition of Anglo-Saxon saints were involved in a cultural conflict where expectations of appropriate cultual attributes clashed. The Barking nuns had Goscelin provide the Latin *vita* which Norman clerics, like most on the Continent, expected of *bona fide* saints. Without written Latin testimony, Continental clerics could automatically express doubt, particularly with regard to the new Wulfhild cult's validity.

Proper Norman cultual practice required a wider variety of Latin texts than usual by Anglo-Saxon standards, yet the Essex community of holy women was possibly also involved in a battle to maintain legitimate traditions of gender roles, also culturally defined. Norman nunneries were distinctly under episcopal control, just as male Norman cenobites were under episcopal direction to a far greater extent than normal among Anglo-Saxon monks.[33] In Normandy nunneries thus had far fewer independent traditions, and through close contact with episcopal authority obtained early outside verification and approval of local cultual developments. Expectations of such Norman standards might indeed create disquiet with the quite independent (and at times unsubstantiated) instances of cults which the inhabitants of Anglo-Saxon monasteries claimed to perpetuate in time-honoured traditions of reverence. Women's communities would have been far less well-placed to have the cult

---

[30] Links of the bishopric with the translation possibilities are discussed by Colker in Goscelin, *History of Barking* (1965), 387–8. London episcopal landholding links to Essex are discussed in Pamela J. Taylor, 'The Endowment and Military Obligations of the See of London: a Reassessment of Three Sources', *Anglo-Norman Studies*, 14 (1991), 287–312 (300–3).

[31] Underlined by Colker in Goscelin, *History of Barking* (1965), 391. This name change could be part of the introduction of monastic vocational names into England, possibly creating problems in assessing the normanity of post-Conquest inhabitants of nunneries and monasteries.

[32] Goscelin, *Vie de Sainte Vulfhilde* (1913), 12: 'Videre hodiernæ filiæ grandevas matres suæ institutionis testantissimas suae sanctitatis. Notissima est adolescentioribus eius sanctimonialis discipula Vulfruna, Iudith cognominata, a primevo flore sub ipsa educata, quæ ad nostri regis Vuilielmi supervixit sceptra. Hec vero tantæ fidei viguisse probatur industria, ut gloriosæ virgines, tam ista quam beata Aethelburga, nonnulla signa ostenderint ipsius instantia. Huius quoque generis fidelia testimonia non respuenda docet prima et angelica nuncia resurrectionis Domini Maria sanctarumque prophetissarum turba. Hec igitur decet tuam paternam excellentiam, o Lundonicæ metropolis ierarcha, ut bonum nummularium et gemmarium Christi non solum probabiliter assumere, verum etiam contra ferocium dentes potenter defendere, qui ante malunt ignota damnare quam prenoscere. Sed sicut rebellis infidelitas reatum, ita benivola fides sortitur caritatis meritum, quæ amabiliter credit indiciis virtutum.' The text *Vita et virtutes sanctae Vulfidae uirginis* is also in Goscelin, *History of Barking* (1965), 418–34.

[33] Sally Vaughn shows Bec as an exception in staying outside that mould, even under Anselm who, as archbishop of Canterbury, would promote it: Vaughn, *Anselm of Bec* (1987), 28–9, 53–4, 61–3.

of their particular saint confirmed by cathedral authorities than men's communities, since a century of Benedictine reform had not led their inmates and leaders to occupy the majority of episcopal seats in the English kingdom.[34] Monk bishops frequently imported the cults which their training rendered familiar. This second purely Anglo-Saxon bar to legitimacy which the women's monasteries faced might prove more difficult to overcome than the ethnic and cultural divergences which contemporaries realized they had to address; the issue of gender opportunities and divergences is a very infrequent topic of debate among the invading clerics, who were more concerned with the richer male monasteries upon their first arrival in England.[35]

No warning about the gender of witnesses is deemed necessary in Goscelin's *Vita Mildrethae*. This abbatial saint's body was removed from her seventh-century Thanet foundation (a local parish or canonry by the mid-eleventh century) to St Augustine's, Canterbury, with the permission of king Cnut. In the *Translatio sancte milidrethe virginis cum miraculorum attestatione*, Goscelin has Cnut describing Mildreth's reception into heaven: 'now in happiness the divine fathers, archbishops and abbots lead her to them, they whom the girl emulated in all virtue and love'.[36] Writing for St Augustine's monks who had appropriated the relics and lands of Mildreth and her foundation thanks to the disturbances of the Viking invasions,[37] the whole discourse is placed in a male monastic context and well attested by male witnesses. Goscelin has what he presents as the saint's male-modelled power forcefully expressed to king Cnut in a testing storm (*Translatio*, ch. 11). The prologue to Mildreth's *vita* stresses the importance of ancient texts (which, for contemporaries, would obviously include Bede)[38] in giving adequate witness to the

---

[34] Frank Barlow, *The English Church 1000–1066* (London, 1979), 62–4, 101–4; while Lawson, *Cnut* (1993), 149–51, shows how Cnut began to favour court clerics (see also n. 8 above).

[35] Indeed, it would seem that links to female monasteries in England were only developed by the generation of Normans born after the Conquest. See Elkins, *Holy Women* (1988), 3 n. 5, comparing attitudes to male and female monastic professions.

[36] Goscelin, *Translation and Miracles of St Mildrith* (1986); Rollason's transl. is from p. 168, n. 73 for a passage given as spoken by Cnut: 'Iam illam, credo, huc inuitant ipsi progenitores sui reges, quorum purpuras condecorat eternaliter uernans rosa quorumque ipsa est corona. Iam adducunt sibi diuini patres, archipresules et abbates in letitia, quos tota uirtute ac dilectione emulata est filia. Dignius itaque in hac arce preclara, inter tanta luminaria ueneratorumque officia, lucebit hec lampas siderea quam in illa desolata ubi iam uilescit ecclesia.'

[37] The late tradition of a last abbess, Leofrune, murdered by Danes when in Canterbury for protection with Ælfheah provides a reason for Cnut's support first found in Florence of Worcester, *Chronicon ex chronicis*, ed. Benjamin Thorpe (London, English Historical Society, 1848–1849, rep. 1964), 164, s.a. 1011; though the nature of the 1030s religious presence at Thanet is difficult to establish, it is certainly male. R. Emms suggests that the abbess could be based at the church of St Mildred's in Canterbury by the turn of the millenium in Brooks, *The Church of Canterbury* (1984), 34 n. 62.

[38] An example of the high regard is the inspiration he provides to the new founders of Jarrow in the late 11th century, pointed out with scepticism, though not contested, by David Rollason, 'Symeon of Durham and the Community of Durham in the Eleventh Century', in *England in the Eleventh Century: Proceedings of the 1990 Harlaxton Medieval Symposium*, ed. Carola Hicks

deeds of the saint.[39] There is no strong recourse to New Testament validation to explain the male witnesses to the 'dear brothers' of St Augustine's for whom Goscelin wrote at the end of his career. In this male, as in the female communities, many voices rush forward to support the heavenly patron and her link to a variety of estates. An important monastery like St Augustine's relied on the sense of self-interest of its new Norman clergy[40] to ensure the promotion of existing cults; however, automatic questioning of such testimony was not expected to be of a sort which would build on theologically unsound social prejudices.

Goscelin dedicates his life of Mildreth (in so far as it is a dedication) to the members of the Canterbury community. St Augustine's Canterbury did not need to remind episcopal authorities of its saintly patrons or history of patronage as did Wilton and Barking.[41] And Goscelin clearly expected most of the audience beyond the monastery walls to concur with a traditional classical respect for ancient texts to help promote this saintly abbess.

Goscelin's life of Barking's founding abbess, Æthelburg, was also able to draw on Bede's account, and he places that authority front and centre in his prologue, again dedicating the *vita* to bishop Maurice. This allows him to pass over in silence the gender of his informants which does not need to stand on its own (though he does point out that people of worthy repute outside the

---

(Stamford, 1992), 183–98 (183–6, 193–4); and the number of imitators of his style found in 12th century monastic houses; see Antonia Gransden, *Traditionalism and Continuity* (1989), 201–3, and 'Bede's reputation as an historian in Medieval England.' *Journal of Ecclesiastical History*, 32 (1981), 397–418 (403–12).

[39] Goscelin, 'Vita Deo dilectae virginis Mildrethae', ed. David W. Rollason, in his *The Mildrith Legend: A Study in Early Medieval Hagiography in England* (Leicester, 1982), 105–43, prologue, p. 108: 'Res digne preconio iacent scriptore sub tepido, sordent sub garrulo, lucent claritate sua sub diserto. Quocirca, O karissimi mei, in uita beatissime uirginis Mildrithe mortalem sensum superante, cum non sufficiam beneuolentie uestre satisfacere, sit tamen aliquid me dulci amicitie obedisse. Parui non ut uolui sed ut modo inter innumeras mentis et temporis ablationes raptim et cursim ualui – si gratiam non meretur repulsa facultas, uel ueniam habeat prompta uoluntas. Sententiam autem ueritatis obnixe exequimur, non ex nouis testibus, sed ex ipsa uita eius et meritis antiquitus descriptis uel ab antiquis historiis collectis. Valeant qui hec fastidiunt tamquam ad se non pertinentia, dummodo uobis domesticis a Deo date domine dilectoribus sint parata. Satis uero docent presentia uel assidua eius signa quam sint prisca credenda.'

[40] Richard Sharpe, 'Goscelin's St Augustine and St Mildreth: Hagiography and Liturgy in Context', *Journal of Theological Studies* (n.s.) 41 (1990), 502–16 (502–5, 509), refers to the replacement of the monks of the community in the late 11th century from Christ Church Canterbury and other houses mentioned in Rollason, *The Mildrith Legend* (1982), and his article *The Translation and Miracles of St Mildrith* (1986), 145.

[41] Or arguably, it does so on a much grander scale, in the translations of 1091 to the new abbey building of abbot Scotland, which Goscelin was commemorating with a whole series of *vitae*, and which therefore needs mention in a less overt way in each individual life; discussed by Sharpe, *Goscelin's St Augustine* (1990), and Richard Gem, 'The significance of the 11th-century Rebuilding of Christ Church and St Augustine's Canterbury in the Development of Romanesque Architecture', *Medieval Art and Architecture at Canterbury before 1220: Transactions of the British Archaeological Association*, 5 (1982), 1–19 (1–2, 15–16).

monastery were witnesses, and these *aliorum* include men who were not normally within it).[42] With the authoritative texts, and with male witnesses, the situation differs from writings for more recently elevated members of the saintly community. Even if, for a women's monastery, a more hostile audience was expected,[43] the Flemish monk need not resort to biblical authority where that of a reader learned in the classical tradition might suffice.

The late Anglo-Saxon men Goscelin celebrated in hagiography were men whose recent elevation to sainthood followed their episcopal promotions, and thus who had more numerous links with the authorities to whom the texts were dedicated. Bishop Osmund of Sarum had worked with several of Goscelin's key informants, and thus a justification for his life of bishop Wulfsige III of Sherborne may not have seemed necessary to the hagiographer.[44] (However, Osmund's Norman tastes might have inclined him to prefer a more orthodox reference to the use of written accounts for his late-tenth-century predecessor.) The presentation of his informants as trusted administrators of the bishop's cathedral community clearly in itself warranted respect in a way the presentable and public activities of senior members of a women's monastic community would not be able to equal, thus removing a difficulty for the hagiographer intent on presenting a highly authoritative account.

Monasteries ever dependent on patronage used hagiographical texts in promotion of the cult within the confines of the local community, while keeping an eye on the transitory and greater community. In England after the Norman Conquest the new foreign élites did not show much interest in existing institutions for women, though historians of male monasticism can cite many conflicts behind male cloister walls which might superficially make this seem a good thing.[45] Note that there is little evidence of a rush to appoint Norman abbesses; for instance, Bryhtgifa succeeded her sister Ælfgifu as abbess of Wilton around 1067, and so was able to commission Goscelin many years later.[46] However a lack of interest could soon translate into a lack of revenue, and diminish the resources available to protect traditional revenues, though protection was a commodity greatly risen in value in England after 1066. Thus the heavily female quotient of Goscelin's list of patrons may reflect a rapid reaction to an astute appraisal of the dire situation which the Conquest

---

[42] Goscelin, *Vita et uirtutes sanctae Ethelburgae uirginis*, ed. M. L. Colker, in *History of Barking* (1967), 398.

[43] As seen in n. 32.

[44] Goscelin, 'The Life of St. Wulfsin of Sherborne by Goscelin', ed. C. H. Talbot, *Revue Bénédictine*, 69 (1959), 73–85, though the period of Wulfsige's episcopacy is established in P. Grosjean's review of the Talbot edn in *Analecta Bollandiana*, 78 (1960), 202–3.

[45] For St Augustine's own turmoil, see n. 40 above. Also in conflict with their abbot were the monks of Abingdon, reviewed in Ridyard, *Condigna Veneratio* (1986), 190–2.

[46] Meyer, *West Saxon Royal Nunneries* (1981), 357, ascribes the delay to dowager Queen Edith's influence, but, as in men's monasteries, the names of the inmates do eventually become normanized.

brought about, since the mid-eleventh century, for what has already been described as the precarious opportunities for female monastic life.[47] Male monastics of conquered and conquering cultural groups could afford to squabble over the direction of their institutions, since their economic, political and spiritual importance guaranteed a healthy survival. Female monastic houses, demonstrably well-off though they might be, were far less able to be complacent in these matters. No divisions are recorded of royal Anglo-Saxon women monastics fighting over the relics of the victims of their own power struggles, as was the case in their heyday in Æthelred II's reign, which the narrator of the *Passio sancti Edwardi regis et martyris* reminisces over as the good old days, for his commissioners, the community of nuns of Shaftesbury.[48] King Edward's *Passio* pays more attention to claiming written sources, and less to the contact with the nuns who clearly provided the author with information about some of the miracles recounted.

The late eleventh-century internal conflicts of which we are informed for women's monastic houses in post-Conquest England are those which involved the 'refugee' women, who desired to leave the refuge provided when their men had been killed or dispossessed and they were viewed as possible legitimizers of Norman succession.[49] Evolving ecclesiastical legalism may account for the greater difficulty in getting nuns out of the cloister (principally for marriage) – though the strictures against such departures in the laws of Cnut and Æthelred make such an assertion dubious.[50] And the Conquest might have put women in the monastic setting who had few other options, but were willing to cultivate them from within. However, the presence of such activity does lead one to suspect that the narrowing scope of power exercised from within Anglo-Saxon nunneries was further shrunk by the Norman disinterest, and that it is symptomatic of a restriction on the tradition of monastic independence which also prompted the commissioning of many, if not all, of Goscelin's hagiographic works.

Goscelin seems to have been, throughout his writings, a hagiographer

---

[47] Of Goscelin's known *vitae*, far more concern women than the 15% average female representation in saintly groups, which is noted by Jane Tibbetts Schulenburg, 'Female Sanctity: Public and Private Roles, ca. 500–1100', in *Women and Power in the Middle Ages*, ed. Mary Erler and Maryanne Kowaleski (Athens, Ga., 1988), 102–25 (103–5), his *vitae* of women total closer to 40% of his production according to Hamilton, *Goscelin of Canterbury* (1973), 76–124. Of his hagiographic oeuvre 25% was written for women's monasteries, over-representing institutions which do not form as high a proportion of late 11th-century England's monastic institutions, listed in Knowles, *Monastic Houses* (1940), App. VI, 702.

[48] Fell's introduction to the *Passio* (1971), which is categorized as possibly written by Goscelin (p. xx); the author details the fight between the mothers of Edgar's children, now abbesses, Wulfthryth of Wilton and Ælfthryth of Wherwell and Barking (mother to Æthelred II) for the possession of Edward's relics, which Wulfthryth wins for Shaftesbury (7–10).

[49] Eleanor Searle, 'Women and the legitimisation of succession at the Norman Conquest', *Anglo-Norman Studies*, 3 (1980), 159–70.

[50] See e.g. the law code sections ICnut 6a, 7.1, and IICnut 50.1, in Felix Liebermann, *Gesetze der Angelsachsen* (Halle, 1903) i, 288, 290, 346.

sensitive to the needs of his patrons, a sensitivity which no doubt helped inspire confidence among his informants. When he turns to his audience, as medieval hagiographers and historians did most tellingly in their prologues,[51] the monk of St-Bertin shows a fine appreciation of a gradation of social situations and attitudes requiring adjustments to what might be thought a series of similar straightforward tasks. In these prefaces to *vitae* and translation accounts, both in his choice of buttressing arguments and in their judicious use, the Flemish monk informs us across the centuries of a definite degradation in the situation of women's monastic communities in England after the Norman Conquest; a degradation which owes more to a change in cultural values than to economic or political situations.

[51] Recent work on the light which prologues throw on the work of 12th-century historians helps us also to reconsider the importance of topos-filled hagiographic prefaces. See Antonia Gransden, 'Prologues in the Historiography of Twelfth-Century England', in *England in the Twelfth Century: Proceedings of the 1988 Harlaxton Symposium*, ed. Daniel Williams (Woodbridge, Suffolk, 1990) 55–81 (76–81); Bernard Guenée, 'L'Histoire entre l'éloquence et la science. Quelques remarques sur le prologue de Guillaume de Malmesbury à ses *Gesta Regum Anglorum*', *Comptes Rendus de l'Académie des Inscriptions et Belles-Lettres* (1982), 357–70, and Guenée's 'Les premiers pas de l'histoire de l'historiographie en occident au XIIe siècle', *Comptes Rendus de l'Académie des Inscriptions et Belles-Lettres* (1983), 136–51.

ANCRENE WISSE AND ÞE WOHUNGE OF URE LAUERD: THE THIRTEENTH-CENTURY FEMALE READER AND THE LOVER-KNIGHT

Catherine Innes-Parker

One of the most difficult problems facing the modern critic is how to reconstruct a historical reading of a text from which we are separated by time and
ideology, lacking, as we often do, even the most basic information about either
author or audience. For this reason, we tend to concentrate on sources and
how they are used in order to reconstruct a reliable reading. Examining the
way in which any given text draws upon and alters its sources is one way of
establishing its thrust, and gives a clearer understanding of how the ideas and
images were meant to be read. We tend, therefore, to interpret texts 'backwards,' attempting to read them through the eyes of the educated reader, a
reader conversant with the tradition out of which the texts emerged, who
would understand them in the light of all that has come before.

There is an additional problem, however, in reconstructing a historical reading of texts such as those of the Katherine Group, written by men for women.
How does one arrive at a reading of these texts which reflects, not the views of
the male author, but the way in which their female audience would have
understood them? The examination of sources which works so well for texts
written for educated men by their peers is often inadequate in the case of an
audience made up primarily of women, many (or most) of whom would not
have had access to a Latin education and would therefore be unfamiliar with
Latin sources. In addition, it seems clear that even women who were familiar
with the Latin tradition did not always think or write according to that tradition. One method of reconstructing a feminine reading is to compare texts
written *for* women (by men) with other texts written *by* women. However,
while there is a relatively large body of literature written by women on the
Continent in the twelfth and thirteenth centuries, there is a dearth of contemporary English texts written by women which express a woman's perception
of issues and imagery similar to those found in *Ancrene Wisse* and its sister
texts. It is therefore difficult to determine how these texts would have been
read by the women for whom they were written.

For this reason, even feminist critiques of these texts tend to approach them
from the point of view of the male author(s): his sources, his ideas, his

'misogyny'. In the case of *Ancrene Wisse*, however, the scholar is presented with a unique opportunity, for a contemporary reading of the parable of the lover-knight (*AW* vii) is available to us in Þe *Wohunge of Ure Lauerd*, an expansion of and meditation on the parable, written shortly after *Ancrene Wisse*.[1] Although there is no way of determining whether *Wohunge* was written by a woman, this possibility cannot be dismissed. Whoever the author was, *Wohunge* was clearly written for an anchoress; it is specifically addressed to a 'dear sister' and the first-person speaker is clearly female. Recent work on the lyrics of the troubadours has suggested that the female audience had a more significant influence on the texts written for them than has previously been assumed, creating a 'demand' which the male troubadours then fulfilled in a sort of 'supply and demand' economy of texts.[2] *Wohunge*, therefore, represents its author's perception of the way in which an anchoress would read the parable, if not a woman's reading, providing a unique opportunity to explore the parable of the lover-knight from the point of view of the thirteenth-century female reader.[3]

When these two texts are read together it becomes apparent that the elements for which the *Ancrene Wisse* author has been most stridently rebuked by modern feminist readers are elements which are either overlooked or read in different ways by the thirteenth-century audience represented in *Wohunge*. Feminist critics have focused on two related issues in the *Ancrene Wisse* passage: the emphasis on the romance tradition and the resultant passive role imposed upon the female reader. The author of *Ancrene Wisse* has been charged with assuming that his readers are mindless consumers of romance, capable only of a passive, emotional relationship with God which is assumed to be vastly inferior to the 'intellectual' male tradition of Bernard and his followers.[4] It should be noted that this reading falls into the patriarchal assumption that the masculine mystical tradition is in some way 'superior'. Yet *Ancrene Wisse* was extremely popular in its own time, and clearly provided its female audience with a message they wished to hear, a message which they

---

[1] All citations from *Ancrene Wisse* (abbr. *AW*) are from J. R. R. Tolkien, *The English Text of the Ancrene Riwle: Ancrene Wisse, MS Corpus Christi College Cambridge 402*, EETS 249 (1962). Citations from *Wohunge* (abbr. *WLd*) are from W. Meredith Thompson, Þe *Wohunge of Ure Lauerd*, EETS 241 (1958). All translations are from Anne Savage and Nicholas Watson, *Anchoritic Spirituality: Ancrene Wisse and Associated Works* (New York, 1991), abbr. *S/W*.

[2] See Pierre Bec, ' "Trobairitz" et chansons de femme. Contribution à la connaissance du lyrisme féminin au moyen âge', *Cahiers de Civilisation Médiévale*, 22 (1979), 235–62.

[3] The idea of interpreting medieval texts through the medium of other texts which draw upon them is not new; e.g., Lee Patterson devotes a chapter of a recent book to this precise method of constructing a 'history of reading', using *Troilus and Criseyde* as an example (*Negotiating the Past: The Historical Understanding of Medieval Literature* (Madison, Wisconsin, 1987), 115–53. This method has not, however, been specifically applied to texts written for women in an attempt to reconstruct a 'feminine' reading.

[4] See e.g., Elizabeth Robertson, *Early English Devotional Prose and the Female Audience* (Knoxville, 1990), 72; and Ritamary Bradley, 'In the Jaws of the Bear: Journeys of Transformation by Women Mystics', *Vox Benedictina*, 8 (1991), 116–75.

did not perceive as limiting or 'circumscribed'. Not only does *Ancrene Wisse* survive in seventeen manuscripts and fragments,[5] it was translated into both French and Latin and incorporated into a number of later texts.[6] In addition, feminine mysticism in general tends to be affective and personal, rooted in daily experience, rather than 'intellectual'. How, then, would the thirteenth-century female audience represented in *Wohunge* read the parable of the lover-knight?

The parable of the lover-knight is one of the most frequently anthologized and profoundly criticized passages in *Ancrene Wisse*. The point of the parable is clear enough: Christ is the mighty king who woos the lady anchoress, besieged in her castle and surrounded by her enemies. The lady is unmoved by beautiful gifts and the promise of an army, the king's beautiful face, sweet words, acts of power, and promises of a kingdom (a feature of the parable which, incidentally, weakens Bradley's argument that the parable focuses on material enticements).[7] Although the male author of *Ancrene Wisse* finds this contempt strange, considering the lowly estate of the lady, the anchoress in *Wohunge* sees it differently. *Wohunge* begins with a lengthy catalogue of the reasons one might choose a lover, listing beauty, wealth, generosity, wisdom, strength, nobility, gentleness and kinship, and declaring Christ's superiority over all human lovers in each category (as does Christ himself in *Ancrene Wisse*). However, the one thing which makes Christ's love irrefutably superior to all human loves is his death on the cross:

> Ah ouer alle oðre þinges makes te luuewurði to me þa harde atele hurtes . þa schomeliche wohes ꝥ tu þoledes for me . þi bittre pine 7 passiun . þi derue deað o rode . telles riht in al mi luue . calenges al mi heorte . (*WLd* 27. 262–9)

> But over all other things those hard, bitter hurts make you worthy of my love, the shameful pains you suffered for me, your bitter torment and passion: your cruel death on the cross weighs heavily in all my love, challenges all my heart. (*S/W* 251)

Here, it is not the *unworthiness* of the anchoress that is at issue, but the *worthiness* of Christ as a claimant for her love.[8] The author of *Ancrene Wisse* himself makes this shift as he moves into the interpretation of his parable:

---

[5] For a description of the manuscripts, see Roger Dahood, '*Ancrene Wisse*, the Katherine Group, and the *Wohunge* Group', in *Middle English Prose: A Critical Guide to Major Authors and Genres*, ed. A. S. G. Edwards (New Jersey, 1984).

[6] As well as *Wohunge*, *Ancrene Wisse* is a source for such texts as *The Chastising of God's Children*, *A Talking of The Love of God* and *A Treatise of Love*. See H. E. Allen, 'Some Fourteenth Century Borrowings from "Ancrene Riwle" ', *Modern Language Review*, 18 (1923), 1–8; Roger Dahood, '*Ancrene Wisse*, the Katherine Group, and the *Wohunge* Group', in *Middle English Prose: A Critical Guide*, 15, 17; and Anne Savage and Nicholas Watson, *Anchoritic Spirituality*, 378 n. 61 and 429 n.7.

[7] Ritamary Bradley, 'In the Jaws of the Bear', 135–6.

[8] This is not to say that the anchoress in *Wohunge* does not candidly confess her unworthiness

Þes king is iesu godes sune. þ al o þisse wise wohede ure sawle þe deoflen hefden biset. Ant he as noble wohere efter monie messagers 7 feole god deden; com to pruuien his luue. 7 schawde þurh cnihtschipe þ he wes luue wurðe. as weren sumhwile cnihtes iwunet to donne. (AW vii.199, f.105b. 21–5)

This king is Jesus, God's Son, who in just this way wooed our souls, which the devil had surrounded; and he, like a noble wooer, after many messengers and many presents, came to prove his love, and showed through chivalry that he was worthy of love, as knights were at one time accustomed to do. (S/W 191)

In addition, it is made clear that, while Christ is superior to human lovers on the material and worldly level, it is not on this level that the anchoress seeks love, and it is not the material gifts offered by Christ which win her love. This point is made in the parable by the actions of the king in response to the lady's contempt for his worldly offerings. Finding that she does not want his power or possessions, he offers her himself:

ah swa þurh his deboneírte luue hefde ouercumen him; þ he seide on ende. Dame þu art iweorret. 7 þine van beoð se stronge ; þ tu ne maht nanesweis wið ute mi sucurs edfleon hare honden. þ ha ne don þe to scheome deað efter al þi weane. Ich chulle for þe luue of þe; neome þ feht up o me. 7 arudde þe of ham þe þi deað secheð. Ich wat þah to soðe þ ich schal bituhen ham neomen deaðes wunde. 7 ich hit wulle heorteliche forte ofgan þin heorte. (AW vii.199, f.105b. 6–13)

But in his graciousness love had so overcome him that in the end he said: 'Lady, you are beleaguered, and your enemies are so strong that you can in no way escape from their hands without my help. So that they do not put you to shameful death after all your grief, for the love of you I will take this fight upon myself, and rid you of those who seek your death. Yet I know it to be true that I will receive from them my death-wound – and I wish it with all my heart, to win your heart.' (S/W 191)

The narrator of the parable then relates that the king did just as he had promised, defeating the lady's enemies through his own death. The narrator adds, however, the fact that the king, through a miracle, rose from death to life. He then appeals to the reader: 'Nere þeos ilke leafdi of uueles cunnes cunde. 3ef ha ouer alle þing ne luuede him her efter?' (AW vii.199, f. 105b.19–20) [Would not this same lady be of an evil sort of nature if she did not love him ever after over all things? (S/W 191)].

There are several interesting points here. First of all, it is the king's *deboneírte*, his graciousness or gentleness, which prompts him to take on the fight himself. In *Wohunge*, Christ's *deboneirschipe* is associated with his gentle

in the face of Christ's great love. Indeed, she acknowledges that Christ's purchase of her soul was accomplished at great cost, of which she is unworthy (WLd 32. 446–50; S/W 254).

meekness, his silence in the face of his shame and misery in the passion. This, a passive feature, is the attribute which prompts the king to take an active role in the battle for the lady's soul, and it should alert the reader to the fact that active and passive qualities are not to be assigned to either the king or the lady without careful consideration. This is reinforced by the treatment of this passage in *Wohunge*, where the anchoress declares:

> Arh ich was meself 7 wah 7 neh dune fallen . 7 mine fan derue . swa bucchede 7 swa kene þ hwen þai sehen me swa wak 7 swa forhuhande 7 buhande toward ham . þei swiðre sohten uppo me . 7 wenden of me wrecche haue maked al hare ahen 7 hefden forsoðe maked . nere helpe nere þe nerre . Þai grennede for gladschipe euchan toward oðer as wode wulues þ fainen of hare praie . Bote þer þurh understonde i þ tu wult hauei me to lefmon 7 to spuse . þ tu ne þoledes ham noht fulli fainen of me . 7 alle gate haue wurpen me in schome 7 in sinne 7 ter after in to pine . Bote þer þe bale was alre meast . swa was te bote nehest . Þu biheld al þis 7 tu allegate seh þ ine mihte stonde aʒain hare wilfulle crokes þurh wit oðer strengðe þ wes in me seluen . Bot neh hefde i fulliche buhed til alle mine þre fan . þu com me to helpe . feng to fihte for me . 7 riddes me fram deaðes hus sorhe 7 pine of helle . (*WLd* 27–8. 279–308).

> By myself I was a coward, and weak, and nearly fallen down – and my enemies cruel, and so fierce and so keen that when they saw me so weak, so desperate and yielding to them, they attacked me even harder. And they thought to have made me, a sinner, all their own. And they would have had me in reality if your help had not been nearer. They grinned for gladness at each other, like mad wolves joyful of their prey.
> Yet through this I understand that you will have me for lover and spouse: that you did not let them rejoice in me altogether, and throw me finally into shame and sin, and after into torment. But where danger was greatest of all, so was help nearest.
> You saw all this, and you clearly saw that I could not stand against their determined deceptions, through any wit or strength that was in me, but had nearly given in altogether to all three of my enemies.
> You came to my help, took on the fight for me, and freed me from the pain of the house of death and the torment of hell. (*S/W* 252)

As this passage makes clear, it is Christ's deed on the cross which establishes the magnitude of his love, and it is through his taking on the battle himself that the anchoress understands that he has chosen her for his lover and spouse. Just as in the parable of the lover-knight, it is Christ's gift of himself, his body and his life, that will finally win the lady's heart.

In *Wohunge*, however, Christ is presented more as a heroic warrior than a chivalrous knight. Apart from the opening invocation to Christ and the meditation upon the reasons why one chooses a lover,[9] the imagery is drawn from the English vernacular tradition rather than from the conventions of

---

[9] Even here, the imagery of the 'brave and famous champion,' the 'stalwart lover,' is

continental romance. The battle is presented in true heroic style, complete with the beasts of battle who 'grinned for gladness at each other, like mad wolves joyful of their prey'. Christ is the heroic champion who binds the 'hell-dogs' and deprives them of their prey, defeating the devil and harrowing hell with one hand tied behind his back (literally, 'wið þi deorewurðe hond nailet on rode' (WLd 23. 137–8) [with your precious hand nailed to the cross (S/W 249)]). This seems to reflect the Germanic image of the unarmed hero, identified by Alison Finlay with the image of the warrior Christ in *The Dream of the Rood*.[10]

The female speaker, however, is not merely a passive observer; she is an active participant in the drama of her own salvation. In the *Wohunge* passage, we see the lady actively engaged in the battle for her own soul, not cowering in her castle waiting passively to be redeemed. Although she has need of Christ's aid to win the war, she takes a vigorous part in the conflict. We first see her, not besieged in a tower, but falling under the superior strength of cruel enemies which surround her as she battles desperately for her soul. Her enemies, perceiving her weakness, redouble their efforts, 'but where danger was greatest of all, so was help nearest.' Christ, perceiving the anchoress's plight, comes to her aid and takes on the fight for her, just as he does in the parable of the lover-knight. And, just as in *Ancrene Wisse*, Christ's combat on her behalf is seen as an indication of his great love for her.

This should, perhaps, prompt us to reassess the lady's position in *Ancrene Wisse*. It is generally assumed that, because the lady is introduced as besieged and destitute in her castle, she is simply waiting passively to be redeemed. However, the fact that she refuses the aid of the king who wishes to redeem her suggests that she is still, however mistakenly, convinced of at least the possibility of redeeming herself through her own efforts, and willing to make the attempt. Alternatively, and more radically, one might suggest that she sees the pointlessness of the king's gifts and army, recognizing that only in his own person can he give her the aid she requires. While there is little suggestion of such perspicacity on the lady's part in the parable, throughout *Ancrene Wisse* the anchoress is encouraged to pursue Christ's aid aggressively until he gives her what she requires, and the lady in *Wohunge* is acutely aware that only through Christ's taking on the battle himself can she be saved.

Christ asks the anchoress to consider how he fought for her, but she is not thereby transformed into a passive observer. As she meditates upon the battle it becomes clear that it is fought and won with the weapons of her own ascetic, enclosed life: poverty, shame, suffering, and enclosure upon the cross.

intertwined with the wealth, nobility, gentleness, beauty and generosity which makes Christ supremely worthy of the anchoress's love.

[10] Alison Finlay, 'The Warrior Christ and the Unarmed Hero', in Gregory Kratzmann and James Simpson (eds.), *Medieval English Religious and Ethical Literature: Essays in Honour of G. H. Russell* (Cambridge, 1986), 19–29.

Drawing on several passages from *Ancrene Wisse*,[11] *Wohunge* presents Christ's battle using the images which parallel the anchoress's enclosure with Christ's enclosure in his mother's womb, in the manger, on the cross, and in the tomb.[12]

This reading is not inimical to the presentation of the anchoress in the parable of the lover-knight, in spite of the insistence of critics like Robertson that the anchoress, 'like the lady in the castle, can only wait passively to be rescued from the castle of her body or wait for that body to be redeemed through Christ's entry into it'.[13] Although the subject of the parable is the love which Christ displays in the battle for the lady's soul, the main focus is on the subsequent response of the lady, or lack thereof. From the beginning of the parable, the lady enclosed in her earthen castle is clearly identified with the anchoress enclosed within her body and her anchorhold. At all points, the language of the parable compels the anchoress to identify herself with the lady. When, after the first episode, the lady is unmoved, the author addresses the anchoress directly, asking not 'what more does *she* want?' but 'what more do *you* want?' The central issue, therefore, is the response of the anchoress to the love of Christ exemplified by the parable. The lady's response to the king is left unspecified at the end, precisely because it is the anchoress who must now take up the action of the parable and respond in her place.

What the response of the anchoress should be is made clear in the interpretation which follows the parable. It begins with a brief passion meditation, to which we will return, which once again stresses the love of Christ displayed on the cross. There follows an extended comparison of Christ's love to the four greatest loves on earth, focusing on the superiority of Christ's love. Finally, Christ himself speaks, wooing the anchoress in person in a forceful speech which repeats the question of the parable, 'what more do you want?' Whatever the anchoress may want, Christ will give more. If she will not give her love, he will buy it; if it is not to be bought, he will take it by force.

After Christ's impassioned wooing, the text returns to the anchoress's response, represented by the image of fire. Here it becomes clear that the response which the author seeks to evoke in the anchoress is not guilt, as Robertson and others argue, but love and devotion. In addition, the response of love expected by the author of *Ancrene Wisse* is anything but passive: Christ's unbounded love demands a response of love which is equally unreserved. The anchoress is faced with an active choice between earthly and heavenly love, and if she chooses the love of Christ, as indeed she must, she embarks upon an active course of kindling the fire of love in her heart using two pieces of the wood, the cross on which Christ hangs. This passage is

---

[11] E.g. *AW* iv.133–4 (*S/W* 143); *AW* vi.181–2 (*S/W* 178–9); *AW* vi.184–5 (*S/W* 180–1); *AW* vi.192–3 (*S/W* 186–7).

[12] Indeed, throughout *Ancrene Wisse* the anchoress's enclosure is described using the metaphor of spiritual combat, drawing on conventional images of the devil's army, the weapons of sin, the castle of the body (and of Christ), and the wounds of the soul, among others.

[13] Elizabeth Robertson, *Early English Devotional Prose*, 72.

dominated by the image of Greek fire, a kind of medieval 'napalm'[14] which was used in siege warfare, an image which brings us back again to the parable, with the lady under siege. The aid of the king, representing Christ's crucifixion and death, is embodied in the Greek fire, made from the blood of a red man (i.e. Christ's blood shed on the cross), the main weapon used to defeat the lady's enemies. However, as in *Wohunge*, the lady/anchoress does not sit passively waiting for Christ to redeem her: rather she kindles Greek fire within her heart and pours it down upon the heads of her enemies, becoming an active participant in the battle. In addition, the anchoress's participation in this spiritual battle is presented in both *Ancrene Wisse* and *Wohunge* as a participation in Christ's battle, the crucifixion. Thus, the anchoress participates in the battle for her own salvation as she is crucified with Christ in her cell, in an active suffering which is described in passionate terms.

It is for this reason that both *Ancrene Wisse* and *Wohunge* present the battle for the anchoress's soul as a metaphorical passion meditation. In *Ancrene Wisse*, the author gives an interpretation of the parable which focuses on the image of the knight's shield. The shield represents Christ's crucified body, pierced in battle for love of the lady/anchoress. Once again, the author of *Wohunge* picks up on this image, as Christ's body becomes not only his shield but his weapon: 'for þu þe ane dreddes nawt wið þin anre deore bodi to fihte aȝaines alle þe ahefulle deueles of helle' (*WLd* 23. 123–7) [For you did not fear to fight alone with your own dear body against all the awesome devils of hell (*S/W* 249)].

After an explication of the allegorical significance of the shield, the author of *Ancrene Wisse* once again emphasises the magnitude of Christ's love and the appropriate response:

Me lauerd þu seist hwerto. ne mahte he wið leasse gref habben arud us? ȝeoi iwiss ful lihtliche. ah he nalde. for hwi? forte bineomen us euch bitellunge aȝein hím of ure luue þ he se deore bohte. Me buð lihtliche þing þ me luueð lutel. He bohte us wið his heorte blod; deorre pris nes neauer. forte ofdrahen of us ure luue toward hím. þ costnede him se sare. (*AW* vii.200, f. 106a.13–19)

'But Lord,' you say, 'why? Could he not have delivered us with less pain?' Yes indeed, very easily, but he would not. Why not? To deprive us of every excuse for not giving him our love, which he so dearly bought. A thing little loved is easily bought. He bought us with his heart's blood – never was a price dearer – to draw out our love toward him, that cost him so bitterly. (*S/W* 192)[15]

---

[14] See Anne Savage and Nicholas Watson, *Anchoritic Spirituality*, 401 n. 33.

[15] In *Wohunge* the anchoress interprets not only Christ's death on the cross, but his entire life as the purchase price of her soul: 'A . deore cheap hefdes tu on me . ne was neauer unwurði þing chepet swa deore. Al þi lif on eorðe wes iswink for me swa lengre swa mare' (*WLd* 32. 446–50) [Ah, you had an expensive buy in me! Never was an unworthy thing bought so dearly. Your whole life on earth was labour for me, all the more as it went on (*S/W* 254)].

For this reason, as a knight's shield is hung in the church after his death to keep his memory alive, so too the crucifix, Christ's shield, is

> ichirche iset i swuch stude; þer me hit sonest seo. forte þenchen þer bi o iesu cristes cnihtschipe ꝥ he dude o rode. his leofmon bihalde þron hu he bohte hire luue. lette þurlín his scheld openín his side. to schawín hire his heorte. to schawin híre openliche hu inwardliche he luuede hire. 7 to ofdrahen hire heorte. (*AW* vii.200, f.106a. 24–9)

> set high in church in such a place where it is soonest seen, to bring to mind Jesus Christ's chivalry, which he performed on the cross. His beloved should see by it how he bought her love, letting his shield be pierced, his side opened to show her his heart, to show her openly how deeply he loved her, and to draw out her heart. (*S/W* 192)

The anchoress's meditation focuses on the suffering body of Christ, stretched on the cross with his arms outspread to embrace her. The only possible response to such suffering love is to love in return (*AW* vii.208, f.110a. 23–5 [*S/W* 197]).

That this love is not a passive love is made clear by the expansion of the passion meditation in *Wohunge*. Here, as in *Ancrene Wisse*, the focus is upon Christ's body which, as weapon and shield, is the means by which the battle is fought:

> Iesu swete iesu þus tu faht for me aȝaines mine sawle fan . þu me derennedes wið like . 7 makedes of me wrecche þi leofmon 7 spuse . Broht tu haues me fra þe world to bur of þi burðe . steked me i chaumbre . . . A swete iesu mi liues luue wið þi blod þu haues me boht . 7 fram þe world þu haues me broht . (*WLd* 35. 568–80)

> Jesus, sweet Jesus, in this way you fought for me against the enemies of my soul. You vindicated me with your body, and made of me, a wretch, your lover and spouse. You have brought me from the world to the bower of your birth, locked me in a chamber. . . . Ah, sweet Jesus, my life's love, with your blood you have bought me, and from the world you have brought me. (*S/W* 256)

As in *Ancrene Wisse*, the emphasis is on the response of the anchoress to Christ's love. The image of the piercing of the shield, the opening of Christ's side, as testimony to the depth of the love on which the anchoress meditates is enlarged as through the wound in Christ's side the anchoress 'reads' Christ's body as a love letter.

> A swete iesu þu oppnes me þin herte for to cnawe witerliche 7 in to redden trewe luue lettres . for þer i mai openliche seo hu muchel þu me luuedes . Wið wrange schuldi þe min heorte wearnen siðen ꝥ tu bohtes herte for herte . (*WLd* 35. 546–53)

> Ah! sweet Jesus, you open your heart to me, so that I may know it inwardly, and read inside it true love-letters; for there I may see openly how

much you loved me. Wrong would it be to refuse you my heart, since you have bought heart with heart. (S/W 255)

Once again, the only response to such suffering love is to love in return, completely, unstintingly, and eternally. The gift of her heart is inadequate, and so the anchoress offers her body to suffer with Christ's:

Mi bodi henge wið þi bodi neiled o rode . sperred querfaste wið inne fowr wahes 7 henge i wile wið þe 7 neauer mare of mi rode cume til þ i deie . For þenne schal i lepen fra rode in to reste . fra wa to wele 7 to eche blisse. (WLd 36. 590–97)

My body will hang with your body, nailed on the cross, fastened, trans-fixed within four walls. And I will hang with you and nevermore come from my cross until I die – for then shall I leap from the cross into rest, from grief into joy and eternal happiness. (S/W 256)

Here, the anchoress's response to Christ's suffering love is an active suffering depicted in terms of participation in Christ's crucifixion. So too, in *Ancrene Wisse*, part vi, which immediately precedes the parable of the lover-knight and in the light of which the parable must be read, the dominant symbol for the anchoress's enclosure is crucifixion. The anchoress's ascetic life is presented as active suffering through which she hangs on the cross with Christ, a crucifix-ion which is described as toil and labour. As Christ laboured on the cross, the anchoress labours in her cell, re-enacting the battle for the redemption of the world.

The end of the anchoress's suffering and toil is described in *Wohunge* with the introduction of the image of 'leaping' which dominates *Ancrene Wisse*, part ii. Here, however, instead of the light leap *into* the world, the anchoress antici-pates the joyful leap *out of* the world, as she leaps with Christ 'from the cross into rest, from grief into joy'. This is indeed not a passive image. In fact, this passage would challenge Robertson's assertion that 'unlike her male counter-part, the anchoress can never escape her body by climbing an allegorical ladder to God',[16] but can only wait passively to be redeemed. Instead, it would appear that the suffering body of the anchoress, when united with the suffer-ing body of Christ in the crucifixion of her enclosure, becomes the means by which the anchoress climbs on to the cross with Christ and ascends to God. And, in *Ancrene Wisse*, part vi, the shame and pain which characterize the anchoress's crucifixion with Christ are specifically identified with the allegori-cal ladder of Bernard which leads straight to heaven (*AW* vi.181–2; S/W 178–9).

It is clear, from the comparison of these two texts, that the role they offer to the female reader in her spiritual life is not simply a devout version of the passive lady of continental romance. The romance heroine is only active and, indeed, only present during the process of courtship, when she often acts as a

---

[16] Elizabeth Robertson, *Early English Devotional Prose*, 72.

means of upward social movement for the knight who woos her. Once her love is won, she marries and disappears from the scene, while her knight continues in his active role. In contrast, in *Ancrene Wisse* and *Wohunge* it is the noble wooer, Christ, who raises the anchoress to the status of his queen. But the anchoress is not thereby simply encouraged to transfer her love to a divine counterpart of the chivalric knight, who will sweep her off her feet and consign her to the oblivion of the romance lady who, once the wooing is over, is never heard from again.[17] Rather, both texts focus on the active response of the female anchoritic reader to the love of Christ enacted in the crucifixion, stressing the anchoress's role after the wooing, when her labour truly begins. Far from imprisoning the anchoress in an inferior spiritual role which is subordinated to a superior, intellectual male tradition, these texts allow for a feminine response to a masculine God, offering the anchoress a spirituality which she can (re)claim as her own.

---

[17] This point was made by Michael Peterson in 'Reconsidering Gender in Middle English Romance', a paper presented to the 19th Annual Symposium of the Ottawa-Carleton Medieval-Renaissance Club, 28 Mar. 1992.

REWRITING THE FALL: JULIAN OF NORWICH AND THE *CHEVALIER DES DAMES*

Helen Phillips

This paper concerns two passages, Julian of Norwich's parable of the lord and the servant (*The Revelation of Divine Love*, long version, ch. 51) and the allegory of the tree of men and women in the *Chevalier des Dames* (lines 1836–2651).[1] Both can be seen, in different ways, as women's rewritings of the Fall: Julian's is a rewriting *by* a woman writer and the *Chevalier* is a pro-feminist work, rewriting the Fall *for* women. It is a plea for the equality of the sexes and the essential holiness of sexual love. Though very different, the two passages use similar strategies, with similar effect: both passages dislodge traditional ideas of culpability for Original Sin, both remove or de-emphasise Eve, and both read back retrospectively onto an image of our first parent(s) a figure of re-deemed humanity. Most crucially of all, both narratives play with two kinds of time, instantive and continual: they depict the instant when sin happened, when primordial innocence turned into sin, as an event which is contained within a larger, continuing event.[2] For Julian the continuing event is God's unceasing tender beholding; in the *Chevalier* it is the flowers which remain continually on the tree of men and women.

It is interesting that these two versions of the Fall that de-emphasize culpa-bility for sin should have been written by a woman and for women, for it was a particularly problematic issue for medieval women. The problems medieval feminists faced differed from those addressed by modern feminists.[3] In par-ticular, they faced the issue of woman's moral status and dignity. Eve's special culpability for Original Sin, and the ensuing miseries in the world, was a

---

[1] Julian of Norwich, *A Revelation of Love*, ed. M. Glasscoe (Exeter, 1976); *Le Chevalier des dames du Dolant Fortuné: allégorie en vers de la fin du XVe siècle*, ed. J. Miquet (Ottawa, 1990).

[2] Though the narratives talk of instantive events and continuous events, these stand, of course, for temporal events and eternal events.

[3] The name of feminist has sometimes been denied Christine de Pizan because her concerns are not identical with those of 19th- and 20th-century feminism: e.g. L. M. Richardson, *The Forerunners of Feminism in French Literature of the Renaissance*, Pt. I, Studies in Romance Lit-eratures and Languages 12 (Baltimore, 1929), 12–34; S. Delany, 'Mothers to Think Back Through: Who are They? The Ambiguous Example of Christine de Pizan', in *Medieval Texts and Contemporary Readers*, ed. Laurie Finke and Martin Shichtman (Ithaca, NY, 1987), 77–97.

favourite *topos* of anti-feminist rhetoric. It is often the first attack trotted out: one clearly felt to be a strong card.[4]

The Parable of the Lord and the Servant

Julian's parable of the lord and servant, like her use of the theme of God as mother, is part of her wider theology: each may owe something to the fact that she was a woman and they are images benign to women. But they are also images benign to humanity in general. They arise, above all, from her vision of God's benign vision: he sees that 'Althyng shal be wele.'[5] It is central to Julian's theology that God has a way of looking that is also loving (it is, among other things, a mother-like way of looking). It is in this divine beholding that he sees the 'godly wil that never assentid to synne ne never shal'.[6] Julian's transformation of the Fall involves looking at it from the point of view of God's mercy, not humanity's guilt.

In chapters 50 and 51, Julian is puzzling over the paradox that, although she and the 'common techyng of holy church' know that humanity sins and that blame 'continuly hangith upon us', from the first man on, yet God does not show blame towards humanity.[7] In her parable, the servant runs out, eager to do his lord's bidding. He falls into a slade and cannot rise.[8]

Here is the first point which will have its analogue in the *Chevalier* passage: sin is presented as an impersonal place, not an act of will by the servant. Sin is pain which befalls him. He suffers seven pains, rather than the traditional seven deadly sins. They involve separation from God, blindness to God's love, enfeeblement, and blindness to what the servant himself is in God's sight (elsewhere Julian says she cannot *see* sin, only the trace it leaves, in pain and harm[9]). His worst pain is that he cannot see God.[10]

The second point is that Julian ignores Eve: this servant is 'Adam' and 'all man',[11] male and female (additionally, as Ritamary Bradley observes, in her treatment of Mary Julian ignores her role as Second Eve[12]). There is no Eve in the scene of the fall into the slade, though later, when the image of the Second

---

4 E.g. *Champion des Dames*, ii, where Eve is the first attack offered by Malebouche's second fighter, Vilain Penser, 4361–528.
5 *Revelation*, ch. 32, p. 33.
6 *Revelation*, ch. 37, p. 38.
7 *Revelation*, ch. 51, p. 53.
8 *Revelation*, ch. 51, p. 54.
9 *Revelation*, ch. 27, p. 29.
10 *Revelation*, ch. 51, pp. 54–55.
11 *Revelation*, ch. 51, p. 58.
12 Ritamary Bradley, *Julian's Way: A Practical Commentary on Julian of Norwich* (New York, 1992), 83; in view of the importance Julian's argument gives to the contrast between the whole and the part, it is interesting that Ritamary Bradley writes of Julian's Mary as 'the Fullness of Creation', 84–7. The dual vision of Mary, at the Crucifixion and glorified in heaven, is one of several dual visions which correspond to the 'two manners of beholding'.

Adam is superimposed upon it, Julian describes the fall into the slade in terms of Christ's fall into the womb of 'the fairest dauter of Adam'.[13]

The third point is that Julian reads back onto the figure of the fallen servant the figure of the incarnate servant. When we first read, the fall is Adam's Fall; gradually it becomes also Christ's 'leap' into Mary's womb. The *Chevalier*, too, will superimpose a figure of redeemed humanity, Mary, onto an image of creation and fallen humanity, the tree and its dark well. Both Julian and the *Chevalier* fuse an image of humanity falling, at one instance in time, with an eternal image of the lasting goodness of humanity and its continual closeness with God.

In chapter 51 the element in the narrative that symbolizes that eternal perspective is the continual gaze of the lord: at the start of events, 'The lord sittith solemly in rest and in peace . . . The lord lookith upon his servant ful lovely and swetely'.[14] There follows the incident in which the servant falls, but the narrative insists that all the time the lord has been continuing to look with love: 'And ryth thus continualy his lovand lord ful tenderly beholdyth him; and now with a double cher'.[15] For Julian the revelation of the special kind of continual looking on the part of God is the key to her understanding of sin.

The parable of the servant is an instance of Julian's doctrine that there are 'two manner of beholding': the beholding of God and the beholding of man.[16] God's beholding is one of love: man is always loved and always has a godly will which never assents to sin. This beholding is the wholeness of God, the great vision. Man's limited vision, in contrast, is a vision only of the part. Sin and blindness are parts. (In the parable of the lord and servant, the event of the fall is presented as only a part, whereas the continual gaze of the lord is the whole, and surrounds it.) The imagery of the part and the whole, and of humanity 'beclosyd', enclosed, within God's mercy, is as important an element in Julian's pattern of ideas as is her manipulation of the 'continual' and the instant: she expresses the same principle through spatial imagery and through temporal imagery.

This concept of God's manner of seeing is central to Julian's theology. Normally one thinks of a way of seeing as secondary to what is seen: secondary to the content; but when Julian presents God's seeing as loving, the seeing is the content itself. God's love is what we fail to see with our human sight. The parable of the servant is based on these ideas: the two kinds of seeing, on the concepts of the part and the whole, and on a contrast of time and eternity. God's manner of seeing actually makes what seems sin to human eyes into a matter of compassion and even rejoicing. The 'double cher', double vision,

---

[13] *Revelation*, ch. 51, p. 58. On the theme of the Leaps of Christ, see T. D. Hill, ' "Mary the Rosebush" and the Leaps of Christ', *English Studies*, 67, no. 6 (1986), 478–82.

[14] *Revelation*, ch. 51, p. 54.

[15] *Revelation*, ch. 51, p. 55.

[16] *Revelation*, ch. 46, p. 49: 'I had ii manner of beholdyng: that one was endless continuant love with sekirnes of kepyng and blisful salvation' (note the use of 'continuant' here).

with which God observes the Fall into the slade is firstly one of compassion but secondly one of rejoicing, for he transforms the fallen servant into Christ.

Le Chevalier des Dames

Before looking at parallels between the two writers' handling of the Fall, it is necessary to introduce the *Chevalier*. It is an anonymous defence of women, composed between about 1460 and 1477, one of a group of pro-feminist writings inspired by the Querelle de la Rose and Christine de Pizan, which includes Martin le Franc's *Champion des Dames*,[17] It is also one of the late medieval works which takes elements from the Courtly Love tradition, or more specifically, the *Roman de la Rose*, and turns them on their head to serve a chaster purpose: thus Deguilleville reformulates the *Roman de la Rose*, Christine's *L'Epitre de Dieu d'Amours* and Chaucer's *Legend of Good Women* make Cupid the defender of women, le Franc even calls the god Amours the Holy Ghost.[18] The *Chevalier* takes Nature, another figure from the *Roman de la Rose* who had been perceived as promoting sensuality, and makes her into a colleague of the Virgin Mary: together they preside as tutelary deities over the high-minded love of the *Champion*'s two young people, Noble Coeur and Noblesse Feminine.[19] The *Chevalier* is built on sophisticated literary allusion: it is a revision of topics from de Meun's *Roman*, a rewriting of the Genesis story of the Fall, and also, in its opening, reminiscent of Boethius.[20] It is a dream poem, delicate and amusing, its hero a knight errant looking for a cause: Noble Coeur, who sets out to defend Noblesse Feminine from her enemies, Malebouche and Coeur Vilain. The poet reformulates fairy-tale and romance motifs: a giant, an island of maidens, a magic white animal who carries the hero to a wondrous place, a narrator who is rendered magically invisible, a challenge issued by a dwarf under a *sicanor* tree, and so on. He makes them all keep their traditional charm, but he also uses them to explore more serious, adult issues, which include narratological complexities as well as feminist, and associated theological, ideas. It is, all in all, a somewhat Narnia-like literary method.

Its view of women's oppression is robust and intelligent; its view of sexual love is high-minded and optimistic. Whereas even in the *Champion des Dames*

---

[17] On the date see *Chevalier*, 8; on the Querelle and the *Champion* see Eric Hicks, *Le débat sur le Roman de la Rose* (Paris, 1972). *Le Champion des Dames*, Pt. I, ed. Arthur Piaget (Lausanne, 1968); the rest of the work remains unedited.

[18] *Champion*, lines 3753–3800. Earlier, Franc Vouloir, the champion of ladies, has replied to Malebouche's advocate's accusation that Amours is Antichrist, in a long declaration about the true nature of Amours, who is the power that governs the cosmos, under the Creator.

[19] In the *Champion*, it is Amours, ably assisted by Lady Reason, who send the Champion off on his errand.

[20] This link is most obvious when the narrator-dreamer, lamenting the blows of Fortune against him, hears a voice which tells him to dry his tears, look up and attend to teaching which will confort him (1–56).

there is much emphasis on the dangers of passion and the need for Franc
Vouloir to keep his steed, Ardant Desir, under control, the *Chevalier* paints an
idyllic picture of idealistic and virtuous young love. Noble Coeur and
Noblesse Feminine are Man and Woman; the first part of the dream is about
their natural impulse to seek each other out. The knight is told by Nature that
the name of the one he seeks is Noblesse Feminine. She is 'franche, nayve,
nette et pure', the pristine, innocent woman, fresh from the hand of God; she is
'Le Paradis d'un vray amant'. She too recognizes him and greets him in a
hymn of praise beginning 'Ha, noble coeur, digne trésor' (872–904). The text
accords him the conventional hero's qualities of valour and courteousness, but
also an untainted human purity and dignity, 'une clarté eslevant . . . dignité
imparfondée' (885–6). He responds with his own hymn of adoration (905–28).
They may be only personifications, but there is something genuinely touching
about their idealism and ardour. The female authority-figures are brisk with
the young man: why doesn't he accord women more sense? They don't have
their hearts in their knees! Noblesse Feminine protests about the effects of
Malebouche on women's lives: if a woman happens to glance at a man people
will say she lusts after him; young women dare not laugh, sing, show pleasure
or even do good to their fellow-men, for fear of slander. Coeur Vilain is trying
to dislodge woman from the throne in the world where God has placed her.
His methods are of the most stupid kind: the claim that all women are like Eve,
and are more culpable than men, liable to bring whole nations to disaster. His
books have influenced many men of little intelligence: the sort who are readier
to believe what they read in books than what they know from experience of
women.

The *Chevalier* keeps insisting on the individuality of humans: they vary in
virtue because of inborn personality and environment and this applies to men
as well as women. Evil, whether found in women or in men (for example in
misogynists) is a property of the individual, not of the sex. Throughout the
work there are traces of a sense that the social dimensions of women's oppression are an important part of the issue: Nature and Noblesse Feminine
allude to the curbs on women's freedom – even to do good. More than once
people's environment and circumstances are blamed for their behaviour: environment and upbringing are prime causes of sin (2600–51), and Nature, speaking specifically of the evil of misogyny, says that people alter according to their
circumstances and generally in life the bad oppress the good (1692–9).
Oppression of women is made part of the world of Fortune, the instability of
worldly happiness. This is a work which approaches antifeminism from a
variety of assumptions about morality: Christian, Boethian, and even – we
might say – embryonically sociological, but expressed with a lightness and
flexibility which gives the arguments an air of common-sense.

The Allegory of the Tree

In the allegory of the Tree, the *Chevalier*'s rewriting of the Fall, Nature shows
Noble Coeur and Noblesse Feminine a wondrous tree, with two equal
branches, covered with flowers, which represent all the men and women who
have ever existed. Each flower is lit by its star. The right-hand branch (the
branch of men) leans constantly towards the left branch (women) which is
surmounted by a great fleur-de-lis piercing heaven, and wreathed by stars: the
Virgin Mary. The right hand branch is often bedewed by dew from the left-
hand branch's flowers: the two branches need each other and cannot exist
without each other. Below the tree is a fountain; four exits carry its water to the
four corners of the earth, and the seeds of the flowers fall into the water, which
is dark, warm and troubled. It is the womb of the mother, troubled because
here the seeds receive the taint of Original Sin. Seeds are nourished here for
nine months by Nature, then leave.

Clearly this complex image is one both of human reproduction and of a kind
of garden of Eden. But it is an innocent tree: neither women nor sex are sources
of evil. Indeed, the traditional images of Original Sin are associated with
Malebouche and Coeur Vilain; they are removed from woman and sex. The
blight upon mankind and the earth which was attributed by antifeminists to
Eve is here blamed on woman's detractors themselves:

> L'air est infait et corrumpu,
> Arbres, fruiz, herbes se perissent;
> Le firmament est desrompu,
> Bestes, oiseaux, tous se gemissent;
> Les poissons des rivieres yssent
> Le souleil devient noir et vain;
> Et toutes choses s'amandrissent
> Par le venin de Cuer Villain. (1796–1903)

> The air is infected and corrupted, trees, fruits and plants die; the
> firmament is disturbed, animals and birds mourn; fish leave the
> rivers, the sun grows dark and weak; and all things are injured by
> Coeur Villain's poison.

The 'puant vermine' and 'faulx rebelle' must be destroyed, and women and
girls saved from the 'dragon enragé' (1811–24).

Nature explains that Adam and Eve, who were once a single body, are the
tree's root out of which the tree grows. Its two sexes are equal:

> Sont d'un estre, d'une substance,
> Et d'une mesmes dignité,
> Sans quelconque difformité,
> Fors sans plus une accidentale:
> Que l'une est femme et l'autre male. (2059–63)

> They are of one essence, one substance, and of identical dignity,

154

without any difference in form apart from the one non-essential
attribute that one is woman and the other male.

Men and women are born from one apple, one liquid, one matter. There are
differences in strength, intelligence, virtue and personality, but these are between individuals; there are no significant differences between the sexes, except
that God has made the left branch softer 'pour sa plus grant perffection' (2136).
Men can be as malevolent or frail as women; if there are male philosophers,
sages and prophets, who teach the faith, there are also female prophetesses
and wise visionaries, whose statements have sometimes seemed to surpass
mere human knowledge (2468–77). The flowers are all the human beings who
have ever existed; their flowers remain continually on the tree, until at the end
of time God will inspect them, and those which have become spoiled will be
pulled off and die and the pure ones will remain, in even greater beauty. Their
seeds, whether of men or woman, fall into the water and become human fruit
'of very diverse qualities and of identical equality' (2156–7).

There are a number of parallels between Julian's parable and the *Chevalier*,
for all its radical differences in genre, decade, language and tone. Firstly, no
special blame or inferiority is imputed to the female (and indeed, visually the
female is given prominence here: the male branch turns continually towards
the female, and the female branch bears a spectacular flower, the fleur de lys,
which towers towards heaven; throughout the work female figures have authority). Male and female are presented as equal, but the female comes across as
more equal. As in Julian's parable, the Fall is literally a fall: here the flowers,
whether male or female, fall into the fountain of troubled waters. The design of
the narrative divides and thus dissipates the potential problems in the Genesis
story. The visual argument splits the female here in two: on one hand, the
womb where the taint of Original Sin is received is 'la mere', but, on the other
hand, into it fall equally male and female flowers. Responsibility does not lie
with any of these flowers. Sin is represented as a place, a pit into which
innocent beings fall (like Julian's slade). Thirdly, like Julian, the *Chevalier* creates a scene in which a figure of redeemed humanity (the flower of Mary) is
read backwards onto the depiction of the Fall. We do meet the accusation
against Eve here, but only in the context of Mary (2240–88).

The author uses the tree, an item from the Eden story usually associated
with sin, then draws on its potentiality for other, more positive images to erase
that association, just as Julian turns the digging, which originally represents
Adam's punishment for sin, into the positive image of Christ the gardener. The
flowers, like the continual loving gaze of God in Julian's parable, remain on
the tree, even though seeds from them fall into the world. The poet thus splits
up the causes of sin and lessens their impact. The causes of sin are depicted as
three agencies which *afflict* people, not acts they themselves *will*. First, Original
Sin is there in the dark water, and each human being is stained at conception
with this; secondly, the stars and, thirdly, upbringing can influence characters,
but wisdom and a good environment can create good characters.

The *Chevalier* allegory reads back Mary into the prelapsarian scene; she is there in the original good Creation. So Creation and Redemption coalesce, as the unchanging flowers on the tree. As in Julian, the essential goodness and glory of humanity remains visible in the allegory: the flowers remain glorious on the tree even while temporarily the seeds descend into the water and go out into the world. Both narratives keep humanity close to God. Although we have noticed the similarities between these two rewritings of the myth of the Fall, there are also significant differences. The *Chevalier*'s narrative concentrates on Creation; it is a myth about origins. It is concerned with the nature of woman, the essential innocence of sexual love, the reasons why individuals differ in their fates and personalities. In as far as the myths about Original Sin are relevant to these concerns, it rewrites them, but there is no interest beyond that point in the nature of human sin or the processes of grace – apart, that is, from the particular crimes of misogynists. Although its rewriting of the Fall is designed to deflect responsibility for sin away from either Adam or Eve, it is content to represent sin as a real stain, which can lead to eternal destruction, whereas Julian continues to hold in paradoxical debate to the end of her chapter 51 (and beyond) the dual proposition that man and God necessarily see sin differently: 'for otherwise is the beholdyng of God, and otherwise is the beholdyng of man; for it longyth to man mekely to accusen hymselfe, and it longyth to the proper goodnes of God curtesly to excusen man'. For Julian, the Eden myth of the Fall is transformed into a myth of Redemption, whereas the *Chevalier* poet keeps it a myth about Creation. That difference directly reflects the ultimate interests of the two works: Julian is, above all, concerned to try to understand the nature of God, whereas the *Chevalier des Dames* is concerned primarily with the nature of women.

LITERACY AND THE GENDER GAP
IN THE LATE MIDDLE AGES:
WOMEN AND READING IN LOLLARD COMMUNITIES[1]

Shannon McSheffrey

Many students of English history and literature see the late Middle Ages, especially the fifteenth century, as a period of steadily rising literacy. Feminism has inspired scholars to examine the place of women in this new lay literate culture, especially women's experience of reading and writing, but they have paid little attention to investigating women's opportunities to learn to read. Most work on medieval reading depends upon evidence about implicit and explicit readers of texts and books, a method which naturally concentrates on those who owned books and were literate. But it is also necessary to approach the question of literacy from the other side – who among medieval people read the medieval books which survive? Uncovering who was able to read in the Middle Ages is a notoriously difficult exercise, given the limited evidence, but it is essential to the enterprise of investigating late-medieval reading.

The importance of thinking more about exactly who were the readers in late-medieval English society is highlighted when we consider that historians like David Cressy and L. R. Poos, studying the documentary evidence for literacy in England, have emphasized how rare the ability to read was.[2] Systemic barriers running along both socio-economic and gender lines excluded the majority of the late-medieval population from direct access to the written word. Cressy's and Poos' work has served to emphasize social and economic differences in opportunities for acquiring reading ability. In this essay I hope to underscore the gender gap in late-medieval literacy. While many scholars have argued that women participated fully in advances in lay literacy,[3] a study of surviving evidence for women's reading in fifteenth-

[1] I would like to thank those who commented on this paper (both at the conference and in written form), especially Judith Bennett, Anne Hudson, Eric Reiter and Robert Tittler.

[2] David Cressy, *Literacy and the Social Order: Reading and Writing in Tudor and Stuart England* (Cambridge, 1980); L. R. Poos, *A Rural Society after the Black Death: Essex 1350–1525* (Cambridge, 1991), 280–7.

[3] Herbert Grundmann's pioneering work on the question of women and literacy hypothesized that in Germany literacy in the vernacular was much more common in laywomen than in laymen (his examples coming from the upper sector of society). 'Die Frauen und die

century sources shows that literacy was much less common among women than among men.

This question is brought into relief by an examination of the place of literacy among a group of late-medieval English people who were unusually interested in reading: the Lollards.[4] This heretical sect, made up primarily of artisan families with a few adherents of somewhat higher station, was active from about the 1380s to the 1530s in the southern half of England. Lollard communities were, in Brian Stock's terms, textual communities, groups whose activities are formed around texts and their interpretation.[5] In their gatherings or conventicles, Lollards heard sermons, read to one another and discussed their ideas. Literacy, the ability to convey the written word to the group from a sermon or other text, was clearly an important skill in a book-centred sect like Lollardy. As Stock notes, illiteracy did not prevent access to a text; others could relay the information it provided. But the purveyors of this information were in a position of power.[6] Margaret Aston argues persuasively that those who were literate were most influential in Lollard communities,[7] and important members of the movement were often described as 'principal readers or instructors'.[8] Literacy was a significant factor in attraction to and participation in the movement, especially in the conventicles, although the role the illiterate could play in a textual culture is an important question, and will be addressed below. Aston and Anne Hudson have pursued different aspects of literacy in the Lollard movement; here I would like to explore Lollard literacy with particular attention to gender difference.

Before proceeding, some discussion of the meaning of literacy is needed. Literacy levels clearly ranged along a broad spectrum in which reading and writing, vernacular and Latin were variables. Even using the most elementary definition of literacy, that of reading in the vernacular, does not avoid the

---

Literatur im Mittelalter', *Archiv für Kulturgeschichte*, 26 (1935), 129–61, esp. 133. Others have posited women's equality rather than primacy in lay literacy. Diana M. Webb, for instance, has said that 'clearly women participated fully in the development of lay literacy': 'Woman and Home: The Domestic Setting of Late Medieval Spirituality', *Studies in Church History*, 27 (1990), 172. M. T. Clanchy's influential *From Memory to Written Record: England, 1066–1307* (London, 1979), 188, argues that women's literacy was not dependent on their gender but on their class. See also Kay E. Lacey, 'Women and Work in Fourteenth and Fifteenth Century London', in *Women and Work in Pre-Industrial England*, ed. Lindsey Charles and Lorna Duffin (London, 1985), 24; Suzanne W. Hull, *Chaste, Silent and Obedient: English Books for Women, 1475–1640* (San Marino, CA, 1982), 2–6, 127.

[4] The standard work on Lollardy is Anne Hudson, *The Premature Reformation: Wycliffite Texts and Lollard History* (Oxford, 1988). See also my *Gender and Heresy: Women, Men, and the Lollard Movement, 1420–1530*, forthcoming from the University of Pennsylvania Press.

[5] Brian Stock, *The Implications of Literacy: Written Language and Models of Interpretation in the Eleventh and Twelfth Centuries* (Princeton, 1983), esp. 3–12, 88–150, 522–3.

[6] Stock, *Implications of Literacy*, 6–8. See also Franz H. Bäuml, 'Varieties and Consequences of Medieval Literacy and Illiteracy', *Speculum*, 55 (1980), 237–65.

[7] Margaret Aston, *Lollards and Reformers: Images and Literacy in Late Medieval Religion* (London, 1984), 206; see also Hudson, *Premature Reformation*, 185–7.

[8] For instance, John Foxe, *Acts and Monuments*, ed. George Townsend (London, 1843), iv, 214.

problem of how well a person could read. Designations of literacy in some cases can be tricky at this distant remove, and were no doubt confusing even at the time. Reading was not necessarily easy to learn in the late Middle Ages, particularly for adults, and some Lollards may have been stymied in a position of semi-literacy where, despite attempts to learn, they were unable to decipher the words on the page with any facility. Robert Benet of London's story illustrates different notions of what it meant to be literate. Thomas Walker, also of London, alleged in 1511 that Benet had read a chapter of the gospel of John to him, but Benet himself testified that he was illiterate. He had, he admitted, bought a small book of the 4 gospels from a stationer named Thomas Capon with the object of learning to read it. But he was unable to decipher it and finally put it away, keeping it locked up in his chest for four years. Finally Capon the stationer himself came to live with Benet and read the book to him, explaining its contents. After Capon died, Benet sold the book (it being again of little use) to Thomas Austy for 'a horse lode of hay'.[9] Benet may indeed have been lying about his literacy, although his motive must be questioned: while others probably attempted to conceal their literacy since it was evidence for heresy,[10] he had already admitted ownership of Lollard books, an equally grave sign of Lollardy. It seems more likely that his literacy had not reached the level where he could effectively read and understand his books – the chapter of John he 'read' to Walker may have been memorized. The evidence for Lollard literacy is by no means complete, but unlike some other data (signatures, for instance) it has the advantage of measuring a basic and pragmatic definition of literacy: the ability to read an English book and understand it.

Two aspects of Lollard evidence for reading are particularly striking. First, many of those involved in investigations against the sect – judges, deponents, and the accused themselves – regarded literacy as evidence for adherence to the heresy. Literacy was apparently so unusual among the socio-economic groups which comprised the Lollard sect that many assumed that reading ability could only have been acquired in heretical circles. Second, there was a significant gender gap in Lollard literacy. Evidence for literacy among women Lollards is exceedingly rare; evidence for Lollard men's ability to read survives much more frequently, though the records do not portray them by any means as usually literate. These data indicate that among the middling economic groups represented in Lollard communities literacy among men was relatively uncommon, and that systemic barriers to women's literacy were so high that even in the Lollard sect where reading was highly prized women were only rarely able to learn to read.

I have investigated the records for all the sizeable communities of Lollards uncovered during the period for which we have best evidence, from the 1420s to 1530. The communities encompassed altogether about 1,000 Lollards, a little

---

9   TCD MS 775, ff. 123v–124r.
10   See n. 11.

over one quarter of whom were women. In discussing literacy rates, I wish to emphasize the comparison between men and women rather than the raw numbers, which are admittedly almost certainly underestimations, as they rely on witnesses reporting the literacy of other Lollards. But it also must be said that these reports are by no means arbitrary. The prosecutors of the sect and the deponents themselves both attached a good deal of significance to the fact that an accused person could read, and officials often actively solicited this information.[11] There is no reason to think that the rate of reporting would have been significantly higher for men than for women and, indeed, the rarity of literate women generally might have increased the likelihood that witnesses would remark a heretical woman's ability to read.

The evidence for literacy among the Lollards reveals that only seven women Lollards out of approximately 270 can be positively identified as literate. Remarkably, five of these seven were part of the same heretical circle, in the city of Coventry, while the other two came from Norfolk and London. The only fifteenth-century example of female literacy is the unnamed daughter of Hawise and Thomas Mone of Loddon, Norfolk, of the group of East Anglian heretics prosecuted by the bishop of Norwich in the 1420s.[12] Among the shadowy London heretical community,[13] one woman accused of Lollardy in 1509, Elizabeth Sampson, could read. According to one of her husband's apprentices, she

> had two English books, one large and one small, and he said that he saw Elizabeth very often looking in these books and reading them, but what was in these books, he did not know. But he said that a certain Richard Elwod intimated to him that the small one was the four gospels.[14]

The remaining evidence for female literacy all comes from the early-sixteenth-century Lollard community in Coventry. The Coventry community

---

[11] Given the frequency with which literacy was mentioned in depositions, it is clear that the court often made enquiries about it and that deponents considered it evidence for heresy. Some attempted to deny their literacy: Juliana Yong, for instance, denied that she could read until she was confronted by another witness who maintained that she could. Lichfield Joint Record Office, MS B/C/13 (hereafter Lichfield Court Book), ff. 14r, 3v, 8v. John Pert and Richard Fleccher of Norfolk also claimed they could not read, although other evidence indicated that they could: *Heresy Trials in the Diocese of Norwich, 1428–31*, ed. Norman P. Tanner, Camden Soc. (4th ser.), 20 (1977), 85, 169; *Acts and Monuments*, iii, 596–7. See also John Martin, 'Popular Culture and the Shaping of Popular Heresy in Renaissance Venice', in *Inquisition and Society in Early Modern Europe*, ed. Stephen Haliczer (Totawa, NJ, 1987), 122.

[12] *Acts and Monuments*, iii, 597.

[13] Elizabeth Bate of London, probably not a Lollard, may also have been literate. See TCD MS 775, ff. 122v–123r.

[14] 'Item dicit quod dicta Elisabeth habuit duos libros in Anglico, unum magnum et alium minorem, et dicit quod vidit antefatam Elisabeth saepius inspicientem in illis libris et legentem super eisdem, sed quid continebatur in illis libris nescit deponere. Sed dicit quod quidam Richardus Elwod intimavit et dixit huic jurato quod minor liber erat de 4or Evangelistis.' TCD MS 775, f. 122v.

was uniquely supportive for women, which probably encouraged female literacy as women taught and read to one other. The wife of Villers, for instance, sat in the house of Roger Landesdale for six hours one afternoon reading to her daughter Thomasina from a certain large book.[15] She may have been teaching her daughter to read: William Lodge testified seven years later that Thomasina herself, by this time the wife of Richard Bradley, was literate.[16] Agnes Jonson, according to another woman, 'knew best how to read'.[17] Alice Rowley, in an unparalleled role in the Lollard sect, often read publicly before men.[18] She also taught Juliana Yong, but soon the pupil overtook the teacher: Robert Silkby said that when Alice Rowley read, Juliana Yong corrected her and continued reading herself.[19]

Of the seven literate Lollard women, three at least probably acquired literacy while young,[20] when it was easier to learn. And at least four of the seven (the Mone daughter, Thomasina Bradley, Juliana Yong and Alice Rowley) – and conceivably all seven of them – learned to read in Lollard circles rather than bringing that skill with them into the community.

In addition to the seven women who are positively identified as literate, the evidence about two women described as reading with their husbands is somewhat less clear. Andrew Randall and his wife of Rickmansworth were considered to be Lollards for harbouring a Lollard fugitive and for 'reading Wickliff's Wicket'.[21] Did both read, or did Andrew Randall read to his wife? Similarly, Thomas Spencer of London, 'with his wife', read a book of the Gospels which he had been lent.[22] In neither case is it clear that the wife was actively reading rather than listening to her husband. None the less, we will add the wives of Andrew Randall and Thomas Spencer to our list of literate women, bringing the total to nine.

No women in other Lollard communities can be identified as literate. Even the gentlewoman Lollard, Alice Cottismore of Brightwell, whose social status made literacy much more likely than among Lollard women of lower station, was unable to read. She owned many books, but when she wanted to show her servant what they said, she had to call upon the local parson, John Booth, to read them for her.[23]

---

[15] Lichfield Court Book, f. 11v.

[16] 'Uxor eiusdem Bradeley scit bene legere.' Lichfield Court Book, f. 11r.

[17] 'optime novit legere.' Lichfield Court Book, f. 14v; see also f. 21r.

[18] Lichfield Court Book, ff. 2r, 7r, 8r, 14r.

[19] 'Legente Alicia Rowley, filia dicte Agnetis [Yong] eam correxit et legit continuo.' Lichfield Court Book, ff. 3v, 8v.

[20] The age of the daughter of Hawise and Thomas Mone is unknown, but she was apparently a child; Juliana Yong was twenty years old; the age of Thomasina Bradley is not recorded, but judging by her husband's age in 1511 (33) she was probably either in her teens or twenties in 1502 when she read with her mother. *Acts and Monuments*, iii, 597; Lichfield Court Book, ff. 14r, 10r, 11v.

[21] *Acts and Monuments*, iv, 226.

[22] *Acts and Monuments*, iv, 226, 233.

[23] *Acts and Monuments*, iv, 582.

Dependence on explicit description of literacy produces a female literacy rate of 9 out of 271. This in itself admittedly tells us little, considering the nature of the sources. But when we compare it with the same type of evidence for men, explicit reports of ability to read, the difference is remarkable. According to depositions and abjurations about one-fifth of all Lollard men could read – 113 men (as compared to 9 women) were positively identified as literate.[24] A significant gender gap in evidence for Lollard literacy thus emerges: the records say that about one in 33 women could read, whereas about one in 5 men could. Lollard men were about seven times more likely to learn to read than Lollard women.

What did it mean to be literate or illiterate in a Lollard community? The gender gap in Lollard literacy did not mean that women – or illiterate men, for that matter, still probably the majority of male Lollards – were completely cut off from the literate culture of the heretical sect. Women and men of all social stations, orthodox or heterodox, surely knew what books were, and they were certainly familiar with the numerous pieces of writing posted in public places by the royal government and other agencies. Reading was a vocal, often co-operative activity; those who could read shared their knowledge.[25] Yet the illiterate – almost all women and a large proportion of men – were cut off from the ability to participate directly in written culture, Lollard or Catholic.

Lollard activities revolving around reading provide interesting evidence about the participation of the illiterate and semi-literate in a textual culture. Both men and women, those who could read and those who could not, had access to Lollard writings through the reading of others. In some cases,

---

[24] 113 of 683, or 17%. When members of the clergy not explicitly described as literate are added, the rate climbs to 20% (134 of 683). These numbers do not include ambiguous implications of literacy to large groups; for instance, Roger Dodds noted that Thomas Baker, Robert Livord, John Sympson, Thomas Reiley, John Clemson, James Edmunds, William Gun and John Harris used to gather together to read (*Acts and Monuments*, iv, 237). The only man in this group who is described elsewhere as literate is Roger Dodds himself. All may have been literate, or none but Dodds; for the sake of this calculation, the latter is assumed in order not to inflate unduly male literacy figures.

For male literacy, see *Acts and Monuments*, iii, 585–7, 596–7; iv, 124, 177–8, 180, 207, 214, 217, 221, 226–37, 239, 580, 583–84, 688; *Letters and Papers, Foreign and Domestic, of the Reign of Henry VIII*, ed. J. S. Brewer et al., 21 vols. and Addenda (London, 1862–1932), iv(2), nos. 4029, 4218, 4545, xiii(2), p. 253; John Strype, *Ecclesiastical Memorials . . . under King Henry VIII, King Edward VI, and Queen Mary I*, 3 vols. (Oxford, 1822), i(1), 117, i(2), 56, 62, iii, 53–4, 62; *Heresy Trials*, 38, 47–8, 60, 64, 79, 85, 94; *Fasciculi zizaniorum Magistri Johannis Wyclif cum tritico*, ed. W. W. Shirley, Rolls Series (London, 1858), 423–4; Lincoln, Lincolnshire Archives Office, Episcopal Register XX (Register of John Chedworth), ff. 57v, 61r, 62r; Trowbridge, Wiltshire Record Office [hereafter Wilts.R.O.], Reg. Langton, ff. 35r, 36r, 38v; Wilts. R.O., Reg. Audley, ff. 107v–108v, 144r–144v, 149v, 158v; Winchester, Hampshire Record Office [hereafter H.R.O.], MS A1/20 (Register of Richard Fox, vol. iv), f. 18r; H.R.O. MS A1/16 (Register of Thomas Langton), f. 66r; London, Lambeth Palace Library, Reg. Warham, vol. i, ff. 169v, 171r, 174v; Lichfield Joint Record Office, MS B/A/1/12 (Register of John Hales), f. 166v; Lichfield Court Book, ff. 1v, 2r, 3r, 5r, 5v, 7r, 8v, 15r, 19r, 20r, 24v; TCD MS 775, ff. 122v, 123r–124v, 125r; William Hale, *A Series of Precedents and Proceedings in Criminal Causes, 1475–1640* (London, 1847), 54–5.

[25] Aston, *Lollards and Reformers*, 106–8, 194–5.

illiterate Lollards showed great awareness of texts and the written word, despite their inability to read. Thomas Boughton, an illiterate woolwinder and shoemaker of Hungerford, who appeared before Bishop John Blythe of Salisbury in 1499, confessed that he:

> had a great mynde to here sermouns and prechynges of doctours and lerned men of the church. And as long as they spack the veray wordys of the gospels and epistles such as I had herd afore in our englissh bookys, I herkned wele unto them and had great delight to here them. But assone as they began to declare scripture after their doctouris and brought in other maters and spack of tythes and offrynges, I was sone wery to here them and had no favour in their wordys.[26]

For Thomas Boughton and perhaps for most other fifteenth-century laypeople, books were heard rather than read. None the less, although he could not himself read, Boughton was sophisticated enough to distinguish between the different texts a preacher used to prepare his sermons.

Books were often passed around from person to person (women as well as men) as a way of spreading the Lollard word. As the example of Dame Alice Cottismore shows, not all who possessed books, temporarily or permanently, could read: illiterate men and women who had books arranged for others to read the contents to them. Thomas Abell of Coventry, who received a book from Joan Warde, was unable to read it and inquired about having someone come and read it to him.[27] Joan Smyth borrowed 'a certain book of the passion of Christ and Adam'[28] from Master Longland for three weeks, and Roger Landesdale came to read it to her in her house. Robert Benet, who sold his books for a horse-load of hay, apparently found his books useless unless someone was able to read them to him.

Men were more likely to have custody of books, but women were by no means excluded. Some of the Coventry women, especially those who were literate, were active in the book trade.[29] Women from other Lollard communities also passed books around, but not to the extent of their more literate sisters in Coventry.[30]

Women's custody of books was often transitional. Joan Smyth inherited the books of her first husband, Richard Landesdale, who died about 1502 or 1503. She kept these books, the Acts of the Apostles, the Epistles of Paul, and the Commandments, for three months; but, as she feared they would be discovered in her custody, she then gave them to Roger Landesdale, her

---

[26] Wilts. R.O., Reg. J. Blythe, f. 74v.
[27] Lichfield Court Book, f. 21r.
[28] 'Quemdam librum de passione Christi et Ade', Lichfield Court Book, ff. 4r, 6v.
[29] Lichfield Court Book, ff. 4r, 5v, 6v, 7r, 7v, 14r, 14v, 15v, 16v, 17r, 20r, 21r, 26v. On the book trade, see Hudson, *Premature Reformation*, 166–8, 200–25.
[30] *Acts and Monuments*, iv, 230–31; *Heresy Trials*, 48.

husband's relative.[31] Joan Austy of Essex, like Joan Smyth, inherited *Wycliffe's Wicket* and a book of the Commandments from her first husband, John Redman, and then about 8 weeks after her marriage to her second husband, Thomas Austy, passed the books on to him.[32] Agnes Pykas of Colchester gave her son John a book of Paul's Epistles in order to convert him; later, John gave to her for safekeeping the book of the Epistles and a New Testament which he had subsequently bought, as he felt he was under suspicion.[33]

Women married to other Lollards often also had access to the books their husbands owned. Richard, the husband of Alice Colins of Ginge, for instance, was called a 'great reader' and was said to have had *Wycliffe's Wicket*, the gospel of Luke, a book of Paul, a gloss of the Apocalypse, a book of Our Lady's Matins in English, a book of Solomon in English, *The Prick of Conscience*, *The King of Beeme*, and a book of the Ten Commandments[34] – an impressive book list, and characteristic in its mixture of scripture, Lollard texts and orthodox devotional texts. Alice Colins apparently could not herself read, but she undoubtedly benefited from her husband's book collection.

Even when the books themselves were not immediately available, recitation of memorized passages of scripture was another common means of conveying written texts. Hudson notes that memorization was used extensively by the Lollards and that it was a means of evangelization to those without access to books.[35] Although few Lollard women could read – or perhaps precisely because few Lollard women could read – they were conspicuous among those in the sect who had memorized passages of scripture or prayers. Children, boys and girls, were also taught long passages of the Bible or other devotional texts. While memorization was a means by which illiterate women and girls (as well as some men) could play significant roles in evangelization, such roles did not translate into positions of power in the movement.[36] Even reciting at conventicles did not give women the opportunity to participate fully in discussions of

---

31 Lichfield Court Book, ff. 4r, 5v, 11v. The text says that she brought them to Roger about three months 'a tempore obitus eiusdem Johannis'; an assumption is made here that the Johannis of the text is a scribal error for Ricardi.

32 TCD MS 775, f. 124v.

33 Strype, *Ecclesiastical Memorials*, i(1), 121; *Letters and Papers . . . of . . . Henry VIII*, iv(2), no. 4029.

34 *Acts and Monuments*, iv, 234–6, 238.

35 Hudson, *Premature Reformation*, 190–2. Learning scripture by heart was by no means limited to Lollards and was a common orthodox practice at least among the gentry. Margaret Rocliffe, for instance, granddaughter of Sir William Plumpton, had, according to her father–in–law, 'near hand learned her sawter [psalter].' *Plumpton Correspondence*, ed. T. Stapleton, Camden Soc. 4 (1839), 8; Nicholas Orme, *English Schools in the Middle Ages* (London, 1973), 55.

36 This differs from the interpretation of Claire Cross, who has seen recitation as a significant element of women's power in Lollardy. Claire Cross, ' "Great Reasoners in Scripture": The Activities of Women Lollards 1380–1530', in *Medieval Women*, ed. Derek Baker, Studies in Church History, Subsidia 1 (Oxford, 1978), 370–1.

the text, an activity normally reserved to men.[37] John Foxe, for instance, describes the public recitation of Alice Colins of Ginge thus:

> This Alice likewise was a famous woman among them, and had a good memory, and could recite much of the Scriptures, and other good books; and therefore when any *conventicle of these men* did meet at Burford, commonly she was sent for, to recite unto them the declaration of the Ten Commandments, and the Epistles of Peter and James.[38]

Alice Colins apparently was not a regular attender of the conventicle, which was made up of men, according to Foxe. She made appearances at the group to act as a kind of living book, but there is no indication that she proceeded to explain the readings to the gathering or even discussed them after she had recited; rather, her recitation was like that of a child called upon to recite before guests.

While women's illiteracy thus did not cut them off from the contents of Lollard books, it was undoubtedly a handicap in their participation in the main arena of Lollard activity, the conventicle. Indeed women participated much less often than men in these gatherings and centred their activities instead on private, informal discussions of doctrine. The evidence indicates that almost all women (and most men) were forced to rely on others to read material in Lollard books to them.

The literate were the most powerful in the Lollard communities: they were the primary purveyors of the Lollard word and the leaders of the sect's gatherings. The significant gender gap in Lollard literacy thus materially affected the place of women in the movement. It also must have influenced negatively their attraction to a sect that was so firmly based on the written word. Lollard women were able to play only secondary roles in the literate culture of their sect's communities.

How does Lollard evidence compare with other assessments of late-medieval literacy? It differs sharply with the notion of a steeply rising rate of lay literacy in the late Middle Ages, a phenomenon which some scholars take as a given.[39] Because of the fragmentary nature of the sources, most

---

[37] The role of men and women in Lollard conventicles is discussed fully in McSheffrey, *Gender and Heresy*.

[38] *Acts and Monuments*, iv, 238 (my emphasis).

[39] Sylvia Thrupp, *The Merchant Class of Late Medieval London* (Ann Arbor, Mich., 1968), 156–8 (see Poos' questioning of her figures, *A Rural Society*, 284); M. B. Parkes, 'The Literacy of the Laity', in *Literature and Western Civilization: The Mediaeval World*, ed. David Daiches and Anthony Thorlby (London, 1973), 555–77; Clanchy, *From Memory to Written Record*, 175–201; Orme, *English Schools*, 43–51; Jo Ann Hoeppner Moran, *The Growth of English Schooling, 1340–1548: Learning, Literacy, and Laicization in Pre-Reformation York Diocese* (Princeton, 1985), 17–20, 177–9; Eamon Duffy, *The Stripping of the Altars* (New Haven, Conn., 1992), 68, 212, 281–2; Aston, *Lollards and Reformers*, 193; Margaret Spufford, *Contrasting Communities: English Villagers in the Sixteenth and Seventeenth Centuries* (Cambridge, 1974), 206–8.

approaches to the subject of reading have been by necessity anecdotal and impressionistic, concentrating on books and the individuals who owned them and generalizing from there. The growing number of books available in the fifteenth century has led scholars to extrapolate from them an increasingly literate population – more books, more readers. But the question of how many more readers and at what social level is not so easy to answer from the books that survive. Anecdotal evidence on book ownership has been used with too little sensitivity to gender and social position – male grocers at the pinnacle of the urban élite, for instance, too often stand for the 'ordinary lay person'.[40]

Evidence for this explosion of literacy among the laity is in fact by no means firm. Attempts to quantify literacy – to look at literate people rather than implied readers of texts – have served to question its extent. David Cressy's statistical analysis of signature evidence in England, for instance, is very pessimistic, estimating that 99% of women and 90% of men were illiterate in 1500.[41] While many have criticized Cressy's evidentiary base and definition of literacy (the ability to write), other methods have revealed broadly similar findings. In particular, L. R. Poos' recent discussion using ecclesiastical court records corroborates Cressy's very low rates among men in fifteenth-century Essex.[42]

Poos' assessments of literacy among the male population of Essex was made possible by two consistory and commissary court deposition books from the diocese of London, where the testimony of witnesses to suits heard by the courts (mostly marriage and defamation cases) were recorded.[43] A further look at these sources to investigate women's reading is instructive. While the scribe designated most deponents as literate or illiterate (literacy arguably meaning here a minimal ability to read English[44]), the omission of this personal detail in the identification of most clerics and most female deponents revealingly illustrates the court's expectations about reading abilities. Presumably in both cases the scribe considered the information obvious and redundant: clerics were, by definition, literate while women were, by definition, illiterate. The

---

[40] Eamon Duffy, in his discussion of widespread lay literacy in his recent *The Stripping of the Altars*, refers to a grocer as an example of the 'middling and lower sorts' who owned books in the 15th century (212). See also Janet Coleman, *Medieval Readers and Writers, 1350–1400* (New York, 1981), 16–17 and passim; Grundmann, 'Die Frauen und die Literatur', 133.

[41] Cressy, *Literacy*, 128, 144, 158, 177.

[42] Poos, *A Rural Society*, 284, 286–7. Jo Ann Hoeppner Moran's work on education in the diocese of York estimated that about 12% of the lay population (almost entirely concentrated among men) could read; Moran, *The Growth of English Schooling*, 69–70, 152–62, 177–81.

[43] London, Greater London Record Office (GLRO) MS DL/C/205, Consistory Court of London Deposition Book, 1467–76; London, Guildhall Library (GL) MS 9065, Commissary Court of London Deposition Book, 1489–97.

[44] Poos cites a reference found in an ecclesiastical court record from 1527 which noted that a witness called himself literate because he could pick out a word here and there in English and read no Latin at all. Poos, *A Rural Society*, 285.

presumption of women's illiteracy could be incorrect: one female deponent actually described herself reading a document in the course of her testimony.[45] One scribe did not make the presumption; unaccountably, for a time he noted the literacy of women deponents as well as of men.[46] This slender information can provide some clues about the nature of female literacy, especially along gender, socio-economic, and geographical lines. Of 21 female witnesses designated by ability to read, 3 were recorded to be literate (about one in 7). In comparison, among male deponents in the same deposition book (a much larger sample of over 300), about one in 3 were literate. Geography was also a significant factor in both men's and women's literacy. The diocese in question comprised both the city of London and the largely rural county of Essex. Not surprisingly, literacy rates were higher in the city: of the 8 rural women, none were literate, while 3 of 13 urban women could read. Similarly, rural men were less likely to be literate than urban men (25% as opposed to 41%). Social station was perhaps the most important variable. All these samples of deponents are skewed towards those of higher status: plaintiffs in cases attempted to choose witnesses of substantial stature, presumably because they were seen as more trustworthy. (Related to this is a strong bias towards male rather than female deponents.) Poos, in his analysis of the male witnesses from Essex, points out that almost all the literate deponents came from the gentry or the upper ranks of the agricultural world.[47] Correspondingly, at least two of the three literate female deponents apparently came from London's merchant élite (the status of the third cannot be determined).[48] The evidence from the deposition books, however thin, corroborates the view that men were much more likely to be literate than women, and that literacy was confined, for the most part, to those of high status. It also suggests that urban women and men had more opportunities to learn how to read than those in rural areas.

Why were medieval English women less literate than medieval English men? Recent work on the social history of late-medieval England tells us that women's economic and social lives were clearly distinct from men's, and so

---

[45] GLRO MS DL/C/205, f. 100r.

[46] GL MS 9065, ff. 136v–254r. No female deponents in GLRO MS DL/C/205 were identified as literate or illiterate.

[47] Poos, *A Rural Society*, 284–7.

[48] Alice Spencer and Joan Dawbeney both testified in the same case, Agnes Eston *v.* John Crosby; both were social equals to the evidently wealthy principals in the case (some of the testimony involved the sale of a piece of gold belonging to John Crosby worth £50 sterling, a very large sum). Joan Dawbeney's husband, William Dawbeney, was styled 'Magister' by the scribe (a title he usually reserved for clerics with MAs and the most substantial laymen), and may have been the same as the William Dabeney, notary public, who was named in 1476. The depositions of William and Joan Dawbeney were taken in their private residence, perhaps in recognition of their status. See GL MS 9065, ff. 201r–201v and 207r–207v (and ff. 186r–186v for the deposition of the third literate woman, Alice Reed); and GLRO MS DL/C/205, f. 321v.

their opportunities to learn to read must also have differed. Jo Ann Hoeppner Moran and Nicholas Orme, in their studies of education in late-medieval England, have argued that women outside the highest classes had little occasion to learn to read.[49] Although women of the nobility, gentry and perhaps haute bourgeoisie could acquire literacy through household instruction and in some cases in nunneries, there is almost no evidence that women below the highest classes had any formal means of learning to read. Possibly girls were included among the 'pueri' educated in elementary and song schools, but the evidence is unclear and Moran and others argue that it is unlikely for this to be usual.[50]

Women's slender opportunities to acquire literacy were no doubt a reflection of the overall restrictions on their economic and social lives. Many scholars argue that literacy was acquired in the late-medieval world for pragmatic, business-oriented reasons,[51] and few women required any knowledge of the written word to fulfill their economic roles. Recent scholarship on gender and work emphasizes that medieval women's work, often complementary to the work of the head of the household, tended to be unskilled, ill-paid, low-status, flexible, and part-time[52] – and unlikely to require literacy. While a few women of high social status, such as gentlewomen and wives of merchants, may have needed to be able to read and write in order to accomplish the complicated administrative work that was their economic lot in life,[53] this cannot be seen as representative of women's work as a whole. While the late Middle Ages saw a greater emphasis on the written word, and literacy probably rose among laymen (although this too has been exaggerated), indications are that below the highest social levels literacy among laywomen was uncommon and perhaps exceptional.

Restrictions on women's literacy may also have had ideological aspects.[54]

---

[49] Moran, *Growth of English Schooling*, 69–70, 152–62, 177–81; Orme, *English Schools*, 52–5.

[50] Moran, *Growth of English Schooling*, 69–70, 152–62; Eileen Power, *Medieval English Nunneries* (Cambridge, 1922), 260–84, esp. 260–2; Margaret King, *Women of the Renaissance* (Chicago, 1991), 164–72.

[51] See esp. Parkes, 'The Literacy of the Laity', 555.

[52] See Judith M. Bennett, 'Medieval Women, Modern Women: Across the Great Divide', in *Culture and History, 1350–1600: Essays on English Communities, Identities and Writing*, ed. David Aers (London, 1992), 147–75, and refs. there.

[53] See, for instance, Rowena E. Archer, ' "How ladies . . . who live on their manors ought to manage their households and estates": Women as Landholders and Administrators in the Later Middle Ages', in *Woman is a Worthy Wight: Women in English Society, c.1200–1500*, ed. P. J. P. Goldberg (Gloucester, 1992), 149–81; Linda E. Mitchell, 'The Lady is a Lord: Noble Widows and Land in Thirteenth-Century Britain', *Historical Reflections/Réflexions historiques*, 18 (1992), 71–97.

[54] For ideological attitudes restricting women's learning, see *Le Ménagier de Paris*, ed. Georgine E. Brereton and Janet M. Ferrier (Oxford, 1981), 56 (I. iv. 24–25); King, *Women of the Renaissance*, 168; Patricia H. Labalme, 'Introduction', and Margaret L. King, 'Book-lined Cells: Women and Humanism in the Early Italian Renaissance', both in *Beyond Their Sex: Learned Women of the European Past*, ed. Patricia Labalme (New York and London, 1980), 2–7, 75–80; Michael H. Shank, 'A Female University Student in Late Medieval Kraków', in *Sisters and Workers in the Middle Ages*, ed. Judith M. Bennett et al. (Chicago, 1989), 190–7.

While literacy was a pragmatic skill, it gave the person who possessed it a certain power: the ability to attain directly the information contained in written texts. Indeed, secular and religious authorities feared the power that literacy gave people of lower socio-economic stations and sometimes attempted to curb their access to reading. Women were sometimes particularly targeted. After the Henrician Reformation of the 1530s made English scriptures much more widely available than they had been previously, Stephen Gardiner's 1543 'Act for the Advancement of the True Religion' forbade the reading of scriptures in public or private by certain groups. Gardiner's categories remind us that questions of literacy and religious practice were differentiated by fifteenth- and sixteenth-century people along both gender and socio-economic lines. The Act forbade the reading of scripture publicly or privately by 'woomen . . . artificers, prentises, journeymen, serving men of the degrees of yeomen or undre, husbandemen, [or] laborers'. Noble- and gentlewomen were exempted from the blanket ban on women's biblical reading, as long as they did their reading privately.[55] Women, except those of the highest status, were grouped together with men of lower-status occupations as the sorts of people who were not to be trusted with the responsibility of interpreting scripture for themselves. Gardiner's Act, promulgated a generation or so after the latest evidence adduced here for the Lollard movement, may reflect a fear that literacy was beginning to pass over the gender and socio-economic barriers it had not previously breached.[56]

Thus Lollard evidence and depositions from ecclesiastical court cases generally corroborate the more pessimistic view of lay literacy in late-medieval England, restricted according to gender and social position. Lollard men, to be sure, were more likely to be literate than their orthodox counterparts, at least according to Cressy's and Poos' findings. Poos' evidence for Essex, home of a considerable Lollard community in the early sixteenth century, indicates that literacy among craftsmen, Lollardy's main constituency, was particularly low.[57] This suggests that Lollard men's literacy was – just as the prosecutors assumed – unusual and probably acquired within the movement. Those few Lollard women who were literate were also probably taught within the Lollard communities. This was the case even for women of high social status, reminding us that female literacy was not automatic at any level: Alice Rowley, widow of a Coventry mayor, learned to read as a Lollard and not before, and Alice Cottismore, gentlewoman, was illiterate. Outside the Lollard community, opportunities for most women to acquire literacy were virtually non-existent. Even within the Lollard sect, women were rarely able to learn how to

---

[55] 'An Acte for thadvauncement of true Religion', 34 and 35 Henry VIII, ch. I, *Statutes of the Realm*, vol. iii (London, 1817; rept. 1963), 896; Duffy, *The Stripping of the Altars*, 433.

[56] Cressy's evidence indicates an increase in literacy in the 1530s and 1540s, particularly among tradesmen. Cressy, *Literacy*, 159–66.

[57] Poos finds that no craftsmen or retailers out of his Essex sample were literate. *A Rural Society*, 286–7.

read. Only in Coventry, where women taught one another, were a significant number able to become literate.[58]

Scholars have approached the subject of literacy in late-medieval England from two directions. The study of surviving texts tends to emphasize rising literacy, but investigation of documentary evidence for how or whether late-medieval English people learned to read has so far produced a less optimistic view. At this stage the two paths of enquiry on this single subject do not meet up: clearly more research is needed. But further discussions of literacy in the late Middle Ages, from either perspective, must take gender and socio-economic status into account. Too frequently, anachronistic terms like middle class[59] mask the fact that the social groups in which all agree literacy was taking hold – the nobility, the gentry, the merchant élites of the towns, and even the upper ranks of the agricultural world – made up no more than a small fraction at the top of English society. And even among these restricted social groups, it must be acknowledged that women were not accorded the opportunity to participate equally with men in the acquisition of literacy. Literacy was perhaps only normally acquired by women at the very highest social level, where private tutors taught girls as well as boys. Outside the nobility, gentry, and the gentry-aping merchant élite, women had almost no chance, even in a context like the literacy-conscious Lollard movement, to learn how to read.

---

[58] William Monter has argued that another book-conscious culture, 17th- and 18th-century Calvinist Geneva, also witnessed a significant gender gap in literacy. E. William Monter, 'Women in Calvinist Geneva', *Signs*, 6 (1980), 189–209.

[59] E.g. by Coleman, *Medieval Readers and Writers*, 16–7 and passim.

WOMEN AND TEXTS
IN LANGUEDOCIAN CATHARISM

Peter Biller

The relation between women and texts in the Catharism which existed in Languedoc from some time in the twelfth century to about 1320 is a subject which we are likely to approach with some expectations and questions. Thinking of Catharism as a 'heresy', we may reflect comparatively about the main heresy of later-medieval northern Europe, Lollardy, where the legal records used by Anne Hudson and others clearly show some role played by literate women,[1] whatever doubt may be cast on their proportional importance.[2] Lingering in the back of our minds will be the association between pious laywomen, religious women, literacy and reading in the works of Herbert Grundmann, who principally used northern European, especially German, sources.[3] When we turn back to think about Catharism there will be two things in our minds, one of which will be the enduring theme,[4] or enduring myth (despite attempts to demolish it),[5] of the prominence of women in Languedocian Catharism; the other will be the romantic pictures, which appear in earlier accounts of Catharism, of the role played in Catharism by a cultivated female aristocracy.[6] Both may encourage us to expect to find among women in

---

[1] A. Hudson, *The Premature Reformation. Wycliffite Texts and Lollard History* (Oxford, 1988), 136–7, 183, 189, 191; see the studies by Cross and Aston cited p. 137 n. 123.
[2] See S. McSheffrey's paper, above, in which she questions the numbers of literate women in Lollardy.
[3] H. Grundmann, 'Religiöse Frauenbewegung und volkssprachliche Literatur', in his *Religiöse Bewegungen im Mittelalter*, 2nd edn (Hildesheim, 1961), 452–75; in his *Ausgewählte Aufsätze*, Schriften der Monumenta Germaniae Historica, 25/3 (Stuttgart, 1978): 'Litteratus-illitteratus. Der Wandel einer Bildungsnorm vom Altertum zum Mittelalter', 1–66 (10), and 'Die Frauen und die Literatur im Mittelalter. Ein Beitrag zur Frage nach der Entstehung des Schrifttums in der Volkssprache', 67–95 (especially from 70).
[4] The most recent presentation is by the *directrice* of the Centre National des Etudes Cathares, A. Brenon, in her *Les Femmes cathares* (Paris, 1992).
[5] J. Duvernoy, *Le Catharisme. La Religion des cathares* (Toulouse, 1976), 264–5; most solidly, R. Abels and E. Harrison, 'The participation of women in Languedocian catharism', *Mediaeval Studies*, 41 (1979), 215–51.
[6] A question-mark about literacy among the Languedocian aristocratic women is suggested by Brenon's comment, 171, n. 1: 'cette aristocratie occitane née avant la conquête française, cette *intelligentsia* au sein de laquelle on sait fréquemment lire et écrire, du moins parmi les mâles il est vrai [. . .]'.

Languedocian Catharism parallels with what is found among the pious and heretical women of northern Europe. What in fact do we find?

The answer given here rests mainly upon a reading of the principal surviving trial material.[7] Along with the letters, chronicles and treatises which bear upon Catharism, there are also the records of interrogations in front of inquisitors and inquisitors' sentences, which go back to the late 1230s and, through the long memories of old people interrogated at that date, take one back at least to the 1190s. The hundreds of vignettes of ordinary people's lives, revealed in this legal material as they intersected with Catharism, provide the historian with the (partly illusory) confidence that much of a past 'reality' can be reconstructed.

We need to recall two fundamental characteristics of Languedocian Catharism. In its organization it was a Church, and it had support in all sectors of society – even, until a surprisingly late date, among the wealthy and influential both in city and countryside. It was organized into dioceses, which were manned by a clerical personnel of bishops and deacons. Where these can be envisaged in important ways as approximations to Catholic secular clergy, those others, both men and women, who had received the Cathar sacrament of *consolamentum* and led their lives in communities, can be seen rather more roughly as equivalents to Catholic religious, monks and nuns. However, their communities were quite fluid and informal, especially in the case of female religious, and seem to have existed at various points on a continuum between family households and formal religious communities. Followers and supporters, designated by inquisitors as *credentes*, believers, were not, according to Cathar theology, part of the Cathar Church; but their sharing of Cathar belief, participation in ritual and material support for the Cathar Church, made them, broadly speaking, Cathar 'parishioners'.

Let us now examine the presence and uses of written materials in this

---

7 Since many of the statements in this paper are about *absence* of reference to women and books or literacy, it needs to be noted that these statements are based on a reading *in toto* of the following trial texts: Paris, Bibliothèque Nationale, Collection Doat MSS 21–6; Toulouse, Bibliothèque Municipale MS 609 (apart from some folios which are blurred in my microfilm – Professor W. L. Wakefield has kindly helped me with his transcripts of parts of these); *Documents pour servir à l'histoire de l'inquisition dans le Languedoc*, ed. C. Douais, 2 pts. (Paris, 1900); BN MS Lat 12856; *The Inquisition at Albi 1299–1300. Text of Register and Analysis*, ed. G. W. Davis (New York, 1948); *L'Inquisiteur Geoffroy d'Ablis et les cathares du comté de Foix (1308–1309). Texte édité, traduit et annoté*, ed. A. Pales-Gobilliard (Paris, 1984); *Liber sententiarum inquisitionis Tholosanae ab anno Christi 1307 ad annum 1323*, ed. P. van Limborch as the second part of his *Historia inquisitionis* (Amsterdam, 1692); *Le registre d'inquisition de Jacques Fournier 1318–1325*, ed. J. Duvernoy, 3 vols. (Toulouse, 1965), together with the same editor's *Le registre d'inquisition . . . Corrections* (Toulouse, 1972). To be added to these are the fragments which have been edited by J. Duvernoy in *Heresis*, 1 (1983), 9–31, and 3 (1984), 5–33, and in a special number of *Bulletin de la Société Ariégeoise des Sciences, Lettres et Arts* (1990), and by H. Blaquière in *Cahiers de Fanjeaux*, 3 (1968), 259–77. A small but important exception is Toulouse, Archives Départementales de la Haute-Garonne MS 124 (see on this Abels and Harrison, 223), of which I have only read the extracts in 'Documents inédits sur l'hérésie des Albigeois', ed. G. Belhomme, *Mémoires de la Société archéologique du Midi de la France*, 6 (1847–52), 101–46 (133–46).

Church, from the point of view of women as distinct from men.[8] First, embedded in a wealthy sector of a society which was penetrated by a notariate, the Cathar Church's organization and finance used and generated adminstrative documents. In relation to the conciliar assemblies held by the bishops and deacons there is a fragmentary survival, the report of a commission on diocesan boundaries, and a reference to a petition for a new diocese which suggests written petition. Notaries were used, who drew up wills in which wealthy *credentes* bequeathed money to the Cathars. Records of debts were kept, and letters used for the demanding of payment. Scattered trial references suggest the inference that religious houses will have had deposits of written instruments, such as a charter for the granting of land.

What has been described so far was an entirely male world. Men only were the members of the Cathar hierarchy, bishops and deacons, and men only were witnesses on a diocesan boundary commission, notaries drawing up wills, testators, and bearers of letters demanding payment. Here is a world of the written document and organization and finance, of which the majority is entirely male, although one qualification and one exception need to be noted. The internal life and organization of early Cathar religious houses are only fragmentarily known, and obviously no cartulary survives. We have just one reference relating to some Cathar *perfectae* from Auriac who had been taken prisoner, who commissioned a document, an *ordinatio*, to regularize their affairs.[9] There is no obvious objection to the conjecture that during the early open period of Catharism the houses and property occupied by Cathar female religious will have generated charters.

Women and men who became *perfectae* and *perfecti* seem first to have gone to spend time with Cathar religious, living with them and joining in their form of life, in a way which suggests a novitiate. References to this period, which must have included instruction, are frustratingly allusive or brief. There are examples of *perfecti* trying to persuade young men to become *perfecti* by using education as a lure, to leave off looking after oxen and be instructed in *grammatica*, or become a *clericus*. At least some communities of male religious provided, then, this sort of education. The existence of learned theologians among the Cathars of the late twelfth and early thirteenth centuries, authors of theological treatises, can be used to speculate further about the level of instruction provided by these Cathar schools. Some *perfectae* tried by inquisitors recounted the outlines of their religious curriculum vitae, beginning with

---

[8] The general picture given here is based on P. Biller, 'The Cathars of Languedoc and written materials', in *Heresy and Literacy, 1000–1530*, ed. P. Biller and A. Hudson (Cambridge, 1994), 61–82.

[9] Toulouse, BM MS 609, fol. 94v: 'Petrus de Devesa scolaris dicti capellani reddidit se familiarem predictis hereticabus in tantum quod fecerunt scribi per dictum Petrum testamentum id est ordinationem rerum suarum; et hoc facto dicte heretice retinuerunt scripturam prefatam.' For the transcript of this I am indebted to Professor W. L. Wakefield, who discussed this case in his 'Heretics and inquisitors: The Case of Auriac and Cambiac', *Journal of Medieval History*, 12 (1986), 225–36 (231).

going off to live with women who were already *perfectae*.[10] However, although these young girls somehow learnt Cathar faith and ritual, there is never any direct evidence that their instruction involved hearing books being read, reading books, learning how to read or possessing books, and no indication that it was other than oral. There is no equivalent of the notion that a boy or young man would become literate through becoming a *perfectus*, nor positive and clear evidence that the instruction given by *perfectae* included teaching how to read and write.[11] Apart from one lone and ambiguous reference by Stephen of Bourbon – to a woman, convicted of heresy, who had denied and then admitted going to Cathar schools (*scolas Albigensium*)[12] – there is silence in the evidence.

Depositions preserve for us vignettes of hundreds of perfects of both sexes, travelling, visiting, living in houses, administering ritual or participating in services, talking to people. There are many hundreds of examples of the males, *perfecti*, administering the *consolamentum*, and while doing so holding the book, called the 'Text', over the head of the recipient. There are many instances described of the book's role in the administration of the Kiss of Peace, where the males, *perfecti*, give the Kiss to men, who in order to avoid contact of flesh pass the Kiss on to women through the intermediary of the book.[13] There are many examples of *perfecti* carrying books, holding books, reading from books, preaching from books. The word-pictures which survive in the depositions of a *perfectus* holding a book and reading from it almost suggest this as a stereotypical mental image of *perfecti* in the minds of *credentes*. The contrast with the women, the *perfectae*, is stark: there is not a single instance where a *perfecta* is

---

10 J. Guiraud, *Histoire de l'inquisition au moyen âge*, 2 vols. (Paris, 1935–8), i, 150; G. Koch, *Frauenfrage und Ketzertum im Mittelalter. Die Frauenbewegung im Rahmen des Katharismus und des Waldensertums und ihre sozialen Wurzeln (12.–14. Jahrhundert)*, Forschungen zur mittelalterlichen Geschichte, 9 (Berlin, 1962), 59; Abels and Harrison, 231.

11 Brenon, 214–5, raises the general question of the literacy of the *perfectae*, suggesting that the evidence does not allow certainty and that it would be unwise to generalize on this point. Koch's account, 61–2, gives the impression that the *perfectae*'s instruction included teaching how to read and write, mainly through citing a passage from Toulouse BM MS 609, fol. 30r, about two *perfectae* who pressed a mother to hand her twelve-year-old son to them, 'quod recederent cum eis et facerent ipsum discere litteras'. Koch quoted this from J. Guiraud, *Cartulaire de Notre-Dame de Prouille*, 2 vols. (Paris, 1907), i, p. cclxxvii. Guiraud seems to misrepresent the incident, in which a group of Cathar religious, headed by two men but including women, tried to persuade the boy to go with them. Described twice by witnesses (fols. 29r and 42r, not 30r), the incident is more accurately depicted in W. L. Wakefield's 'Heretics and Inquisitors: The Case of Le Mas-Saintes-Puelles', *Catholic Historical Review*, 69 (1983), 209–26 (217 and n. 30).

12 *Anecdotes historiques, légendes et apologues tirés du recueil inédit d'Etienne de Bourbon dominicain du XIIIe siècle*, ed. A. Lecoy de la Marche, Société de l'Histoire de France (Paris, 1877), 289.

13 A. Borst, *Die Katharer*, Monumenta Germaniae Historica, Schriften 12 (Stuttgart, 1953), p. 198 n. 27; Duvernoy, *Religion des cathares*, 212. See an example in BN Doat MS 23, fols. 123v–4r: 'ipsa testis et alii supradicti acceperunt pacem ab haereticis scilicet homines osculantes haereticos bis in ore ex transuerso, deinde osculabantur sese inuicem bis in ore ex transuerso; mulieres uero acceperunt pacem a libro, deinde osculabantur sese inuicem bis in ore similiter ex transuerso'.

explicitly noticed as carrying, reading or in any way using a book. Occasionally women, *perfectae*, are noted preaching[14] – but use of a book is never mentioned.

Now, this contrast must be a little too stark. Among the hundreds of occasions of administration of the *consolamentum* described or alluded to in the depositions, there are three where women conferred the sacrament.[15] On each of these occasions these *perfectae* must have held the text in their hands and imposed it on the head of the recipient, since this was the core of the ritual – though the three depositions do not spell this out.[16] These few examples show that it was very rare for *perfectae* to confer the *consolamentum*. At the same time we lack any positive evidence about the literacy of any single *perfecta*. It seems likely, then, that it was not the norm for a pair of *perfectae* to carry books about with them, and that they obtained a text temporarily for such occasions. Some corroboration of this comes from the cases of *credentes* who looked after the goods of *perfecti* and *perfectae*. Take the example which is provided by the confession in 1319 of a *credens* called Jeanne of Sainte-Foy, who looked after possessions of both a male and female perfect.[17] After the death of the *perfecta* Jacoba, some of Jacoba's things and utensils were brought for safekeeping to her and her mother's house in Toulouse ('fuerunt aportate alique res & utensilia dicte heretice ad domum ipsius & matris sue ad custodiendum'). She and her mother also looked after the possessions of an unnamed male heretic, a *perfectus*, and these were a shirt, a purse with money, and a heretical book ('ipsa & mater sua tenuerunt & custodierunt quendam librum hereticorum & quandam camisiam cujusdam heretici, & quandam bursam'). In all the deposition references to such safekeeping, the pattern is always like this: a *credens* who looks after the goods of a perfect temporarily, or, on the perfect's death or capture, may look after a book or books if the perfect is male, but not if the perfect is female.

Credentes provided support of various sorts to the perfects, and they shared their beliefs. One can see this tending to vary according to sex, men being more likely to provide money, for example, women being more likely to provide food, and, especially in the late interrogations glimpsed by Gui's sentences, far more likely to make the beds and wash the clothing of the *perfecti*.[18]

---

14 Abels and Harrison, 228, 239–40 (where some increase of women preaching in the 1240s and 1250s is suggested).

15 Ibid. 227 n. 61.

16 There is an apparent exception in Brenon, 50, where Arnaude of Lamothe is described administering the *consolamentum* – 'Arnaude prit en mains son livre des Evangiles' – but Arnaude's use of the New Testament in this rite (probable) and her possession of it (possible) are no more than conjectures, since there is no reference to a book in the deposition where Arnaude is described as conferring the *consolamentum*.

17 Limborch, *Liber sententiarum*, 70.

18 P. Biller, 'The Common Woman in the Western Church in the Thirteenth and Early Fourteenth Centuries', in W. J. Sheils and D. Wood, ed., *Women in the Church*, Studies in Church History 27 (Oxford, 1990), 127–57 (149).

Where letters and books were concerned, it was men who acted as bearers of written messages, but both men and women who were concerned with books. All the scribes referred to were male, and the few instances of purchasing books only involve men. However, one of Gui's sentences preserves a conversation between one female *credens* and some men about dealing with a heretic's book which lacked two folios, and it was the woman who was taking the initiative in this matter.[19] Much earlier, in a deposition of 1243, we have the brief vignette of a female *credens*, an unnamed woman, who was looking after the so-called text, belonging to heretics, which she was carrying in a bag. In the chaos of the siege of the castle of Montredon by the army of Lautrec, as she was carrying this bag with her, it was seized, but she got it back again.[20] However, most of the safekeeping of books was in men's hands.

One among several reasons for this may lie in the literacy and ability to read books of the *credentes* themselves. Among the male *credentes* there is a steady trickle of the literate. But among female *credentes*? In all the trial material I have encountered two possible cases: Alazaïs, a married woman of Moussoulens, appearing before the bishop in Carcassonne in 1250 and asking for a written copy of evidence of heresy which had been given against her;[21] and the *credens* Peter of Beauville sending a letter to his wife Guillelma, a *credens* and living in Avignonet, asking her to join him in Narbonne.[22] These women may have been literate; they may also have had someone to read for them. Otherwise the contrast is black and white. The inquisition material coming from Quercy around 1240 and from the late Catharism of just after 1300 shows male *credentes* who would keep a heretic's book for a while, and read Cathar doctrine in it; but there is never a single instance of a female *credens* doing this. One direct example of a female *credens*'s curiosity about the contents of these books may be quite significant. It comes in the confession made by *Domina* Finas of Tauriac in 1244. She described one sighting of heretics where there was one Hugo Boers, *litteratus*, whom she, Lady Finas, took along with her 'in order to read the books of the heretics, so that she could hear what they said and try out whether they spoke good or evil' ('et hugo Boers litteratus quem duxit secum illa quae loquitur ut legeret libros haereticorum, et audiret quid dicerent, et probaret utrum bonum vel malum dicerent').[23] Are we to presume that both her own lack of literacy and her rank's habit of employing others are suggested in this action of hers, in getting a literate man to do her reading? And was the lack of literacy of this noblewoman, sister of the Lord of

---

[19] Limborch, *Liber sententiarum*, 169–70.
[20] BN Doat MS 23, fol. 115r–v.
[21] Douais, *Documents*, pt. 2, 139.
[22] BN Doat MS 25, fol. 312v.
[23] BN Doat MS 22, fol. 67r–v. Lady Finas has been discussed by E. Griffe, *Le Languedoc cathare au temps de la croisade (1209–1229)* (Paris, 1973), 179, J. Duvernoy, *Le Catharisme. Histoire des cathares* (Toulouse, 1979), 239–40, Brenon, 169–71.

Rabastens and married to the Lord of Tauriac, typical of women in general in the aristocracy of Languedoc at this time?

We must qualify the picture which has been presented so far. Something much more complex than literacy and illiteracy may be implied by men, but not women, holding and reading books. Take the example where a man, Raymond Vayssière of Ax-les-Thermes, testifies in 1320 about his memory of nineteen or twenty years before when he was behind his house, standing in the sunshine, and four or five arm-lengths away there was a man called William Andorran and his mother, Galharda. William was holding a book and reading it, and his mother was listening. Raymond asked him what it was, so William brought the book over, and Raymond read in it, recognizing as he read what he had heard from two *perfecti*.[24] Here we have two men holding a book, two men reading in it, and a woman who always listens. So far this represents what we always see – that is, never a woman reading. Now, in this late Catharism we find a strong vein of men from the notariate, men used to handling texts in all sorts of ways. At an earlier stage we find instances of notaries having a formal role in reading a book in Cathar ceremonies, where this reading is followed by a heretic expounding the text. The literate heretic could have read the text, but a notary was preferred, presumably because of the authenticating role which a notary performed. Something similar may have been at work in other contexts. The choice of who read a Cathar text may have been based not just on literacy, but on other added assumptions about the reader's role and ascribed authority.

Catholic accounts of Languedocian Catharism usually bear indirectly, and only once directly, on this theme. Authors throughout, from Alain de Lille around 1200 to Bernard Gui in the early fourteenth century, provide a picture of literate and book-using Cathar *perfecti*; but they are silent on women. There is an interesting polarity on an allied theme, that of women preaching. From the late twelfth to the mid-thirteenth century there is a row of Catholic authors writing about heretics in southern France, Bernard of Fontcaude,[25] Alain de Lille,[26] an early thirteenth-century anonymous,[27] and Stephen of Bourbon,[28] all of whom harp on about Waldensian women preaching: the fact of women

---

[24] Duvernoy, *Registre d'inquisition*, i, 285.

[25] Bernard of Fontcaude, *Adversus Waldensium Sectam* viii, PL 204, cols. 825–8. Bernard is clear on the fact which he is opposing, entitling the chapter 'Contra hoc, quod mulieres praedicare posse dicunt', and referring to the fact that 'feminas, quas suo consortio admittunt, docere permittunt', viii. 1, col. 825. Bernard reports the Waldensian proposition, that 'mulieres debere docere', and the supporting arguments, which are the references to old women teaching in Titus 2:3 (viii. 5, col. 826), and the prophetess Anna speaking about Christ in Luke 2:38 (viii. 6, col. 827).

[26] Alain de Lille, *De fide catholica* ii, 1, PL 210, col. 379: 'mulierculas secum ducunt, et eas in conventu fidelium praedicare faciunt'.

[27] *De valdensibus*, ed. G. Gonnet, *Enchiridion fontium valdensium* (only vol. 1 published, Torre Pellice, 1958), i, 155: 'Affirmunt etiam quod tam laici quam femine sine scientia litterarum possunt predicare.'

[28] Stephen of Bourbon, *Tractatus de diversis materiis praedicabilibus*, in *Quellen zur Geschichte der*

preaching and/or teaching, the Waldensian claim that this is licit, and (on occasion) the arguments advanced by Waldensians to support this. There is a strong contrast here with the Cathars. There is the report of a single famous occasion when a Cistercian told off a Cathar *perfecta*, Esclarmonde, sister of the Count of Foix, for entering theological debate,[29] and there is an Occitan text, discussed below, which refers to a Cathar group, in which women predominate, expounding the gospel and preaching a particular dogma. Apart from these two instances, Catholic authors are silent on Cathar women preaching. It does not figure, as with the Waldensians, as an issue for formal polemical statement and refutation. It is not, as with the Waldensians ('among them women preach'), described as a general practice, as a norm. It may be that some of the contrast between orthodox interest and orthodox silence is rooted in a more fundamental contrast between Waldensians, who issued from the Church as an order of religious, and Cathars, members of a counter-Church. That is to say, the legitimacy of Waldensian preaching was an issue inside the Roman Church, where Cathar preaching was not. It may also have been possible – this comment is additional, not alternative – that Catholic authors were accurately reflecting the fact that the Waldensians were simply keener on this than the Cathars both in doctrine and in practice.

The one Catholic source to deal with the theme in a way which implies generalization is an Occitan text of the mid-thirteenth century which purports to be a dialogue between a Catholic and a Cathar.[30] Izarn is a Catholic religious, possibly a Dominican, and Sicard is a captured *perfectus*. In their theological discussion the Catholic heaps polemical abuse on a Catharism which, in his simplified picture, is represented by two persons or groups: on the one hand, Sicard himself, an itinerant male preacher, a *perfectus*, and on the other hand a group or community of five named Cathars, three of whom are women, one of whose names, Lady Domergua, heads the list and may head the community. Sicard has been to an evil school ('malvaiz escola'), and Izarn marvels at where Sicard could have found a master to instruct him ('maistre que t'aia enssenhat').[31] When we peel off the polemicist's scepticism, what is left is this. Sicard has been at something called a school where a master has instructed him in Cathar doctrine; and he carries in a bag or by his chest the Holy Spirit ('Aquel sant esperit . . . Sil portas en ta borsa ol tenes en ton se'),[32] in other words what the Cathars called the 'Text', the New Testament. When the Catholic author turns to the community, Lady Domergua, Garsens, Peironelle, and two men, he describes how one weaves, another spins, another

Waldenser, ed. A. Patschovsky and K.-V. Selge, Texte zur Kirchen- und Theologiegeschichte, 18 (Gütersloh, 1973), 16: 'Qui eciam, tam homines quam mulieres [. . .] predicantes'.

[29] Abels and Harrison, 227–8.

[30] 'Le débat d'Izarn et de Sicard de Figueiras', ed. P. Meyer, *Annuaire-Bulletin de la Société de l'Histoire de France* (1879), 232–92.

[31] Ibid. 245 l. 9, 248 l. 113.

[32] Ibid. 246 l. 30–31.

expounds the Gospel and another makes a sermon about how the Devil made all creation ('Desponen l'avangeli . . . l'autra fai so sermo, Cossi a fag diable tota creatio'),[33] then comes to his main charge: they do this, but 'know not grammar nor how to form letters' ('no saupro gramatica ni de letra ques fo').[34] The *perfectus* is an educated man who carries a book and has been taught evil things, while another group of Cathars of uncertain status, in whom women and one aristocratic woman in particular predominate, discuss scripture and expound theology despite their utter illiteracy. The Catholic author's stereotypes fit roughly with the many male Cathars, *perfecti*, whom we glimpse in the depositions, who were literate, used books, and used bags for their portable vade-mecum books. And they fit the absence of any glimpse of a literate book-using female Cathar, whether *perfecta* or *credens*.

The picture put forward here has concentrated on texts and literacy as opposed to the oral culture of the illiterate in order to establish a point. A few men, *perfecti*, were literate, used books, and in a few cases wrote theological treatises. One book, the Text, had a central place in the Cathar sacrament of the *consolamentum*, something which will have been highlighted by the almost total absence of any other objects that acted as props in Cathar ritual. It was also the mediating instrument in the Kiss of Peace which will have reminded men and women of the necessity for perfects of either sex to avoid the slightest physical contact with the other sex. A small minority of male followers, principally notaries, a few knights and town business folk, had enough literacy to read directly the Cathars' books. Cathar women, whether *perfectae* or *credentes*, seem to have been outside the written documents of the Cathar church's organization and finance, and outside its written theology, although the early houses of female religious may well have possessed deeds. Women who were *perfectae* discussed scripture and theology, as did female *credentes*; often the circles were predominantly female. They were not always female, and groups who discussed theology with reference only to what they heard were often male, because, of course, the majority of male *credentes* were also illiterate, also outside the world of texts and also eager discussers of theology. It would seem that female remoteness from books and a picture of parallel and overlapping textual and oral worlds is a useful simplifying *hypothèse de travail* which we should use when investigating women's role in Languedocian Catharism. It would be interesting to see how far we could emerge with different Catharisms in the sermons of the men, the *perfecti*, based on books which arranged lists of scriptural authorities under formally articulated Cathar dogmas, and the conversational and less formal Catharism of women – and of many illiterate men.

'Women', of course, is a term which can bar the way to envisaging the ideas

[33] Ibid. 247 l. 60–64.
[34] Ibid. 247 l. 66.

of many individuals.[35] Consider three sorts of 'women'. There are, firstly, those women whom the truth (or myth) about women and Catharism has hidden from history, namely those among ordinary women who (like many ordinary men) did not like Catharism. For these women the most significant facet of Cathar books may have been that they were read and expounded by men, and were possibly the sources for expressions of repugnance for the female body which they were unlikely to have found parallelled in Catholic sermons in thirteenth-century Languedoc. Whereas there had been many *perfectae* early in the century, their numbers had been reduced to only one by around 1300[36] – and it is tempting to connect this fact with the ease with which one can encounter misogyny in the very late Cathar sermons.[37] 'Women', secondly, includes lukewarm Cathars, affiliated to Catharism mainly for reasons of tradition and family. In their minds the books will have had a small and unimportant place. 'Women' includes the enthusiasts for Catharism, but among these includes women who had had close contact with books, seeing and earnestly listening to their exposition, together with those for whom book or a book were much more remote but still very important; and also those for whom what counted was a spoken Catharism, known to them mainly through what women in their families and neighbourhoods said. These three categories, however, simplify a phenomenon whose complexity we only dimly perceive. Consider an odd confession from the 1270s in which a man describes the statement of a woman called Anglesia, that is to say, Englishwoman. Anglesia's commitment is clear: her firmness in her faith had led to her being burnt to death. In the context of conversations about the good weather which prevailed when the *perfecti* had still been living in the country, and the bad weather one had now they had gone, she was reported to have made a very peculiar statement. Heretics – *perfecti* – had a book, which they looked at when there were storms, 'and this' (presumably the book) 'in Bulgaria'.[38] Elements in this myth seem to include some ignorance and lack of ordinary observation of the *perfecti* and what they did with books, allied to extraordinary respect for the mysterious and wondrous power of the heretics' book, all the more extreme for its very remoteness to this particular woman, Anglesia.

When we turn the pages of inquisitors' trials from southern France in this period we encounter men and women who followed the Waldensians, and

---

[35] An earlier attempt to emphasize variety of individual response to Catharism among ordinary women was made in Biller, 'Common Woman', 154–6.

[36] There are references to *Jacoba heretica* in Limborch, *Liber sententiarum*, 14, 30, 32, 35, 70, 76, 77 and 86. Not all these are used in the discussions of Jacoba in Koch, 85 and nn. 91–93, and Abels and Harrison, 240 and nn. 126–9. Brenon, 332–5, also provides an account of Jacoba.

[37] The principal early evidence – the notion that women will have to change sex to enter the heaven of the good God – comes from a text of c.1200 which contains material relating to northern French Catharism, about which we know so little; Biller, 'Common Woman', 151 n. 99.

[38] BN Doat MS fol. 216v: 'audivit Anglesiam uxorem quondam Petri Raterii, quae fuit combusta propter haeresim, quod haeretici habebant quendam librum quem respiciebant, quando videbant tale[m] temp[estatem – conjectural], et hoc in Bulgaria'.

also men and women who professed such beliefs as the world having no beginning or end, people having no souls after the deaths of their bodies, and their being no afterlife, whom we can call materialist atheists. When we turn to the extracts from sentences on several hundred male and female followers of Waldensians from Quercy, we see that a small handful of the males and none of the women read books. This evidence is very thin, unlike that collected eighty years later by Jacques Fournier. Consider the pair of materialist atheists whose depositions are next to each other in his register, a woman, Jacoba Carot,[39] and a man, Arnaut of Savinhan. Jacoba has some very coherent doctrines. When asked about their source she says they came from inside herself, from her fatuity and from doubt she had in her heart; the doctrines are never related to texts. She talks about doctrine, talks a lot to women, and snatches of her vernacular survive in the Latin proceedings. She also talks to men, and it is a man, a miller from Ax called William Caux, who claims to have argued with her, saying when controverting her on one point, 'I have heard it thus from chaplains and the friars minor, and it is found written thus in charters and books, as the chaplains say'.[40] The next case is of a man, Arnaud Savinhan.[41] By contrast, when he is asked about the source of his doctrines his reply is that he learnt letters, read, and from what he read he formed his belief.[42] Are these two mental worlds – the female oral and the male textual? Only up to a point. While a further examination of other materialist atheists would not entirely remove the contrast, it would erode it considerably: for most of the other males were also illiterate, and in discussions referred to their own thoughts, proverbs and other conversations in much the same way as Jacoba.

Two suggestions seem to emerge. First, we encounter broadly similar patterns, more or less fragmentarily, among people who were very diverse in outlook, members of the Cathar Church, followers of the Brothers and Sisters of a banned mendicant order, the Waldensians, and materialist atheists. Ordinary Catholic laymen and women are mainly, though not entirely, missing from the pages of inquisition trials, but they are not missing from the notarial material from Toulouse which has been so deeply studied by John Mundy, and whose picture of very restricted female literacy broadly fits what we have been seeing.[43] Catharism was a Church, deeply embedded in Languedocian society, and it seems to reflect the cultural patterns of that society. An example introduces the second suggestion, drawn from Waldensian followers. We have seen that we cannot find book-reading and book-owning female followers of the Waldensians in southern France, though we can find males. When we move northwards, however, to the German-speaking followers of Waldensians, we

---

[39] Duvernoy, *Registre d'inquisition*, i, 154–62.

[40] Ibid. 152: 'ita audivi ego a capellanis et Fratribus Minoribus, et ita invenitur scriptum in cartis et libris, ut dicunt capellani'.

[41] Ibid. 163–8.

[42] Ibid. 164.

[43] See n. 45 below.

are able to find female (but not male) *credentes* owning books, reading books, and sending books to each other.[44] The example is tiny, and is only used here as a leitmotif for the suggestion of a contrast between ordinary women in northern and southern Europe. With the necessary simplicity of a question for research, and the tentativeness of a hypothesis, the suggestion here is that there was a contrast in the education and culture of ordinary women – of any variety of Christianity, of any degree of zeal or lukewarmness – in different parts of Europe. The hypothesis for testing is this: that ordinary women in parts of north-western Europe were to quite a large degree excluded from literacy, but that this 'degree' was significantly milder than the brutal extensiveness of the exclusion from literacy of ordinary women in southern Europe.[45]

---

[44] G. F. Ochsenbein, *Aus dem schweizerischen Volksleben. Der Inquisitionsprozess wider die Waldenser zu Freiburg i. U. im Jahre 1430 nach den Akten dargestellt* (Bern, 1881), 187, 189, 191, 220, 250–1.
[45] Note the positive elements in the accounts of women in literacy in German sources studied by Grundmann (see n. 3 above) and in England by M. T. Clanchy, *From Memory to Written Record. England 1066–1307*, 2nd edn (Oxford, 1993) – see index entry, 406. Note the pessimism in two examples from southern Europe: J. H. Mundy, *Men and Women at Toulouse in the Age of the Cathars*, Studies and Texts 101 (Toronto, 1990), 117–18, and Christine Meek's comment to the author of this paper that she has never encountered positive evidence about female literacy in the archives of medieval Lucca.

INDEX OF MANUSCRIPTS

GENERAL INDEX